How a Century of War Changed the Lives of W~

Counterfire

Series Editor: Neil Faulkner

Counterfire is a socialist organisation which campaigns against capitalism, war, and injustice. It organises nationally, locally, and through its website and print publications, operating as part of broader mass movements, for a society based on democracy, equality, and human need. Counterfire stands in the revolutionary Marxist tradition, believing that radical change can come only through the mass action of ordinary people. To find out more, visit www.counterfire.org

This series aims to present radical perspectives on history, society, and current affairs to a general audience of trade unionists, students, and other activists. The best measure of its success will be the degree to which it inspires readers to be active in the struggle to change the world.

Also available:

The Second World War:
A Marxist History
Chris Bambery

A Marxist History of the World:
From Neanderthals to Neoliberals
Neil Faulkner

How a Century of War Changed the Lives of Women

LINDSEY GERMAN

PlutoPress
www.plutobooks.com

First published 2013 by Pluto Press
345 Archway Road, London N6 5AA

www.plutobooks.com

Distributed in the United States of America exclusively by
Palgrave Macmillan, a division of St. Martin's Press LLC,
175 Fifth Avenue, New York, NY 10010

British Library Cataloguing in Publication Data
A catalogue record for this book is available from the British Library

ISBN   978 0 7453 3251 2   Hardback
ISBN   978 0 7453 3250 5   Paperback
ISBN   978 1 8496 4848 6   PDF eBook
ISBN   978 1 8496 4850 9   Kindle eBook
ISBN   978 1 8496 4849 3   EPUB eBook

Library of Congress Cataloging in Publication Data applied for

10   9   8   7   6   5   4   3   2   1

Typeset from disk by Stanford DTP Services, Northampton, England
Simultaneously printed digitally by CPI Antony Rowe, Chippenham, UK and
Edwards Bros in the United States of America

Contents

Acknowledgements

A number of people have helped me with this book. I would like to thank first the Barry Amiel and Norman Melburn Trust, which kindly helped to fund my research and writing. I am very grateful to them. I hope that in a small way it contributes to advancing 'public education, learning and knowledge in all aspects of the philosophy of Marxism, the history of socialism, and the working- class movement' – the trust's aim.

I would also like to thank all those who agreed to be interviewed and to share their thoughts with me. It has been a great privilege to talk to them, especially to Billie Figg and Angela Sinclair, now both 90 and representatives of a truly remarkable generation. Those interviewed are listed below. The book could not have been written without them, although they may not necessarily agree with all the conclusions that I draw.

Neil Faulkner, Elaine Graham Leigh, Chris Nineham, Kate Connelly, Kate Hudson, Andrew Murray, Sara Farris, Nina Power and Michael Williams read and commented on all or part of the manuscript. Neil Faulkner also gave a detailed and effective 'first edit' of an early manuscript. David Castle and his colleagues at Pluto Press have been very helpful and encouraging, and understanding about deadlines. Elly Badcock compiled the index.

David Shonfield has been generous with his house in Italy, a beautiful and peaceful place to write, and has engaged in numerous stimulating conversations on the topic.

I would like to thank all my work colleagues at Stop the War for their help and patience and in carrying work while I was writing.

Finally, my thanks as always to John Rees, my partner and comrade, who helps me in more ways than I can possibly say.

The Women Interviewed for this Book

Pat Arrowsmith
Carmel Brown
Kate Connelly
Billie Figg
Rose Gentle
Penny Hicks
Tansy Hoskins
Kate Hudson
Joan Humphreys
Dahabo Isse
Helen John
Jenny Jones

Rania Khan
Sinead Kirwan
Henna Malik
Jackie Mulhallen
Nicola Pratt
Yvonne Ridley
Chanie Rosenberg
Elaheh Rostami Povey
Jane Shallice
Angela Sinclair
Rae Street
Carol Turner

Introduction

The Stop the War movement, which began over a decade ago in response to the War on Terror, has become the biggest mass movement in British political history. One of its most remarkable features has been the involvement of women of all ages, races and backgrounds who have been at its centre. Why did this movement become such a vehicle for women's political action, and what does that tell us about the position of women today? To answer these questions we must look not just at the past few years, but at the changes that have taken place over the past century.

Women's liberation and war have often been intertwined in modern history, with the atrocities of war making a dramatic impact on women's role. The history of the two world wars is full of stories of women who broke through stereotypes, worked in unfamiliar jobs, acted with great courage, became feminists, rejected relationships with men and took up arms. Successive wars have shown not just women involved in wars – although in this era of total war it is impossible to ignore the direct involvement of civilians in war and the effect on them – but women taking an increasing part in opposing them.

It is almost 100 years since the world descended into the horror of the first of two world wars. It began in sunshine and patriotic fervour, endured four years of mud, misery, injury and carnage on an unprecedented scale, and ended in revolutions and social upheaval. The First World War was a watershed: it deposed kings and emperors, ushered in universal suffrage and workers' revolution, and changed people's attitude to war forever. Governments of the wealthiest countries have never again been able to preside over such carnage and the death of some ten million young men across Europe and further afield.

But if the war changed the lives of young men and their families, it also had a profound effect on women. By the end of the war they had experienced working in jobs previously reserved for men and been paid wages higher than they were able to earn in domestic service, the biggest single employer of women before 1914. Although they were denied access to some of these jobs when the war ended, they continued to work in greater numbers and in some of the new fields of work that were opening up. They had the vote, or at least some of them did (full female suffrage would have to wait another decade). They started wearing much more comfortable and unrestricted styles of dress. And while marriage and motherhood were still considered women's main roles, the number of children that women had began to decline quite sharply.

The life-changing impact of the Second World War, just a generation later, was even more dramatic. Women worked in essential industries, joined the armed forces and many jettisoned ideas about chastity and taboos on sex before marriage with great enthusiasm. Again, while they were encouraged to return to the home, marriage and family after 1945, women embarked on careers and education which challenged the traditional stereotypes.

Modern industrialised warfare is fundamentally different. We now have wars of total attrition. Industrial mass production creates and sustains vast armies and unprecedented firepower, and results in unparalleled killing and destruction. It is qualitatively different from previous eras. At Waterloo (1815) Britain had 156 guns; at the Somme (1916) the British army had 1,400 guns, and fired nearly two million shells in just a few days. The Prussian army at Waterloo had 60,000 men; by 1914 the German army had 1.5 million men on the Western Front alone. One outcome of modern firepower was often stalemate and wars of attrition. Industrial output was decisive, mobilising not just soldiers but workers in war industries too. Women were crucial on the home front.

This book is an attempt to understand the relationship between women and war in Britain in the twentieth and twenty-first centuries. Unlike most of Europe during the Second World War, Britain escaped Nazi occupation, but it was nonetheless subject to heavy bombardment and high levels of government intervention, as well as conscription to create a war economy.

The Second World War shaped the lives of my generation, born in the postwar era of optimism, when people expected improvements in health, education and housing provision as a reward for the terrible years of war, death and dislocation our parents and grandparents had endured. The second half of the twentieth century offered more opportunities for women than at any time in history, and the basis for many of those opportunities was created in the first half of a century which witnessed not only two world wars, but also the worst economic crisis to date.

War has a terrible impact on all people, but increasingly on women as victims of injury, rape, displacement and death. But in Britain and a number of other countries it has also promoted women's emancipation by breaking down oppressive social structures. Many of the great social changes from which my generation benefited had their genesis in war; others were already in gestation but were advanced by the two world wars.

This was true of the vote for women, equal pay, first raised by trade unionists in the munitions industry and in public transport during the First World War but not granted even in a weakened form until the 1970s, more accessible divorce, education at higher levels, employment in 'men's' jobs, and a falling birth rate.

Although I was born six years after the Second World War ended, the fact of the war was a major feature in my life. 'The war' was a constant reference point. My father, and the fathers of most of my friends, had been in the armed forces. The only time they had been abroad was as a result of the war: to Sicily, Burma, North Africa, Greece. One uncle lost a leg at Nijmegen, Holland in 1944. Another, a merchant seaman, was in the river police during the Blitz, then transported troops across the Channel on D-day. London was peppered with bomb sites. My primary school still had its air raid shelters, now stuffed with old desks and equipment.

However, it struck me from a young age that there was another side to the war and one that I understood especially from my mother. This was in stark contrast to the image of war projected from most sources. It was about going out to work and having enough money to go to the Streatham Locarno, the London

Palladium and especially the Hammersmith Palais with Canadian and American soldiers and airmen, with money in their pockets and only a brief time to enjoy. This lifestyle was not enjoyed by all women, but my mother was a teenager when war broke out and had no family responsibilities or children. However, her experience was typical of many young women and shows how the war gave them opportunities they would have thought impossible only a few years earlier. Most importantly, they paved the way for future generations to seize opportunities which they were only beginning to define and articulate.

This was in unoccupied Britain. Just a short distance across the Channel, women's lives were much more dangerous and repressive. Women in the occupied countries and under the Axis powers faced rape, torture, imprisonment, death on a daily basis. Nevertheless many of them fought bravely in the resistance movements. Even in Britain, death and danger were ever-present, and many, including my mother, lost loved ones. The contradictions expressed in these lives are what this book is about.

The modern form of warfare which sucks civilian lives into its core is a product of an economic system based on industrial competition. Even in the age of globalisation these corporations are tied to nation states or alliances of nation states. Their fates are interlinked. They form part of an international matrix of competition which, periodically, descends into armed conflict. War is a means of safeguarding and extending their markets and geopolitical reach. In this way competition between, say, Ford and Volkswagen or Exxon and Gazprom can become the root of conflicts resolved on the fields of battle – a process that involves destruction and waste on a vast scale.

The beneficiaries of war are not the poor and working class, who fight, work, suffer and die, but those who control the system. Their property, their profits, are at stake. But if they succeed in vanquishing their competitors, they can enjoy the prospect of even greater profits and more lucrative markets. Theirs is an exploitative system, which relies on one class controlling the wealth another class produces. Women are not separate from this process but are themselves part of the class society, and how they respond tends to reflect their position in society.

War is one of the most terrifying aspects of modern capitalism, an all-pervasive war economy which threatens to catapult us back to barbarism. It is also a major force for change: it forces apart old ways of working and living in such a way that women and men are drawn along in its wake, obliged to take on new roles, confront challenges and dangers, revise their ideas and, if fortunate, come out at the other end in one piece.

However, progress for some comes at the cost of the mass annihilation of others. There is no greater mark of a barbarous and dehumanised social system than one that destroys lives, creates wastelands and leaves devastation on such a scale that most people conclude a different system has to be created. It took tens of millions of deaths, the Holocaust, the rise and fall of fascism and nuclear terror before people were ready to try to build a society based on more equal and just principles.

War has also created an odd dialectic for women: their lives have been changed by processes wrought by wars. This has helped them to develop a much deeper understanding of war and a strong commitment, now seen in many women across several generations, to campaign against it. So the consequence of total war has been to build opposition to it and to make women more politically aware and active.

The wars of the twentieth and early twenty-first centuries have played a pivotal role in British politics. Britain's history as an imperial power, its continued interventions in the affairs of other countries (albeit since 1945 as a junior partner of the United States) and its warmongering under successive governments have all helped to create an opposition to war which is one of the touchstones of left-wing politics. Time and again, questions of war have been major political issues: in 1914; in 1938 with appeasement; in 1956 with Suez, the Cold War and nuclear weapons; and in recent years, especially 2002–3, the Middle East. War and domestic politics are interlaced.

In Britain my contemporaries and the men and women of later generations have less direct experience of war, but even so, war has become a permanent fact of life for us. The 'balance of terror', which until recently existed between the United States and Soviet Union, was sometimes justified as the means to ensure that a third world war could never happen. But many who had lived through the First and Second World Wars knew that wasn't necessarily true, that deadly weapons could lead to war even if the consequences seemed too horrific to contemplate. The Cold War always contained within it the threat of a major 'hot war'.

So, relatively soon after the Second World War a new opposition to the threat of war and nuclear weapons emerged internationally, as the implications of armed peace became clear. No one with any awareness could ignore the sometimes very real threat of nuclear annihilation, and this helped lead to the movement against nuclear weapons. The Cuban missile crisis of 1962 was, it was feared, likely to lead to another war less than 20 years after bombs and rockets had devastated London and other major British cities.

Opposition to war has grown since then. This has been specially marked among women. The movement against the Vietnam war took place in a period of social change: women were moving into new jobs, entering higher education, discovering a freer sexuality and engaging in political action. It propelled women's concerns to centre stage, exposing an American Left that was simply incapable of relating to these problems.

If women's political issues took centre stage, they did so at least partly in relation to war; those of us who found the Vietnam war to be overwhelmingly a politicising issue had opposition to war engraved in our DNA. Those who created the women's liberation movement in the late 1960s consciously linked their struggle against oppression with the national liberation movements which were so effective in the 1950s, 1960s and 1970s in some of the former colonies of the Western empires.

The changes in women's lives from the 1960s onwards led to women asserting their right to equality and organisation. One of the main concerns of many has been peace. The peace movement was revived in the early 1980s, this time in opposition to the siting of cruise missiles in Europe. In Britain a major expression of this movement was the Greenham Common peace camp organised by women as a feminist response to militarism, though I felt it was too narrow and too focused on feminism to fulfil its potential. It did however mobilise and galvanise very large numbers of people.

It was only a few years before the 'balance of terror' was overturned by the collapse of one side, leaving a much more unstable situation in which new wars became increasingly frequent and dangerous. Since 1989 there has been a rapid succession of wars involving the United States, Britain and other Western powers. The First Gulf War, the Balkans wars (which brought about the breakup of Yugoslavia) and then the War on Terror all indicated how the United States planned to deal with its declining economic power in the twenty-first century.

All were increasingly described not as wars of aggression – which would have been both illegal and politically unacceptable – but as wars of humanitarian intervention. One justification, especially for the War on Terror, became the need to rescue women from subjugation and oppression. Despite the urgency with which this case was pressed by First Ladies and Secretaries of State, the response from many women was to argue that this liberation was not being carried out in their name.

I was strongly opposed to the Vietnam war and to all the wars that followed. But it was from 11 September 2001 that I played a key organising role in building the movement, helping to form the Stop the War Coalition and being elected as its convenor. The high level of involvement and activism in the movement was obvious, with women of all ages, all nationalities and religions, and very widely differing class backgrounds. The legacy of opposition continues and will no doubt give rise to new movements in the future.

It has been remarkable to see how many women have been involved at every level, often with a sense of purpose not found in other spheres of politics, and I have been increasingly intrigued about how this should happen and what political significance it might have. The answer in part seems to do with the cumulative effect of war on women's lives and consciousness. The twentieth century experienced total war, with civilians increasingly the majority of victims and women expected to play an active part in waging war.

War has infiltrated the home, work and social life in a way that would have been impossible throughout most of history. Women have played a role as combatants, as war workers, defence workers and health workers. They have been direct victims of war. They have also suffered bereavements. The social changes resulting from these developments in turn fed involvement in, and often opposition to, war.

I want to explain the hows and whys of women's role in warfare, and why so many women in the twenty-first century now oppose war. Wars have been motors of change for women, altering the family and women's role within it, transforming the sorts of work that women do and their ideas about themselves. The collective and individual decisions and actions of millions of women and men are how history is made. This book is about some of their decisions, their implications and consequences and – most importantly – how they can be used to shape the future.

I have interviewed women from different generations about the impact of war on their lives. They have varying backgrounds, beliefs and experiences which I have found extremely valuable in illuminating their motivations, decisions and the impact of war on their thinking. I hope that their views, however subjective, have helped to develop insights about wider changes. The Stop the War Coalition, which began in 2001, is looked at through the eyes of some of its participants. They cover a range of ages and backgrounds, and all are people who have experienced war or have some experience of opposing it.

I look at the questions which have arisen out of the War on Terror: the role of 'humanitarian intervention' in modern wars and the way in which arguments about women's equality are used to justify wars. The attitudes to, and of, Muslim women are also considered. Finally, I use women's experiences to understand how war has changed women and their ideas, and what the prospects are for peace and women's liberation in the future.

The experiences are, needless to say, individual. They do not claim to represent all women in the movement or indeed the totality of the movement. There are many organisations and groups within what can be broadly called the peace movement or anti-war movement. These include religious groups, such as the Quakers, who have played a continuing and honourable role in the movement, and groups such as Women in Black which organises internationally for peace. The various groups often focus on specific issues or take different approaches to organising. The book is not a history of women's peace organisation or of peace and anti-war campaigning generally. What it does do is raise two major issues – women's liberation and war – and make connections which I think are relevant and I hope will be useful to those fighting in order to change the world.

The wars that we have witnessed in recent years are not an aberration, but the result of a competitive and crisis-ridden system. Future wars are likely to be about resources, commodities and food and water shortages. They will be about the major powers fighting for market share and strategic control. We will need mass movements to oppose these wars, which endanger the future of humanity. In Britain, governments are demanding austerity and sacrifice from working people while inequality grows and the spending of billions of pounds on waging war every year continues. As the postwar welfare state sees its greatest threat yet from the same people who support wars and the obscenely high levels of military spending which accompany them, a new generation of women activists are coming onto the field of battle. They have already made clear that they are unwilling to countenance war and militarism, and in the course of opposing those dangers, they are asserting their liberation.

1
Women and the Great War

'Although sixteen years of age at the time, England had been at war three months before I knew. I was in domestic service on a farm near the River Humber and one day as I was attending to ducklings a shell whizzed over my head from the direction of the river. This was in November 1914 and I refused to believe a farm boy who told me England was at war.

'Girls who worked as maids on those small farms were completely isolated. The farmers and their wives never talked with the girls except to tell them what to do next. They had no books and never saw a newspaper. They were on duty from five in the morning until ten at night and were not allowed to burn a candle at night.'[1]

When the First World War broke out in 1914, the position of women was defined very narrowly and traditionally. The two major areas of employment were domestic service and in the North the textile industry, where women, even after marriage, worked in large numbers. Among the largest section of the working class, the coal miners, women workers were practically non-existent, prevented by Act of Parliament since 1842 from working in the pits.

While most jobs were not prohibited by law, many were by convention. Women in Britain did not, for example, work as clerks in the Bank of England or as conductors on the London buses. Married women generally were not expected to work in paid employment – the 1911 census recorded only around a tenth of married women as employed outside the home. Instead, they were expected to devote themselves to their family and home, of which the man was undisputedly the head.

Their work at home was onerous. Few homes had electricity or mains water, making women's lives a constant battle with dirt.

Traditionally, families were large, especially within the unskilled working class, although that was beginning to change.

Most women received little education and started working in their early teens. They had no right to vote. The few women who aspired to higher education were only able to gain university degrees from late in the nineteenth century. They could study at purpose-built women's colleges but could not receive a degree from Oxford or Cambridge until 1920 and 1947 respectively.

Few women travelled very far from home, let alone abroad. Their hair was long, as were their skirts, and trousers were rarely worn and considered exotic and dangerous.

War of the sort that was about to consume their lives was unknown. Previous wars involved a professional army fighting in distant countries, whose victories would be marked in the naming of terraced streets but whose day-to-day conduct had little direct impact on most people in Britain. The Boer war just over a decade earlier in distant South Africa had sounded some alarm bells, not over the conduct of the war itself, despite the shocking treatment of Boer civilians, but over the lack of fitness of army recruits.

It would have seemed incomprehensible that war would embroil the whole of Europe and to such an extent that 'Big Bertha', the German howitzer, when fired in France could be heard in Hampstead or that civilians could be bombed from the sky.

But in 1914 everything started to change. The Austro-Hungarian, German, Russian and Ottoman (Turkish) empires all collapsed as a result of the war. The British Empire saw major rebellions. The lives of millions changed: death, disruption and danger became a part of everyday reality. The state came to play a major part of people's lives.

Every aspect of women's lives changed too. Women won the vote. They strove for equal pay. Work changed for women, as did life in the home. There were fewer servants, more factory workers, more women doctors and teachers. Social and sexual attitudes altered. Skirts were worn shorter and hair was bobbed.

Some of these changes had started before 1914, but the war accelerated them, sometimes dramatically. By 1914, Britain was in a state of crisis. Many women were discontented with their lives, a discontent which crystallised in concerted political agitation for the vote. This came against a backdrop of other issues which were also leading to fundamental changes. Irish nationalists were demanding Home Rule (Ireland was governed directly from Westminster) and a Unionist minority was determined to stop them. The Conservative Party was closely allied to the Unionist Ulster Protestants and Britain was close to a very serious conflict over Ireland. Working-class people had also risen up in a huge wave of strikes in the years before 1914. Again, there was every sign of this conflict growing in 1914; class polarisation was intense in these years.

All these issues divided Britain along social and class lines and there seemed no easy resolution to them. They added to a sense of foreboding.[2] Mobilisation for war in Britain and elsewhere in Europe derailed the rising militancy across the continent. Opposition to the government and to the war became very difficult. Militancy went underground, to erupt with even greater force when the war was over.

A Society Worth Fighting For?

'How does a working man's wife bring up a family on 20s a week?' was the question asked by the Fabian Women's Group when in 1909 it began its study into the life of workers in Lambeth.[3] The families investigated were not the poorest or the highly skilled, but those who made up much of the transport, service and labouring jobs whose modern equivalents are still poorly paid. The conclusion drawn by the researchers was that these workers could not be expected to feed and care for their families properly and, despite being waged, were among the working poor.

Maud Pember Reeves and her Fabian colleagues were part of a generation concerned about the future of working people and their families. Their concerns matched those of some in government who feared industrial and imperial decline, especially in relation to Germany and the United States. The years before and during the First World War therefore brought in various reforms. The Liberal government introduced old age pensions, National Insurance,

Labour Exchanges and school meals, while the Conservatives established compulsory secondary education to the age of 14 and local education authorities.

Welcome as these changes were, they were not able to stem the tide of discontent which was swelling among the working class and poor. Strikes over wages and working conditions spread rapidly in the four years before 1914. They involved the miners, transport workers and other groups of unionised workers, but such was their radicalising effect, and such were the conditions in which working people struggled, that the action spread to groups, especially women, not necessarily thought of as militant trade unionists.

Another Fabian writer, Barbara Drake, described how

'The wave of industrial unrest, which swept over the country in 1910, spread … to women. In the East End and in the South of London, the jam and pickle workers, biscuit makers, bottle washers, tin box makers, cocoa makers, distillery workers, rag pickers, "sweated" and unorganised women and girls, earning from 5s to 10s a week, emulated the action of the London transport workers and came out on strike.'[4]

A revolt of charwomen (cleaners) employed by the London County Council won them a minimum wage, holiday pay and direct employment. The women of Cradley Heath in the West Midlands, employed as chain-makers, also went on strike in those years.[5] Such was the scale of revolt that women's trade union membership nearly doubled between 1910 and 1914.[6]

The industrial unrest in the summer of 1911 centred on a dock strike in London which effectively brought the capital to a standstill. Women in Bermondsey also struck over wages and conditions in 1911. Women factory workers organised flying pickets to pull out other groups of women workers. They dressed in their Sunday-best feather boas and fur tippets, as if celebrating. They were part of a growing militancy which was also beginning to connect different political issues.

Life was also changing for middle- and upper-class women. There was a growing political awareness among some, who wanted a purpose in life beyond the decorative idleness which society still decreed, who craved education and who sometimes espoused socialist or feminist ideas.

The phenomenon of the 'New Woman' appeared in literature and political commentary in the late nineteenth century. Women's greater access to secondary education, the opening up of new areas of employment such as clerical work and greater opportunities for mobility created conditions where women began to consider the possibility of individual and wider social change.[7]

The Pankhursts, most famous for their campaign over women's suffrage, were a prominent left-wing Independent Labour Party family. Christabel Pankhurst was one of the first women to graduate from Manchester University and her sister Sylvia was a talented artist who studied at the Royal College of Art. Women such as Maud Pember Reeves, Clementina Black and Barbara Drake dedicated themselves to the study of working women's living and working conditions in order to try to change society. Others, like Isabella Ford and Mary Macarthur, worked in trade union organising.

An increasing number of these women also felt that they had to earn their own living, being unable or unwilling to depend on marriage or family for their future. Some middle-class women had begun to take advantage of new skills like typewriting to enter paid employment. A very small number were also entering higher education, facilitated by the women's colleges developed at Oxford and Cambridge and by the opening up of provincial university colleges to women. A small number of working-class and lower middle-class women went into teaching and became an important part of the education system in the first half of the twentieth century. Shop work also increased.

The major political campaign involving women in the pre-war years was for their right to be full citizens in a democracy. Women were denied the vote in parliamentary elections, although some with property qualifications could vote in local elections or stand for school boards. The campaign for women's right to vote was international. The desire among women for change crystallised in the call for the vote as the key means of achieving this. Demonstrations of women and men took place in different parts of the world to win the demand. It was part of the campaign by socialist women who launched International Women's Day at their Copenhagen conference in 1910.[8] In Britain, the suffragettes entered popular consciousness with their tireless and imaginative campaigns.

The Women's Social and Political Union, popularly known as the suffragettes, was founded in 1903 by Emmeline Pankhurst, widow of Dr Richard Pankhurst, a Manchester radical and campaigner. Their affiliation to the Independent Labour Party put them on the left of the labour movement. There were always feminists in the ILP, which took the issues of women's equality seriously and which had many prominent women as members, including Isabella Ford, Ethel Snowden and Katherine Bruce Glasier.

In October 1905, Emmeline's elder daughter Christabel and her friend, the former millworker Annie Kenney, disrupted a meeting at the Manchester Free Trade Hall where the Liberal politician Sir Edward Grey was speaking. Their arrest for demanding votes for women launched a mass campaign which saw the WSPU intervening directly in politics. Their campaign was particularly aimed at the Liberal government, which had refused even to countenance their demand.

Despite its high profile in the media and its imaginative tactics, the WSPU was not the only show in town. The National Union of Women's Suffrage Societies (NUWSS) – the suffragists – offered an alternative. It adopted more constitutional tactics, such as campaigning for a mass petition, and it had very wide support – much more than the WSPU – in the Lancashire and Cheshire cotton towns among working-class textile workers. By 1910 50,000 people were affiliated to the NUWSS.[9] Many small suffrage societies also were involved in campaigning.

Gradually, divisions emerged in the campaign over the vote. First, there was the argument over whether to campaign for women's suffrage on the same terms as for men or whether to fight for full adult suffrage. Before 1914 a minority of working-class men had the vote, but many unskilled workers did not. To campaign for the status quo to be extended to women would be to enfranchise middle- and upper-class women but leave many working-class men and women disenfranchised.

The argument in favour of adult suffrage was at least partly about class and whether middle-class women should gain the vote before working-class men. 'Perhaps sixty per cent of working people had become disenfranchised by 1914'[10] because a high proportion of the working class did not meet the residence criteria needed to register as they had to move to find work.

Disagreements within the newly formed Labour Party and ILP were partly over adult suffrage. They also reflected a political shift as Emmeline and Christabel Pankhurst moved away from any association with the ILP. The WSPU antagonised Labour with its by-election policy (practised from 1906) and its slogan 'Keep the Liberal out'. It adopted a 'neutral' position so it did not matter if the Labour candidate supported women's suffrage. This often meant the Tory won, or if it was a Tory/Liberal contest the WSPU was *de facto* supporting the more reactionary candidate. From 1912, Christabel tried to extend the policy to make it explicitly anti-Labour, claiming that the party was propping up the government and therefore complicit with it.

Divisions within the labour movement over the tactics and demands for the suffrage therefore widened. There is also some evidence that the style and wealth of some of the WSPU women alienated many ILP women.[11] These schisms only increased as society polarised around the issue.

In 1911 the Liberal Prime Minister Herbert Asquith announced he would introduce a Bill which would extend the vote to men, but did not include women.[12] By this time pro-suffrage opinion was such that his rejection of women's rights only led to more involvement and militancy. The arrests of suffragettes increased as their tactics were met with greater state repression. Imprisoned suffragettes went on hunger strikes as part of their demand to be treated as political prisoners. In response, in 1913 the government introduced the Prisoners (Temporary Discharge for Ill Health) Act, known as the 'Cat and Mouse Act': hunger strikers would be released from prison when the strike began to endanger their lives, only to rearrested when they were no longer at risk.

Many women's health was permanently damaged as a result of the hunger strikes and the force feeding which was often used to try to stop them. Some died as a direct result of their treatment. A conference on the Act in 1913 showed the discontent and anger over the issue, heightened when one suffragette, Emily Wilding Davison, was killed in June that year as she tried to stop the king's horse at the Derby in protest over the refusal to grant the suffrage.[13]

By 1912, Christabel Pankhurst saw the return of a Tory government as the best chance of achieving votes for women. At the same time many radical women, including Christabel's sister Sylvia, were moving in a very different direction, connecting wider issues with that of women's votes. The parting of the ways for the Pankhursts came in 1913 when Sylvia's support for the workers involved in the Dublin lockout led to her speaking at a rally in solidarity with them held in London's Albert Hall.[14] She was ejected from the WSPU and now concentrated on the East London Federation of Suffragettes, which had already developed semi-autonomous status and a very different set of pro-working-class campaigning priorities from that of the main organisation.

There is some evidence too that the majority of the WSPU, unable for the most part to aspire to the high levels of personal sacrifice involved in Christabel's tactics, were becoming less engaged. There was a dramatic fall in dues in 1912–13.[15] The Pethick Lawrences, staunch builders of the WSPU, made their exit in these years.[16]

Effectively, therefore, a split was already in train before the outbreak of the war. It was exacerbated once the war pushed the women's suffrage movement in very different directions.

The War to End All War

It is striking how many of the women involved in the various campaigns over the suffrage rallied to a range of issues during the course of the war. They organised over welfare, against the war itself, against unemployment, high rents and food prices, as well as for the continuation of the suffrage campaign. One suffrage society helped to set up a women's trade union for women welders.[17] The breadth of organisation among women was a tribute to the role of the suffrage movement and the increasing ability of at least some of its supporters to link the vote with other social issues.

However, the war also intensified splits within the suffrage movement. Emmeline and Christabel became some of the most fervent supporters of the war, while Sylvia and women like her saw the war as something in which working people had no interest. The split which had already emerged over class issues now expanded into division on this crucial question. In the face of poverty and rising unemployment, the East London Federation turned its organising talents to the relief of women and children in particular:

'Before August, 1914, was out we had opened our Cost Price restaurants, where twopenny meals to adults and penny meals to children were served to all comers, with free meal tickets for the destitute. The Gunmakers' Arms, a disused public house, we turned into a clinic, day nursery and Montessori school.'[18]

Sylvia Pankhurst's concerns reflected the urgent reality for many families. An immediate consequence of the war was real hardship for many working people. One of its initial effects was women's unemployment, as factories not geared to war production shut down. Women whose husbands enlisted lost their income and the meagre separation allowance which was eventually agreed for them still left many struggling. To make matters worse, prices began to rise.

The Federation set up a League of Rights for Soldiers' and Sailors' Wives and Relatives, agitated through meetings, processions and deputations, and demanded equal pay for women workers. They also campaigned against the Contagious Disease Regulations which penalised and often criminalised women with sexual diseases who had sex with soldiers.

The position taken by Emmeline and Christabel Pankhurst was very different. They became patriotic enthusiasts for the war, helping to initiate the practice of giving white feathers, symbolising cowardice, to young men in civilian clothes to shame them into signing up. The official WSPU paper changed its name to *Britannia* and the movement effectively abandoned all campaigning for the issue which they had held most dear for more than a decade.

Emmeline was one of the organisers of a July 1915 'Right to Serve' demonstration, which demanded that women should be able to do war work and join the armed forces. This was backed by David Lloyd George, who would soon become Prime Minister.[19] Any radicalism shown by the Pankhursts in their earlier years of campaigning disappeared. When a peace conference was called in The Hague in 1915, Emmeline supported the cancelling of the boat service from Tilbury, so that delegates were unable to attend:

> 'What we criticise is the holding of the Congress at all. We are perfectly satisfied, and we have information which supports that belief, that the whole thing has been engineered by agents of Germany. Well-meaning, honourable women have proved to be no match for German agents. I am very glad that the cancelling of the service has made it impossible for Englishwomen to attend.'[20]

Mrs Pankhurst's support for the war never flagged. After the Russian revolution in February 1917, she travelled to Russia to support the government against the growing clamour for the war to end, and supported women's battalions to oppose the workers and soldiers who were demanding it.

All wings of the suffrage movement split. The NUWSS under Mrs Fawcett, long a constitutional campaigner, supported the war, although it was clear that many members had their doubts or were openly opposed to it. The splits reflected divisions among the wider Left and the labour movement and marked a turning point which was to change politics in Britain and which was reflected to different degrees internationally.

This was the position that accompanied the wave of patriotism and jingoism at the outbreak of war. A former suffragette, Sybil Morrison, recalls 1914:

> 'People were excited, they weren't horrified by it as they were in the Second World War – it was *completely* different. They rushed out in the street,

followed the soldiers as they marched through the streets and kissed them, threw flowers and seemed to think it was something to be thrilled about because we were told it was all going to be over by Christmas . . . We were conned. We were made to believe this was a war to end all wars and there'd never be another war.'[21]

The picture changed as the war developed. Growing discontent over the course of the war, its terrible consequences in terms of death and injury and the hardships suffered by the civilian population saw the re-emergence of political campaigning. In 1916, when franchise reform once more became an issue, socialist women 'again took part in the campaign to ensure that women would be included in any new bill'.[22] Women's suffrage was back on the agenda.

Protest and Persecution

The war had a profound effect on women in many ways. The working-class suffragette Hannah Mitchell wrote very movingly about the impact on her of the outbreak of war and the fears for her son, who became a conscientious objector – by no means an easy option given the pro-war climate of the time:[23]

'All my life I had hated war . . . The idea of men killing each other had always seemed so hideous to me, that my first conscious thought after my baby was born was that he should be brought up to resist war. His father fully agreed with me . . . we both believed that war in the main is a struggle for power, territory or trade, to be fought by the workers, who are always the losers.

'By 1914 my son was sixteen; it was clear that he might be soon involved in the war.'[24]

She, like millions of women, feared for her family, but also for the flux and change that war would bring. When her son eventually was allowed to become a conscientious objector, 'for the first time in many, many months I slept soundly that night'.[25]

Despite her relief, COs were subject to imprisonment, where they suffered abuse and hostility. Dorothy Bing described singing outside Wormwood Scrubs one Christmas Eve, where her brother and other COs were jailed. 'We sang carols and they waved their blinds out of the cell windows, so we knew they heard.'[26]

The fear of loss led a number of women into anti-war campaigning. The threat of war had been present internationally for the best part of the previous decade. In the 50 years preceding the First World War, 'women played a substantial role in the international peace movements that existed in increasing strength throughout the fifty years preceding the First World War'.[27]

Campaigning had an international dimension. The international socialist organisation, the Second International, had repeatedly issued statements and threatened strikes in the event of war. Its women's organisations had campaigned against war. When war was declared, however, most of the national components of the International accepted the arguments of their own governments and enthusiastically backed them.

One of the few exceptions was the Russian organisation which opposed the war and led a revolution against it three years later. Women such as Alexandra Kollontai and Inessa Armand played a key role in campaigning against the war. So too did the German socialists Clara Zetkin and Rosa Luxemburg, although the German Socialist Party, the SPD, almost exclusively backed the war.

In Britain the socialist movement was much weaker, though there was some pre-war opposition to the coming carnage. The 1912 conference of the Women's Labour League passed an executive resolution condemning secret diplomacy and the Foreign Office for acting as though war was inevitable. At the 1913 conference Katharine Bruce Glasier moved the first resolution against militarism and an expansion of the war in the Balkans, which was then raging and which many saw, presciently, as a prelude to greater war.

The 1914 conference voted against arms expenditure and conscription and for joint international action by workers against war. The League sent a message of support to Rosa Luxemburg when she was arrested in April 1914. Mary Longman, secretary of the League, spoke at a German peace demonstration in July

1914.[28] In Britain, according to Sheila Rowbotham, 'It was from the feminists that the early anti-war organisations developed'.[29]

The picture, however, was mixed. Ada Nield Chew, a pacifist and member of the Women's International League for Peace and Freedom, played no active part in opposing the war.[30] As we have seen, much of the early opposition to the war focused on the economic effects on working-class women and by and large this did not connect explicitly with pacifist or anti-war campaigning. Fenner Brockway, the well-known pacifist whose wife Lilla formed the No Conscription Fellowship in 1916, regretted that he had failed to ally the anti-war movement with the class struggle.[31]

Anti-war and peace campaigners faced an uphill struggle in the early years of the war. Once trade unions and working-class parties decided to support the war, as many did, it was hard to mount opposition against the cheerleading and jingoism. Any opposition was fragmented and often met quite brutal repression, including imprisonment. However, in Europe events began to take shape as early as 1915. A demonstration for peace was held in Berlin in 1915, Clara Zetkin and the French socialist Louise Saumoneau organised a socialist women's conference in Berne in March 1915, and there was also the larger Hague women's conference in April 1915.[32]

It took a great deal of courage to attend these conferences. The socialist women who met in Berne issued a manifesto which was distributed in Germany by Zetkin and in France by Louise Saumoneau.[33] The Women's Labour League sent delegates to the Labour and Socialist Women's International conference which declared war against war.[34]

The conference was by no means a small thing given that fighting involving German troops was taking place on French soil. Zetkin's socialist politics were uncompromising and in her manifesto to the Berne conference she talked about class war and how the fight against the war had to be taken to the landlords and capitalists as well as the military: 'the entrepreneur lowered your wages, the tradesman and unscrupulous speculator raised prices and the landlord threatens to evict you.'[35]

The Hague congress had a much more pacifist character. It was chaired by the American feminist Jane Addams (at this stage, the United States was not involved directly in the war). Two thousand women attended. The congress expressly adopted less confrontational terms, framing its rules so that all those who registered could speak, but not about the war specifically. Many were privately resentful, especially when the congress concluded by deciding to send flowers to the wounded in all the belligerent countries.[36]

Despite this, the congress was vehemently opposed by the belligerent governments. Most of the British women who wanted to attend were denied passports, and most of those who did were those who were already out of the country for other reasons. The conference led to the formation of the Women's International League (later renamed the Women's International League for Peace and Freedom).

The NUWSS executive, which was already divided over the war, with Millicent Fawcett in favour, saw further divisions: more than half the NUWSS executive resigned in 1915 because they supported the Hague conference.[37] The divisions were similar to those that had split the WSPU. The NUWSS branched into militarist and pacifist wings, the latter becoming the Women's International League for Peace and Freedom. Despite a number of speeches and writings from pacifist and socialist feminists, among then Catherine Marshall's 'Women and War' speech of 1915 and C. K. Ogden and Mary Sargant Florence's 'Militarism versus Feminism', it was hard to make much impact.[38] All that changed as the war progressed.

The introduction of conscription in 1916 was widely opposed. Before that the British army had been a volunteer force, although there was great social pressure to sign up. The death rate in France and Belgium was so high that volunteers alone could not fill the gaps. There was more disillusion with the war, which had brought great hardship especially to working-class people. The Women's Labour League opposed conscription[39] even though it had supported the war in 1914.[40] A Women's Peace Crusade was set up 1916 in response to conscription. Susan Grayzel describes how:

'It explicitly called upon women socialists to take action against the killing of their men, and it organised open air meetings for women to express these views. In Glasgow, which became a centre of the WPC, it mounted an impressive public campaign for a negotiated settlement to the war, and it responded even more vigorously after the Russian revolution.'[41]

Opposing the war was still very difficult in view of the high levels of state repression. A Derby socialist and pacifist, Alice Wheeldon, was arrested with other members of her family for allegedly plotting to assassinate the Prime Minister David Lloyd George. Despite the evidence against them being very flimsy, they were found guilty and served prison sentences.[42] But in general, growing reservations about the war, war-weariness reflected in opposition to price and rent rises, conditions at work and carnage at the front, led to a mood of discontent.

The Russian revolution of February 1917 helped to crystallise that discontent. It was begun by women marking International Women's Day by protesting at food shortages and wartime conditions, and it spread rapidly, leading to the overthrow of the Tsar. The revolution was greeted with much enthusiasm internationally, in part because Russia's reputation for autocracy and repression was well known, in part because the revolution expressed the opposition to war now felt in all the belligerent countries.

A conference was held in June in Leeds in support of the revolution. This attracted a wide range of delegates, including members of the Women's Labour League.[43] The revolution led directly to Russia withdrawing from the war, a point not lost on the millions who also wanted the war to end. This helped to spur political radicalism. In the defeated countries, the imperial monarchies were overthrown by revolutionary movements. Even in Britain victory did little to stem the tide of discontent.

Work: Danger and Dilution

At first women lost their jobs when war was declared – within a month women's employment had contracted by 14 per cent.[44] A Central Committee on Women's Employment was set up to deal with this. Its patron was Queen Mary and trade unionists complained it used volunteers to do work taken from unemployed women. Trade unionists were co-opted onto it, with the National Federation of Women Workers leader Mary Macarthur becoming honorary secretary and leading Labour women such as Susan Lawrence, Margaret Bondfield and Marion Philips joining the committee. It set up local relief committees where wages were paid at 3d an hour for a maximum 40-hour week. The scheme was castigated by Sylvia Pankhurst as Queen Mary's sweat-shops.[45]

The needs of an increasingly demanding war economy led to the setting up of a National Register in August 1915, which recorded the age and occupation of all men and women aged between 16 and 65. This was part of the growing impetus to encourage women to work. Women moved from the textile industry, which was slack, or domestic service into war work.[46]

Between July 1914 and July 1918, 1.25 million more women were in employment; of these 99 per cent were employed to fill the jobs of men who were at war.[47] The range of work women took on was much wider than is sometimes imagined. Despite legislation preventing women working in the mines, some women were employed as surface workers. 'Pitbrow lasses' were employed in the Lancashire pits, with over 3,000 in the South Lancashire coalfield.[48] Women were taken on in optical factories and as Bank of England clerks.[49] Women war workers included post women, Land Army women who worked in agriculture, drivers of butchers' and other delivery carts, members of the timber corps and nurses.[50] Women worked as carpenters at the front, bus and tram conductors and drivers, and clerks. This was in addition to the many women who worked in the intense and dangerous work in the munitions factories.

Nurses at the front were known as Voluntary Aid Detachments (VADs). There were a number of other nursing bodies and in total thousands were involved in this work. It had a major impact on their lives and took them from a sometimes very sheltered middle-class existence into a grim reality which few could have imagined. 'Nursing provided a way for substantial numbers of women who lived miles from the battleground to experience the devastating effects of war.'[51]

Later, specifically female services were established, attached first to the army with the Women's Army Auxiliary Corps in 1917 and then to the navy (WRNS) and air force (WRAFS). These were designed to fulfil support roles to free men for combat.

Few of these jobs had been done by women before. It led to changes in both attitudes and behaviour, including the clothing that women wore, with short skirts and trousers becoming more common. Critically, for the first time many women started to get involved in workplace organisation.

By 1918 women's trade union membership stood at 1,086,000, up from 357,956 in 1914 and 166,803 in 1906.[52] Many of the women employed in these new jobs came from quite different areas of work. The single largest number of women workers at the London General Omnibus Company, working as conductors and drivers during the war, had previously been domestic workers (1,245), followed by former dressmakers (355). At Armstrong Whitworth, the munitions manufacturer, of 12,000 munitions workers 3,486 had come from home, 2,513 from domestic service and 1,158 from shop work.[53]

It seems that women preferred factory work to domestic service, where they were subject to constant supervision, often treated with great indignity, paid extremely low wages and hardly allowed any free time. As Susan Grayzel points out, 'Overwhelmingly . . . women gladly left domestic service for the better pay and greater personal freedom afforded by factory work.'[54]

The best paid women tended to work in munitions, often working incredibly long hours in dangerous conditions. During six months in 1916, 41 munitions workers died as a result of TNT poisoning and in December 1916, 26 women were killed and 30 wounded in an explosion in a northern factory.[55] The huge Woolwich Arsenal munitions factory had 9,484 women working there in 1916 and 24,719 in December 1917. Increasingly, munitions relied on women, with the proportion of women in national shell factories rising from 13 per cent in 1914 to 73 per cent in July 1917. The Scottish munitions factory at Gretna employed 10,867 women in 1917, of whom 5,000–6,000 lived in hostels on site.[56] Women war workers who worked in a munitions factory in London's Grays Inn Road were a big majority: 'The factory made fuses for shells and apart from the toolmakers and the foremen all the staff were female.'[57]

Ethel Dean went into service in 1909 when she was 13 years old. She worked 14-hour days and was one of the 400,000 who went to work in the munitions industry. She had to change into overalls every morning surrounded by barrels of gunpowder. 'You wasn't allowed to wear any hairpins in your hair, no hooks and eyes in your clothes, nothing metal whatever on you, even linen buttons with metal rings.'[58]

Women worked for much lower rates of pay than men. They also came without time served in an apprenticeship, on which skilled engineers prided themselves, or with the degree of control over the job which male workers had. They were often regarded with suspicion by the men and exploited as flexible labour by the employers. As Gail Braybon and Penny Summerfield put it:

'Throughout the war, skilled men faced a dilemma. On the one hand, they wanted women to have equal pay for their own safety. On the other, they resented women earning good money, and particularly disliked married women earning high wages, as it was felt that they should be supported by their husbands, or did not "need" good wages. They saw the solution as being the removal of women from their trades.'[59]

Even before the war, mass production techniques and new technology and machinery leading to automated techniques were being used to alter the labour process in the favour of employers. This was greatly accelerated by the demands of the war itself, which needed a constant supply of shells and under which conditions employers and government were able to make investments in machinery and works facilities such as canteens and toilets for women, which 'could rarely have been undertaken subject to ordinary commercial risks'.

The main pattern of employment in making shells was not to substitute women directly for skilled men. In most cases women would be employed in new factories or new plant.[60] The first dispute over 'dilution' was at Vickers Crayford in Kent, where the company took on women to make shells in 1914 at around half the male rate. The agreement reached between the engineering employers and the unions decreed that women should not replace skilled men but work on automatic machines. This was a local agreement, followed by one between the engineering unions and the engineering employers. The Shells and Fuses agreement of 1915 covered dilution and agreed that women would get the rate for the job if they took over men's jobs, but only for the duration of the war. So women's inequality at work was enshrined in the assumption that at the end of the war they would return to the home or to lower paid 'women's work'. Equal pay only applied to piece rates, not to time rates, which were still below those of the men.[61]

However, the war also led to greater recognition that women could and should work in 'men's jobs' and that they should receive decent wages for doing so. Women themselves were campaigning for better conditions and were joining unions. The Women's Labour League organised a meeting on 'Industrialised Women after the War' which was attended by delegates from 125 trade unions and societies, nine national trade unions, 23 Cooperative Women's Guild branches, 23 ILP branches, twelve trade and labour councils, the London Labour Party, eleven League branches, three British Socialist Party branches and three Adult Schools.[62]

The question of equal pay, though far from won, was now on the agenda as a consequence of women's work in non-traditional jobs and of a growing militancy towards the end of the war. 'The whole issue of equal pay for women workers . . . first came to the fore in the 1918 London bus strike,' according to Andrew Murray.[63]

Home: Poverty and Profiteering

The combatant nations had to find means to help women and children who faced loss of family income as a result of the men going to war. Germany gave financial support to all soldiers' families from the start of the war, but this was greeted with hostility by the rest of the population who were suffering increased deprivation, and was eventually means-tested. In France allowances were means-tested from the outset. In Britain, the initially volunteer nature of the army made a difference, as Susan Grayzel explains:

> 'The combination of the need to recruit men and the power of trade unions means that a consensus emerged in Britain that allowances had to be universal, fairly administered by the state and substantial enough to counter hardship ... However, because this allowance was paid to soldiers' wives (and *de facto* wives) and was granted as a right based on a soldier's labour for the nation, women could and would be disqualified if they failed to fulfil their duty as "wives". In other words, the state saw part of its role as being obliged to scrutinise women, and infidelity and misbehaviour became grounds for the denial of this benefit.'[64]

The state stepped in to ensure that families were supported while the soldiers were at the front, but did so by increasing the state's role in surveillance of and interference in the family. They were aided by voluntary organisations such as the Voluntary Women Patrols, sponsored by the National Federation of Women Workers, and the Women Police Service (originating from the more middle-class suffragettes). 'Women employed in both organisations performed the basic tasks of policing – the street patrol – taking on the job of, among other things, separating couples found in public parks and thoroughfares.'[65]

The Central London branch of the Women's Labour League reported in 1915 that '[League] Activity had included work on the allowances paid to soldiers' and sailors' wives and the supervision of these people by the police; a circular had been issued requiring wives to register at the local police station and giving the police the right to enquire into their behaviour, make reports, visit the women at home and *admonish* them.'[66]

It seems particularly iniquitous that, at the same time as sending their men to fight, the government and its associates were enforcing control and morality on their wives and families. Matters were made worse by the fact that working-class families' living standards were being eroded by price rises in food, rents and other basics, which the government did little initially to alleviate.

One of the biggest problems facing women in particular was profiteering, and they were at the forefront of resistance to it. An increasingly militant response was the rent strike. There was a series of campaigns on housing. Women's Housing Associations were set up in Glasgow and Manchester, and Sylvia Pankhurst tried to organise a rent strike in East London over the rising costs of war.[67]

The most famous action of this campaign was the 1915 Glasgow rent strike. The situation in Glasgow, a major industrial and shipbuilding city, much of whose industry was given over to war production, reached crisis point when landlords raised rents. They could do so because there was a shortage of housing as a result of labourers coming to the city for war work who were willing to pay the higher rents.

Many of those threatened with eviction were the wives of servicemen and this caused great resentment. The women formed pickets to prevent evictions and by December 1915 the government was forced to introduce regulation in the form of the Rent Restriction Act.[68]

The Clydeside socialist Harry McShane described the rent strikes many years later:

'When the war started all the unoccupied houses were taken up by workers drafted into the workshops and shipyards for war production. The landlords immediately started to raise the rents and to apply for eviction orders against the old tenants who couldn't pay. The hardest hit were the unemployed and the elderly, and the soldiers' wives; but it even became difficult for the employed workers, despite increased wages, to meet the demands of the house-factors.

'The struggle against rent increases and evictions became keenest in Govan and Partick, where most of the skilled workers in engineering and shipbuilding lived. New workers were moving into these areas all the time; everyone was looking for a house near his work because of the long hours of overtime. Mrs Barbour organised the women in Govan to resist the rent increases. They got together to resist the sheriff officer when he came to evict anybody, and had processions 200 strong against the house-factors.'[69]

Women were particularly involved in these campaigns because many were now single-handedly trying to balance a household budget, which even before the war had been inadequate and was now stretched beyond breaking point. In addition, it was generally understood in many working-class communities that women would pay the rent out of the household budget,[70] so this particularly affected them. During a Leeds rent strike in 1914 the *Women's Dreadnought* reported: 'The women, it is said, are marching about the streets brandishing pokers, rolling pins and toasting forks, to show that they intend to protect their homes.'[71] Rent strikes led by women also took place in Birmingham, Liverpool, Dundee, Aberdeen and Ayr.[72]

Rent and food became major issues in the early years of the war, and were a focus for women who had campaigned round strikes and the suffrage before the war.

'The concern of women about food prices was so overriding that the women's council of the British Socialist Party left that party to work solely on the issue. There were strikes and agitation in the labour movement in general on rising prices and rent increases: "Shall we pay more rent?" asked the November 1915 *Labour Woman*, and gave its answer: "No".'[73]

Most of the women leaders of the Glasgow rent strike, such as Mrs Barbour and Helen Crawfurd, were members of the Independent Labour Party, which was to achieve substantial electoral success in the city after the war. They led 25,000 on rent strike by October 1915.

On 18 November 1915, in an effort to break the strike, tenants were taken to court in an attempt to get their rent deducted at source from their wages. One was an engineer from the Dalmuir shipyard. Workers there downed tools and marched to the court, joined by the Scottish socialist John Maclean. They held a street meeting and demanded to meet the sheriff of the court, who agreed. Afterwards he phoned Whitehall and was told rent restriction legislation was in the pipeline. When the Act was passed in December 1915 it pegged rents to pre-war levels. Increases would only apply if repairs had been carried out.[74]

Often former suffragists were involved in campaigning which followed on naturally from their pre-war protests. In October 1914 Ada Nield Chew represented the National Federation of Women Workers and Women's Labour League on a delegation to Rochdale Health Committee to call for health centres and a maternity centre. The cotton towns were very hard hit by the war as domestic markets collapsed. Rochdale started a scheme for feeding infants under three and their mothers in 1915, similar to one carried out by Manchester suffragists.[75] These ideas were taken up across the country as the very rudimentary welfare state was found wanting in many areas. 'An experimental model public kitchen, on the lines suggested by Ada Nield Chew, was set up in Westminster Bridge Road and supported by the League. National kitchens, with restaurants attached, were run by the Ministry of Food and local authorities to help overcome war shortages and dislocation.' There was a campaign for free school meals in order to combat problems of poverty and nutrition. Hull began to feed schoolchildren three times a day, seven days a week at the start of the war.[76]

These piecemeal reforms were led from below, often by women with a commitment to socialist or Labour politics (Labour had never been in government, but it did have ministers in the wartime coalition). The rapid rise in prices led to food protests of different sorts. Women campaigned over food supply. Groups ranging from the East London Federation of Suffragettes to the Fabian Women's Group raised issues like milk depots, cost-price restaurants, meals for schoolchildren, prices and food production.[77] This was a continuation of activity that had taken place before the war. Margaretta Hicks from the British Socialist Party argued for direct action on prices from 1912 when there were many strikes over the high cost of living. There was a reported strike in Edmonton over the price of milk where women boycotted fresh milk until its price came down, as 'A strike for better terms is of no utility if the price of bacon and cheese, milk, coal and rent goes up.'[78]

The government belatedly intervened. The first Ministry of Food National Kitchen was opened by Queen Mary on 21 May 1917.

Love: Against the Law?

More work opportunities and changing social attitudes altered women's outlook. By the end of the war, women had modified their appearance and behaviour. They wore shorter skirts and cut their hair, were more likely to go out on their own and took to 'drinking alcohol and smoking cigarettes publicly'.[79]

During the war there was an attempt to limit alcohol consumption with the introduction of licensing hours and the diluting of alcohol. It was felt that all-day pub opening and general drunkenness damaged the war industries and undermined morale. But 'more and more women began to make use of public houses during the war . . . includ[ing] more members of the middle class and respectable working class than previously'.[80] It is likely that this was connected with women's more public role, their increased hours of work, their greater access to independent incomes and simply the strains of war and the fear of the death of family members.

Attitudes to sex and marriage also changed. Again, this process was already underway. By the beginning of the twentieth century women on the Left were discussing limiting the number of children they had by practising birth control, although information on contraception was still considered subversive in most countries and those disseminating it were likely to face at best social ostracism, at worst legal sanction.[81]

Nevertheless, the beginning of the twentieth century saw the start of the long trend towards smaller families and the increasing use of contraception among skilled and white-collar workers. The rapid decline in fertility was most marked among the working classes, a decline achieved mainly by 'natural' means of birth control.[82]

The war led to changed attitudes towards sex, given the level of upheaval and danger now prevalent in society. Some of them were bizarre, as in the case of the cleric in Bristol who wanted to arrange marriages between women and wounded soldiers in 1915.[83] Others reflected the much wider changing social circumstances which affected even upper-class girls. The challenge to pre-war conventions which only affected a minority of New Women in the years before the war now became much more commonplace, despite the reservations of many. 'In all classes war brought about a loosening of social convention, and as time went on, and girls who had never before earned money or been free of chaperonage found themselves independent, their elders were sometimes horrified by their behaviour.'[84]

While sex outside marriage does not appear to have reached anything near the levels seen in the Second World War, it did increase. The number of children born outside marriage in England and Wales nearly doubled between 1914 and 1917, but fell again in 1918.[85]

There were also many scares about prostitution and sexually transmitted diseases. The main line of attack on promiscuity and venereal disease was against the women themselves, who were regarded as prostitutes. Some were referred to as 'amateur girls', meaning that they were unpaid prostitutes. The Bishop of London launched a 'Cleansing London' campaign in 1916, which attacked any woman who might be seen in this light.[86] A Canadian woman journalist referred to women prostitutes as 'vast hordes of vampires who have been allowed to prey upon the soldier on leave'. She demanded night courts to try these women.[87] Margaret Damer Dawson, a woman police commander, reflected that

'It's all so one-sided, so unjust to women. They talk as if men were innocent angels, helpless in the hands of wicked women – many of them have worked for the starvation wages women used to get, and they have found a way of earning as many pounds in a night as they used to earn shillings in a week.'[88]

The state once again imposed draconian measures. The Defence of the Realm Act (DORA) Regulation 13A, introduced in 1916, gave military authorities the power to expel prostitutes from specific areas where they might encounter soldiers. Regulation 40D of March 1918 forbade women with a venereal disease from soliciting or having sexual relations with soldiers. Women could be forcibly examined and imprisoned under these laws. By October 1918 there had been 203 prosecutions. Most suffrage organisations opposed the law.[89]

State intervention could also have a positive side. It enabled those who wanted to achieve change for women, especially in the family and childcare, to press their case for permanent change once the war was over. 'World War One was the turning-point in agitation for state support for maternity. Panic about racial "degeneracy" contributed to a public mood which enabled labour organisations to push for reforms.'[90] It was proposed that there should be an extension of government separation allowances to soldiers' wives so that they became a form of family allowance.[91] As we shall see, some of these reforms did leave a permanent legacy.

After the War: What Happened to Women?

The war led to much greater state direction of industry and society. Laws ranged from those controlling sexual relations to those prohibiting strikes in war industries and limiting the consumption of alcohol. Although some of these laws were repealed after the war, they marked the beginning of greater state intervention in the lives of all citizens. Most women saw changes as a result of the war.

Perhaps the one most anticipated was the vote. Many of the young men dying in the trenches were not entitled to vote – an increasingly anomalous position; nor were many of the women who played such a vital role in war work. The Labour Party conference of 1916 was addressed by the veteran suffrage campaigner Charlotte Despard, who had broken with the Pankhursts in 1907.[92] Sylvia Pankhurst and Catherine Marshall from the NUWSS called for the inclusion of women in any franchise extension.

Demonstrations were held to demand the vote. Sylvia Pankhurst called for human suffrage and in October 1916 the National Council for Adult Suffrage was established.[93] However, there was still disagreement about the age at which women would be granted the vote – a reflection of the determination of some in government to avoid granting them full equality.[94]

The Representation of the People Bill was introduced in Parliament in June 1917 and passed through the House of Lords in 1918. The Act though failed to give women the vote on the same terms as men. All men were now enfranchised from the age of 21 whereas only women aged over 30 with certain property qualifications were given the vote. It took another decade for women to become enfranchised on the same basis as men. The denial of the franchise particularly affected many of the women who had made such a contribution to war work. There was also a certain element of anti-climax about it, given the years of campaigning before the war.

The first sitting woman MP was Constance Markiewicz, though as a Sinn Fein member in Ireland she refused to take her seat, which meant that the first woman MP was the Tory Lady Nancy Astor. The women who had campaigned so hard for the vote failed to get elected.

The government justified giving some women the vote as a tribute to the valuable work they had done during the war. There were in fact more fundamental reasons. It was increasingly untenable to grant all men the vote while denying it to any women. Once the class element was taken out of the franchise, as it was through the recognition that soldiers and workers were entitled to vote, it was difficult to deny it purely on the basis of gender, although the government did try.

There was also the fear of growing radicalisation as a result of the war: the first belligerent nation to give women the vote was revolutionary Russia on 20 July 1917.[95] Defeated Germany, in the middle of its own revolution which swept away the Kaiser and established a republic, issued a decree enfranchising women on 30 November 1918. The lessons were not lost on Lloyd George and his fellow politicians. Finally, while it may have been onerous for suffrage organisations to have to start campaigning again at the end of the war, it would have been even harder for the government to resist them.[96]

The radicalism seen towards the end of the war continued. In 1919 the strikes which had ended so abruptly nearly five years earlier erupted again with increased bitterness. That year soldiers who had not yet been demobbed mutinied.[97] While the immediate threat from the strikes and mutinies was contained, there were political reconfigurations.

Some of the women who had campaigned before and during the war, such as Sylvia Pankhurst and Helen Crawfurd, became revolutionary socialists, linking their campaigning on women's issues to much wider questions of changing society. The British Communist Party was formed, bringing together many of the disparate socialist groups and individuals under the influence of the Russian revolution.

The feminists who had had such an impact, especially through the suffrage movement, now tended to abandon separate organisation. The Women's Trade Union League and National Federation of Women Workers merged with the mainstream unions. The Women's Labour League was incorporated into the Labour Party as the Women's Sections in 1918. By the end of 1922 there were over 1,000 with a membership of 120,000.[98] The women's movement tended to fragment after the war, some women campaigning on birth control, others on peace and internationalism, and still others for the full franchise.[99]

The women who had played such a big part in war work were treated abominably even before its end. Many lost their jobs. Two days before the Armistice, 6,000 women mainly from Woolwich Arsenal marched to Parliament to protest at being laid off. There was a similar huge demonstration in Glasgow.[100] Women like these were removed from the official unemployment figures in February 1919 on the grounds that their normal work no longer existed. Women who worked in engineering or munitions were reclassified according to their pre-war occupations. They were therefore excluded from the unemployed insurance scheme.[101]

Despite manipulating the figures, by early 1919 nearly half a million women and 26,700 girls under 18 were officially unemployed.[102] It was widely accepted that men had priority over jobs that were available and that women should return to the home. There were often considerable battles over this, with much resistance and resentment on the part of the women. Some were able to hang on for a while but eventually lost their jobs. Women tram conductors in Cardiff and Bristol, for example, were eventually forced out in favour of men in 1920.[103]

Women munitions workers were offered lay-off pay at 13 weeks on a benefit of 25 shillings a week (far below their usual wage) in December 1918. To receive this, they had to sign on daily. Women were often denied benefit for refusing domestic work. Yet women did not want to return to the pre-war years, and especially not to the hated, low-paid domestic work. At one Labour Exchange only one woman out of 3,000 registered as willing to go into service.[104]

Yet attitudes were changing, not just in terms of women refusing such work, but also in the growing recognition that women both wanted and often were obliged to work. A conference on Women's Right to Work was organised by the Women's International League in Manchester in September 1919. They demanded equal pay, the right of entry to any trade and the raising of women's minimum wage, and condemned the dismissal of women from government employment.[105]

The war put equal pay on the agenda. Raised in the 1918 bus workers' strike, by the end of the war it was one of Sylvia Pankhurst's aims in East London.[106] Before the war the demand had been opposed by some reformers such as Beatrice Webb, who thought women would lose employment if it happened, and Eleanor Rathbone, because it would lead to job segregation.[107] But women's entry into 'men's work' – even if many of them were peremptorily forced out of it again – weakened these arguments and made it a campaigning point on the trade union and Left agenda. However, it still would not be granted even nominally until well after the Second World War when women's work was even more central to the war effort.

Although women were booted out of men's jobs, more women began to go out to work after the First World War. The expansion of white-collar work absorbed many of them, as did the new industries – electrical engineering and car and aircraft manufacturing. The former in particular employed many young women completely new to industry.[108]

For upper-class women the world was also changing. In 1920 women received degrees from Oxford for the first time. The feminists Winifred Holtby and Vera Brittain were two of the beneficiaries.[109] The breakthrough into higher education was, until the 1960s, only possible for a very small minority. But it did enable an increase in the number of women doctors, teachers and other professionals and gave that minority of women some sense of purpose which had long been denied them.

Many of the women who had campaigned for the vote before the war and a range of welfare issues during it now tried to consolidate some of the gains which had been made. Hannah Mitchell became a Labour councillor and campaigned for a municipal wash-house in Manchester.[110] Agnes Dollan, active in the Glasgow rent strike, became the first woman ILP councillor in 1919. In 1918 the Maternal and Child Welfare Act established clinics for pregnant women and children.[111]

What is sometimes called 'municipal socialism' expanded between 1918 and 1921. This took various forms: the provision of local authority housing, sanctioned by central government (although the new houses were often beyond the reach of the poorest), free school milk in working-class areas and family allowances, which were of special benefit to women.[112]

The motivation for the Poplar councillors in 1921, who defied central government by refusing to set a rate that would penalise their constituents – some of the poorest in London – was the desire to improve the health and welfare of the people of the East End. But it also drew inspiration from the campaigning of the previous decade, from the East London Federation of Suffragettes, from George Lansbury's pacifist socialism and from the Russian revolution of 1917.[113] The decision to defy the law, even though it meant imprisonment, and the mass support the councillors received in the East End, was the result of these long years of campaigning.

A final feature of the postwar world was the number of women who might have expected to marry but who now found that unlikely or much harder to achieve. With nearly one million British war dead alone, it was estimated that there were one million 'surplus women'. The 1921 census revealed that there were 1.75 million more women than men.[114] Women had to find ways of living which accommodated to that fact. Few had the option of not working. The burden of caring for the many physically and mentally injured former soldiers also fell predominantly on women.

No one who lived through the war could fail to be affected by it. It was often called the war to end all wars, but many felt that was more an aspiration than a reality. Those who had campaigned so vehemently against the war continued to do so in a world where peace seemed increasingly precarious. Some did from a socialist or communist stance, others as pacifists, who believed that all wars were immoral. Pacifism was expressed through organisations such as the Peace Pledge Union or the Quakers.

Sylvia Pankhurst devoted her energies during the 1930s to opposing Mussolini's intervention in Abyssinia, while the bulk of the Left and much of the working-class movement saw the civil war in Spain as the dress rehearsal for another world war. In this they were right as fascism's influence spread from Italy and Germany. Some women abandoned their pacifist principles to call for rearmament in the face of the fascist threat. Edith Summerskill won a by-election in Fulham for Labour on that slogan in 1938, as anti-war activists became increasingly horrified at the government's appeasement of Hitler.[115] She, like many others, believed that history was about to repeat itself, only 20 years after the last war had ended.

2
The Home Front, 1939–45

How long ago Hector took off his plume,
Not wanting that his little son should cry,
Then kissed his sad Andromache goodbye –
And now we three in Euston waiting-room.

Frances Cornford, 'Parting in Wartime'

The coming of war in 1939 had long been feared and predicted. In this respect it took on a different character from the First World War. Despite the extravagant claims for the 1919 Treaty of Versailles and the hopes placed in the League of Nations for permanent peace, by the 1930s fascist governments were in power in Italy and Germany. Wars of aggression were being fought in China and Abyssinia, the Spanish civil war had ended in defeat for the democratically elected left-wing government and Hitler's expansionism was met with appeasement, symbolised by the 1938 Munich agreement, which effectively handed Czechoslovakia to Germany.

Military advances meant aerial bombardment was now one of the greatest threats. In the 1930s there were unsuccessful attempts to have aerial bombing made illegal on the grounds that it constituted a war crime.[1] Its devastating use in Spain signalled what was to come.

The Spanish civil war galvanised public opinion in Britain and abroad. Victory in Spain for General Franco, who had staged a military putsch against the Republican government in July 1936, would usher in a fascist dictatorship and strengthen Hitler in his expansionist ambitions.

Around 2,000 British people joined the International Brigades, made up of committed left-wingers and communists, who went

41

to fight in Spain. Among them were women, who also went as nurses and journalists. One early casualty was Felicia Browne, an artist already in Barcelona when war broke out and killed early on during a military advance into Aragon.[2]

The small minority who actually fought were backed by many more at home, who tried to build solidarity for them. Mass meetings were held: 7,000 went to the Albert Hall in November 1936 to support a Spanish Medical Aid rally, where Isobel Brown organised a collection which raised £2,000 in half an hour.[3]

Working-class people, already suffering unemployment and poverty, identified with the Spanish republicans. In West Ham, the Young Communists collecting for a food ship took in 50 tins of milk, 20 tins of coffee and 35lb of sugar in two hours. In the mining communities of South Wales, according to the miners' union leader Will Paynter, 'there wasn't a home, facing the impoverishment that they were facing, that wouldn't make a contribution . . . to help the fight of the Spanish people.'[4] Women played a leading role in this solidarity work, helping to bring orphans from the Basque town of Guernica to Britain in 1937. They were also involved in helping to get Jewish refugees out of Nazi Germany and Austria in 1938 against the background of Chamberlain's policy of appeasement.

Fear of an air war led to emergency measures, although they were often regarded as inadequate. The British government issued the population with gas masks in anticipation of gas attacks on the pattern of the First World War, though in the event none came.

The provision of shelters, recruitment of air raid wardens and, most importantly, the evacuation of children from the cities were all severely tested when war broke out and would have been found wanting without decisive intervention from ordinary people.

The failure of government to adapt quickly enough and with sufficient resources caused discontent. Public sentiment was very different from the jingoism of 1914, and direct experience of the First World War led to much greater scepticism about the second. France's defensive fortification along the Franco-German border – the Maginot Line – anticipated trench warfare, which was rapidly made superfluous by the German *Blitzkrieg* which swept through Belgium and into France. The occupation of most European countries by the Germans for most of the war also changed the pattern of warfare. There was much greater reliance on airpower and on direct repression and conscription of national populations. In the later years of the war in particular, sections of these populations themselves took on the occupying forces. The resistance movements or partisans played decisive roles in France, Italy, Yugoslavia and Greece.

Women, from code-breakers and partisan fighters to those who joined the armed forces, played a direct role in war. They had little choice, for the exceptional circumstances in which they found themselves required an exceptional response. In the process many developed a radical political consciousness about the world and how it could be better ordered in the future.

The Second World War was won industrially as much as militarily. The production of ever more destructive weaponry on a grand scale was essential to victory. The protection and welfare of the state's citizens on the home front was also essential to its success. There was therefore a major role for women, especially in Britain and the United States, who took on work which had previously been done by men or entered new jobs for which a large workforce was needed.

Britain had a unique role in the Second World War. It suffered the threat of invasion, major bombing campaigns, with deadly V2 rockets landing in the final weeks of the war, evacuation, rationing and high levels of war production. This was different from the situation in the United States, which joined the war in 1941 but which suffered virtually no direct attacks and where domestic consumption remained high. It was very different too from the occupied countries or those like the Soviet Union where major battles led to massive losses.

No other country conscripted women on the scale that Britain did, and that had a major impact on how women's roles changed. Unlike both the United States, where women were not obliged to work in war industry, and Germany, where there was little conscription of women, in Britain conscription was introduced almost from the outset.[5] Eighty per cent of the increase in the workforce between 1939 and 1943 comprised women who had never worked before or those who had been housewives.[6]

No Escape: Evacuation, Rationing and Bombing

War disrupted family life, first due to evacuation and then to the bombing itself. Evacuation began even before war was officially declared. On 1 September 1939, children were sent with their teachers to the countryside to be billeted in people's homes. Pregnant women and mothers of under-fives also went. In the first week 1.5 million people were evacuated, although this was around half the pre-war expectation.[7]

There were very ambivalent feelings about evacuation and very mixed experiences. Some children were well looked after and got on well with their hosts. Others found their billets inhospitable if not actually unfriendly. While the scheme was not compulsory, it was strongly encouraged. Women living in others' homes found it stressful; there were sometimes stark class differences. According to one Women's Voluntary Service organiser: 'over and over again . . . it really is the poor people who are willing to take evacuees and . . . the sort of bridge-playing set who live in such places as Chorleywood [a wealthy village in the commuter belt of Hertfordshire] are terribly difficult about it all.'[8] But bombing was relatively light for the first year of the war, and many families brought their children home. By March 1940, a million had returned.[9]

Their reasons were no doubt complex, but as well as the perception that there was not the immediate danger predicted at the outbreak of war, there was clearly a sense among many families that they would rather be together whatever the dangers. Official reports on public opinion during 1940 revealed that in Nottingham on 30 May, 'Bus conductors are stopping alarmist chatter by women about evacuation. Common opinion is that children are not safe anywhere so why bother to evacuate them',[10] while in London on 15 June, following a speech by a government minister on evacuation, 'CAB [Citizens' Advice Bureaux] secretaries report "Terrifying effect" of sentence in

Macdonald's evacuation speech in House, e.g. "the Government cannot absolutely guarantee the children's safety". Women ran about housing estates crying and wanting to get children back.'[11]

According to a report in the summer of 1940, 'Typical remarks made by . . . women are these: the Government have taken our husbands – they won't get our children"'.[12] Some feared that the areas which took evacuees were dangerous, and mothers did not want their children suffering when apart from them. So children evacuated to Wales were brought back in 1940 because of the bombing there.[13] The return of children created many problems, not least that they were perceived as being out of control. Whole schools were evacuated in many cases, so children who stayed at home often missed months of education, as well as missing out on school meals and milk.[14] More children were evacuated again after the Blitz began in London in September 1940 and when other cities experienced heavy bombing raids.[15]

Class issues surfaced during evacuation. Public schools evacuated to comfortable premises with their country-based equivalents. The rich could rent homes many miles from the threat of bombing or invasion. The well-off often evacuated their own children across the Atlantic, to the United States or Canada. Those who headed for the United States read like a rich list: the Guinnesses, Rothschilds and Hambros, a wide section of aristocracy, Lord Mountbatten's wife and children, the son of the politician Duff Cooper and the son of the press baron Lord Rothermere.[16] Vera Brittain, the feminist and pacifist intellectual who had written so movingly of her experiences as a nurse during the First World War, agonised, but eventually sent her two children to stay with friends in the United States.[17]

Rumours that the Princesses Elizabeth and Margaret had taken this route were untrue, although they did live at Windsor during the Blitz, and the King and Queen returned there every night.[18] Newsreel of transatlantic evacuees arriving in the United States was hissed in a Winchester cinema.[19] There were some attempts to extend the scheme to poorer children, but it was unsuccessful, partly because working-class mothers were reluctant to part with their children over such a distance and partly because Churchill feared it would encourage defeatism.[20]

Food rationing was introduced in January 1940. The supply of most basics was controlled and people had to register with particular shopkeepers to receive their ration. Butter, sugar and bacon or ham were the first items to be rationed, followed by meat. Later, tea, margarine and cooking fats were added, then cheese and jam. Tea, rationed from the summer of 1940, hit the working class particularly hard.[21] Shortages of eggs and milk led to the supply of dried eggs.

However, rationing did allow equal distribution of food and there is some evidence that nutritional standards for poorer people improved.[22] Yet rationing imposed a degree of regulation which was unwelcome and food that was not rationed was only available, if at all, after hours of queuing. Still, rationing was widely considered to be fair, even though prices rose rapidly, which caused some discontented grumblings,[23] as in London in July 1940.[24] There was also a great deal of resentment of the rich who could eat in restaurants and who could afford luxury foods. Partly in response to these complaints, in autumn 1940 the first British Restaurants opened. These provided cheap and nutritious food, at first for those bombed out by the Blitz, but later for everyone. Any sizeable town had one and eventually London County Council provided 250.[25]

By the summer of 1940, the war in Britain had reached a critical stage. France had been defeated and Nazi Germany was in control of continental Europe. The British and French armies had been badly defeated, with the British army forced to evacuate from Dunkirk. With the United States and Soviet Union still a long way from joining the war, the only forms of defence Britain had were the Navy and Air Force, which fought a battle of the skies in the summer of 1940 – a battle which it was by no means assured in winning.

The coalition government headed by Winston Churchill but with a number of Labour ministers, replaced the discredited Chamberlain government. Many Tories were still appeasers and there was much ruling-class pressure to sue for peace. But

Churchill, a pro-Empire Tory, was in *de facto* alliance with the anti-fascist Left.

The effect of the war on the consciousness of women, especially in the run-up to the Blitz, shows a level of resentment of bureaucracy and inefficiency, coupled with a growing militancy and determination. It was reported from Scotland on 7 June that 'Working-class Edinburgh women say they will fight the Germans in the streets if men can't stop them.' Days later, 'Nottingham women want to be armed with rifles and hand grenades', while in Leeds on 18 June it was said that 'people demand that whole nation should be armed.'[26]

These sentiments coincided with the formation of the Local Defence Volunteers, who became known as the Home Guard, in the summer of 1940. Women were not allowed to join, although the MP Edith Summerskill was eventually allowed to become a member of the House of Commons Home Guard.[27] Initially, they were not issued with working weapons so the scheme fell somewhat short of arming the whole nation as Leeds people had demanded.

There were constant worries about morale among women in particular, given the dangers they faced. Women were slower to recover from the shock of the news and more prone to mood swings than men, according to a survey taken during the abortive Norwegian campaign in April 1940. Women were more likely to stop reading newspapers or listening to the radio if the news was bad.[28] It was thought that there was more disquiet among middle- and upper-class women, whereas among working-class women there was more likely to be bewilderment.[29] One professional expressed the view that 'It should not be forgotten that working-class women are less well informed, and better able to put aside future fears than women in the better-off classes of the community, but these generalizations do not enable one to express any opinion on possible breakdowns in morale among working class women.'[30] It is hard to see these views as anything other than condescending.

While surveys seem to show women were less familiar with some issues than men and sometimes tried to ignore them, there is also much which points in the other direction. There is some evidence that working-class women were keen to prosecute the war and some also that they resented those who prevented this. One report in June 1940 noted: 'Poplar women angry at able-bodied men spending their time at greyhound racing.'[31]

There was a lot of foot-dragging, obstruction and stupidity from officials in relation to the need for mass mobilisation and a total war economy. This reflected inefficiency in the run-up to war and in its early months, but it also developed from ruling-class divisions. The British government had until May 1940 been headed by appeasers who had wanted to avoid war with Germany and they still maintained strong support in the Conservative Party. Lack of preparations reflected their passivity in the face of military threat. They also feared allowing too much popular mobilisation among ordinary civilians, which they thought could lead to radicalism and socialism. Fears of socialist revolution were greater than the fear of fascism. As the historian A. J. P. Taylor put it, 'It would be the Spanish civil war all over again.'[32]

Many women wanted to contribute but were prevented from doing so. In London in June 1940, 'Business and professional women [are] extremely annoyed at their non-mobilisation by Government.' In the same month, the 'Federation of Women's Employment reports "inundated with enquiries about employment from women of professional class and well educated type – ages 25 to 60. Discontent felt when no employment available".'[33]

The ever-present threat of bombing was the main danger for those not in the armed forces. The provision of safe shelters was of immediate concern. The government-approved Anderson shelters were built in many gardens and enabled people to take shelter without massive disruption to domestic life. But Anderson shelters offered poor protection and anyone living in flats or homes without gardens had to rely on communal shelters.

Government fears about a 'shelter mentality', which would lead to Londoners staying in the shelters, cost many lives. The plan in the Borough of Finsbury for a mass deep shelter which could accommodate the whole population was rejected by the government because it would concentrate too many people in one place.[34] But talk about air raid precautions and shelters could not hide the fact that a sustained heavy air attack would show many shelters to be inadequate. Some areas attempted to organise systems for coping with air raids. In London in June 1940 it was reported that 'Fulham Housing Estate has a democratic system in operation of shelter marshals and their helpers chosen by tenants', while 'Hackney women [are] arranging to take in each other's families if blocks of flats are hit; less neighbourliness shown in streets of private houses.'[35] These informal arrangements were often in advance of the authorities and there was rising criticism of the failure to make sufficient provision. People began to take action. In Newcastle in the summer of 1940 'successful communist demonstrations demanding better ARP shelters, etc. were held'.[36] By early September 'people in poor areas [were] using makeshift shelters.'[37]

The London Blitz began on 7 September 1940. A night of repeated bombing, mainly of the docks and the surrounding areas in east London, left 430 dead and 1,600 seriously injured. The bombing continued every night for several months and struck many parts of London. In the first three weeks the fire brigades tackled 10,000 fires.[38] A shelter in Columbia Road in east London took a direct hit, killing 40 people.[39] The next night another 412 were killed and 747 injured, and on the third night 370 died, including 73 killed in a Canning Town school where families already made homeless by bombing were sheltering; a further 1,400 were wounded.[40]

While fire-fighters and defence workers demonstrated considerable courage, as did the local population, many of those able to leave London did so. 9 September marked an exodus, with Paddington Station crammed with people heading west.[41] It was clear that the East End was being hit by far the hardest and also that the shelters there were much worse than those in the wealthier areas. There was talk of marching on the clubs and hotels in the West End from Stepney and the Isle of Dogs. Reports on 12 September noted that 'many people [are] taking rugs and cushions from poor districts to spend [the] nights in

West End shelters'.[42] The public shelters were often cramped, with rudimentary or no sanitation.

Angela Sinclair, an Oxford undergraduate, felt she could not continue studying when the war broke out and initially trained as nurse, but did not take to it:

> 'A young man I'd met at Oxford wrote to me and said, "I've found something I really like doing called the Friends Ambulance Unit in London". This was the beginning of the Blitz and I thought, that's just the stuff, so I joined the FAU [Friends' Ambulance Unit] who of course were Quakers. I realised it was a pacifist movement and I discovered pacifism. It was called that because in the First World War they drove ambulances, but in the Second World War they didn't. It wasn't that sort of war so they had people working in hospitals and in the air raid shelters and rest centres looking after people. I worked in the shelters in Wapping.'

Angela worked in great danger:

> 'I remember going to work one night, we worked all night, I was taking the underground and an incendiary bomb fell onto the rails in front of me. I didn't know what to do because they could explode, I couldn't see any station staff and I didn't know whether the driver would see it.
>
> 'I remember one quite exciting incident. I don't remember which night, but there were several nights during the Blitz which were famous for real carpet bombing. I remember the London ones – there were bombs everywhere and fires everywhere and a wounded fireman (I think he fell off his ladder) was brought to our shelter so we could help him get care. We wanted to take him to hospital but he refused saying his wife would be worried.
>
> 'I went to the nearest phone box to telephone his wife. Like an idiot it didn't occur to me whether the phones would be working or not but quite amazingly they were. I didn't have a torch with me. But I could see because there were fires all around. What was strange was it looked like there was snow on the ground – it was all white. It was beer: they'd hit a brewery and there was foaming beer running down the street. So I put in my 2d and made my phone call.'[43]

The city was devastated: buildings were destroyed, whole streets disappeared, water and gas mains ruptured and railway lines were bombed. It was clear that the authorities were incapable of coping with such a massive bombardment. Indeed, the local authorities in parts of East London, Stepney and West Ham were regarded as so inefficient that their functions were taken over by central government.

Resources were minimal in the poorest areas, where food, shelter and other necessities of life were woefully inadequate. Homelessness was a major problem. Many volunteer workers, journalists and campaigners were bitterly critical of local and central government which presided over this. The journalist 'Ritchie Calder brings sad tales back from the Isle of Dogs where people are just wandering around like unclaimed mongrels, too stunned to even ask where they can get food and a new home and dragging their bits of bedding and children about with them.'[44] Perhaps the greatest government failure was the refusal to open the London underground stations as shelters until the government was forced to do so. East Enders had demanded this from the beginning of the Blitz. The author Bernard Kops, then a teenager living in Whitechapel, describes how on 8 September he joined

'thousands upon thousands . . . that pushed their way into Liverpool Street Station, demanded to be let down to shelter. At first the authorities wouldn't agree to it and they called out the soldiers to bar the way . . . The people would not give up and would not disperse, would not take no for an answer. A great yell went up and the gates were opened . . . "It's a great victory for the working class," a man said. "One of our big victories."'[45]

The Communist Party led the campaign to open the London stations, arguing that the rich in the West End had superb shelters in the basements of hotels and clubs, and that the refusal of the government to provide protection from air raids was due to its class outlook and its priority of profit. The view from the government and the civil service was that they did not want to encourage a 'shelter mentality'. But there was no such a mentality. Their concern was one more illustration of a condescending and bureaucratic attitude, especially to working-class people, which at the beginning of the war led to inefficient and therefore counterproductive responses to the air raids. This caused growing class anger and radicalisation, which heightened as the war went on.

The first weeks of the Blitz saw many people taking direct action by refusing to leave the stations and simply occupying them. The Communist Party continued its agitation, keeping the stations open and organising the homeless to occupy the Savoy Hotel shelters. Phil Piratin, an East End communist who was elected MP in 1945, described how they demanded tea and bread and butter at the price charged in Lyons Corner Houses. At first they were refused, but it was impossible for management to evict them during an air raid, and soon 'the trollies and the silver trays laden with pots of tea and bread and butter' were delivered.[46] It was another victory.

In early October the government bowed to pressure and gradually allowed Londoners to take shelter in the tube stations. Over the following months money was spent on making a number of the stations sanitary and habitable with the erection of bunks and the provision of food and entertainment, despite the class instincts of those in government. A report sent to the Labour MP Herbert Morrison, Minister of Supply in the coalition government, for example, claimed that it was 'undesirable to give excessive publicity regarding Christmas festivities and general amenities provided in shelters'.[47] Angela Sinclair, working in the Stepney shelters, recalls the problems:

'In the East End there were a lot of Jews. There were a lot of Irish who built the docks who were on one side of the Commercial Road and there were a lot of Jewish immigrants who came mostly from Russia around 1905; you could tell because the shops mostly had different names like The Star, not the names of persons, but where they did they had Russian or German names. The Jews and Irish didn't mix at all and in the air raids they had their own shelters.

'The shelters were pretty terrible because the Home Office had already invented Anderson shelters which were very unpopular – they were cold, with just corrugated iron over your head.

'People did feel safe in the docks because they had these enormous warehouses but the Home Office wouldn't supply them as shelters because they were so close to the river. So we were in these unheated shelters.

'That's when I started smoking, because they used charcoal to heat the shelters and these braziers would smoke terribly and the smoke gets in your throat.'[48]

In fact, two things encouraged her to take up smoking:

'First of all, I couldn't understand what these Cockneys were saying: in wartime there was always this pally feeling and they were very sweet to me and would offer me cigarettes. I didn't want to refuse because that would have looked unfriendly. So it was partly that and partly the fumes from the charcoal that started me smoking.'[49]

Bombing hit many of the major cities in Britain. In the autumn of 1940 there were attacks on Liverpool, Birmingham, Plymouth, Swansea and Coventry. The bombing of Coventry on 14–15 November 1940 was the worst. The intense bombardment which destroyed much of the city became known as Coventration and left 568 dead and 1,200 injured. 'A civilian had a 60 per cent greater chance of being killed or seriously wounded during that one night in Coventry than during the whole six years of the war elsewhere.'[50]

The effect of this bombing was devastating: the physical and mental injury alone had a profound impact on everyday life and women bore the brunt of it. Children were evacuated, and this continued in waves after intensified periods of bombing; and they were often kept out of education for this reason or because the schools had closed. There was extensive homelessness and water supplies were disrupted, replacement furniture or cooking utensils were hard to obtain, food expensive and in short supply. The blackout, during which no house lights could be seen from the street and there was no street lighting, was reportedly one of the things women especially found most irritating.[51]

Increasing numbers of women were in paid work and both they and men worked very long hours. The sheer grind of trying to maintain a family routine needed much more work than usual.

One woman in a working-class area of Birmingham wrote in October 1940 shortly after one of the worst raids in the city about her preparation to go to the Anderson shelter: 'If there is a meal imminent I lay it on the tray as I prepare it. If we are expecting a raid we sit down to the table with the meal on the tray but if we are all having a meal I lay the table and have the tray handy where I can just put the things on it. Our eating habits are just the same.'[52]

Yet behind this attempt to carrying on as normal, many women, especially mothers, were deeply apprehensive. As one Mass Observation report from December 1940 stated:

'But all the time, behind their grumbles about the war and its prosecution, or determination not to complain, there still appeared the constant worry as to how to make ends meet; economic worries about prices, wages, shopping; psychological anxieties about blackout, parting from husbands and children.'[53]

Women were on the front line much of the time. They were, in effect, combatants, since the battle of London of 1940–41 was an attempt to destroy the social and economic existence of the city, and everyone who worked during the bombing was both under fire and part of the struggle to save the city. This was immensely empowering.

Many women put themselves in even greater danger by working in civil defence and the various occupations created to deal with the air raids and their impact, as well as the general crisis and dislocation which accompanied the war. Around one sixth of those who became Air Raid Precaution wardens were women although, like the women who joined the armed forces, they were paid lower rates than the men: in 1943 ARP women received £2 15s a week whereas men got £3 18s 6d.[54] Others worked as ambulance drivers, in shelters like Angela Sinclair, as fire watchers, on observation posts, organised mobile canteens for men clearing the bomb sites or staffed reception centres for those bombed out. A Mass Observation writer who worked as a volunteer on mobile canteens spoke of driving a large and unwieldy van round the ruins of Bloomsbury and Soho to hand out meat pies and cakes in the autumn of 1940:

> 'At one of our last pitches of the day in Charing Cross Road again, we had a bit of excitement. There was a raid on again – about the fourth of the day, I think – and suddenly we heard planes and loud gunfire. Each detonation swayed the van astonishingly, and I saw a number of people running on the pavements.'[55]

The bombing affected even those whose direct experience was not the worst. Vera Brittain's 1940 diary recalls her driving with some difficulty from her privileged home in west London to see for herself the bomb damage in the East End and the City. She commented on the children playing amidst the devastation created by the miles of bomb sites and wondered at parents who refused to evacuate their children.[56]

The worst period was 1940–41 and it affected many of the urban areas. People left to live in the countryside, so poor was the provision of shelters and so great the fear. In Clydebank outside Glasgow, bombing in March 1941 left 35,000 out of a total population of 47,000 homeless; only seven out of a total 12,000 tenements were undamaged.[57] Liverpool, a major Atlantic port where much convoy food and equipment was loaded, was raided for seven nights in May 1941. Heavy air raids took place in Plymouth, Belfast, Newcastle, Hull, Bristol and many other cities.

Jackie Mulhallen, a Stop the War activist from King's Lynn, describes her family's experience when she was an infant:

> 'I do not remember the event, but the story will show that I was conscious of it. My mother told me that my grandfather, who had cancer, was outside shutting an outbuilding for the night when a German plane coming back from bombing Plymouth started shooting at him. She was watching with me in her arms, with her mother. They were terrified for him, as he couldn't run, and when they looked at me they realised that I was very shocked. My mother dates my astigmatism from then. He eventually got back into the house safely. My other grandfather was killed when a bomb fell on his house in 1943. The plane was just emptying their bombs on the way

back from Plymouth. It was not a strategic area and was the only house to be bombed.'[58]

From the summer of 1941 the intensive daily bombing declined, but there were still the retaliatory ('Baedeker') raids in 1942, which targeted historic towns, then resumed bombing from 1943 in London and finally the rocket attacks, which began in the summer of 1944 with the doodlebugs (V1s) and continued with the V2s until 1945. Florence Davy described a rocket attack on Dalston library which killed a number of staff and the vicar's wife.[59]

Bombing remained a part of people's everyday reality throughout the war in London. A teenager in Hoxton described doodlebugs hitting her estate in 1944, but that after the alarm the women continued to prepare their Sunday lunch. She was certain a doodlebug was heading for their flats:

'I was getting hysterical, I just knew that the bloody thing was coming; the fact that you don't hear it tells you it's heading for you, you see because all the noise is sort of carried away . . . I virtually got hold of my mother and I dragged her . . . we just about got to the shelter, when there was this terrible noise . . .we all rushed into the shelter . . . and then there was this terrible noise like a whip crack.'

The windows in her block of flats were blown out and the adjacent block collapsed. Her friend's parents were dug out from the rubble after they were hit while walking home.[60]

Billie Figg, a young woman working in central London in 1944–45, describes a major attack near her office at Australia House where she worked on deciphering shipping codes:

'There was a doodlebug which fell on Ad Astral House which was the air force headquarters in Aldwych. Then when I worked at the Amalgamated Press a bomb fell on the market down Farringdon Street. The junior had gone out from the dressmaking department because we used to make clothes to feature in the magazine about make do and mend. She sadly was lost in that, she didn't come back. I think that was a V2 in Farringdon market.'[61]

The Farringdon bomb in March 1945 killed 110 people. Morale collapsed again and people tried to leave the city rather than suffer even more. It seemed terrible after five years of war and with the tide turning against Hitler that new weapons were being used against them. Yet people continued to work and get on with their lives. As Billie Figg explained:

> 'Isn't it extraordinary, now we've had our lives, coming up to 88, we're so much more scared of everything than ever we were when we were 18 or 20 and still had our lives to come. We'd say, oh dear there's been a doodlebug on Ad Astral House but we had to work the next day. I don't remember sitting in the train coming up from Woodford and particularly worrying when I saw all the bombed out houses. I think you're insulated, you don't think it's going to happen to you. There isn't an alternative; there was nothing we could do about it.'[62]

The New Workers

The war brought big changes for women at work. Whereas before the war it was largely single women who worked outside the home and married women were largely marginal to the paid economy, things changed in the 1940s. By 1943, 7.5 million women were in paid employment, compared with 1.25 million in 1931, and the proportion of married working women almost trebled from 16 per cent to 43 per cent.[63] The number of women employed in engineering rose from 97,000 to 602,000 between 1939 and 1943, making them a third of all workers in the section. They also rose to a third of employees in shipbuilding, transport, vehicle building, chemicals, water, gas and electricity.[64] However, this process was not always smooth or quick. It took a great deal of government regulation – far more than had ever been seen before.

As with the First World War, initially women's unemployment levels rose. Some areas of work began to dry up relatively quickly, as workers were laid off in boot and shoe manufacturing, the potteries and textiles.[65] Women also lost their jobs in the luxury trades and in jobs less essential to the war effort. As a result in 1940 more women were out of work than in 1939 and unemployment continued to rise in some areas.[66]

Women were often keen to work, yet there seemed to be a mismatch between their willingness and work being available.

In London in July 1940, 'Harrow: Labour Exchange Manager reports [it is] "difficult to pacify [the] spate of women wanting to undertake war work."' At the same time, many women were registering for work without success in Dagenham.[67] Vera Brittain observed in 1940 that women in Birmingham had taken on more dirty work than the men.[68] One problem facing married women was the need for childcare in the form of crèches and nurseries. In London in July 1940 the 'need for crèches in factory areas [was] considered imperative by observers'– and this a year after the outbreak of war and in a period before the Blitz. In Willesden, voluntary small crèches were set up to enable women to work.[69]

Still, many women were determined to engage in some sort of war work. The list of prior occupations of women at a training school for engineers in Lambeth in September 1940 consisted of: 'Office workers, 58; housewife or no specified occupation, 138; dressmaker, milliner, tailor, 21; cutter or designer, 7; saleswoman, 23; teacher, 16; journalist, 13; beauty specialist, 11; supervisor, 14; artist, 10; actress, 8; catering or domestic, 17; ARP, 8; nurse, 5.'[70] This reflects the pool of women outside employment but also the decline of the personal service trades.

It was clear by the end of 1940 that a voluntary approach to war work, which left the labour market unregulated, would not meet the military and industrial requirements of the war economy. The following year marked a major change with the introduction of laws which made certain occupations essential to war work and for the first time introduced conscription for women, into the armed forces, civil defence or war industry. The first step in this process was the law requiring all women aged between 20 and 40 to register at employment exchanges. The age of registration was extended in 1943 to include women aged between 19 and 50. Single women could be directed to certain jobs in different parts of the country.

The Essential Work (Registration for Employment) Order released women from work in areas such as retail. They were not allowed to change jobs without permission, but their employers also had to keep them in work and could not reject employees sent from the labour exchanges. Young women were directly conscripted from December 1941, when the National Service No. 2 Act allowed for women aged between 20 and 30 to be conscripted (the age being lowered to 19 in 1943). The mobilisation of women was encouraged by an official Women's Consultative Committee in the House of Commons which was set up following a debate on Woman-Power in March 1941. Members included MPs, trade union and Labour women.[71]

Regulation of women's work created circumstances which were to have more lasting effects on women's consciousness and employment. Women did jobs that they had never done before and which would once have been regarded as unthinkable. They worked in munitions factories and shipyards, made aircraft and transported steel rods and coal on the network of canals. There were more than half a million extra clerical workers compared to pre-war figures.

By 1943 half a million women were in civil defence and a similar number in the women's branches of the armed services. A further 80,000 were in the Women's Land Army, which did essential work in agriculture.[72] While many of these jobs did not outlast the war, they proved beyond dispute that women were capable of doing work of this nature. In many instances men were forced to address – and overcome – at least some of their prejudices.

The women's sections of the armed forces now expanded from their origins in the First World War. Women could choose one of the forces, the Land Army, civil defence or industry. The women's forces were widely regarded as unequal, with the WRNS (naval Wrens) having the most attractive uniform and not being under military discipline, which meant that women could legally quit. The women's branch of the Royal Air Force, the WAAF (Women's Auxiliary Air Force), was also seen as more glamorous than the women's branch of the army, the ATS (Auxiliary Territorial Service). The ATS was the usual destination of those who were conscripted, as opposed to volunteering. Called the 'Cinderella service', its brown uniform was unpopular.

The women's services were not directly engaged in combat roles and were sometimes seen as fulfilling sexual services for men in the forces. The ATS had the worst reputation.[73] This meant that the very valuable and taxing work which women in the armed forces performed was often discredited.

Shortage of manpower especially from 1941 expanded the remit of women in the armed services from the original auxiliary roles of driving, cooking and clerical work. Women were admitted to mixed anti-aircraft batteries from 1941, first in Richmond Park. Crowds would gather to look at the first women to take a combat role in the British armed forces. Wrens learnt welding, mine spotting and radar. WAAFs took charge of barrage balloons.[74]

Another change brought about by the war was the increase in married women working. The conscription introduced in 1941 was for single women only and there was great reluctance to make too many demands on married women, but it was soon recognised that large numbers of married women would be needed to fulfil the demands of the economy. Married women were encouraged to work, although they were not assessed as 'mobile' and so were not required to relocate. More and more married women went into work, some on a part-time basis. 'By the end of 1942, 10 million women aged between 19 and 50 were registered for war work; 7.5 million were in full-time paid work and there were around 380,000 part-timers.' Government intervention ensured that part-time workers numbered nearly 900,000 a year later.[75] This set the pattern for much of women's work after the war, with growing numbers of married women working and very high levels of part-time work. One recognition of this change were two Acts of Parliament passed in 1944 and 1946 which lifted the 'marriage bar', so allowing women to continue to work as teachers and civil servants after marriage.[76]

One obstacle to married women, especially mothers, working was their domestic responsibilities. The burden of childcare was the greatest, but alongside it went shopping in difficult circumstances, cooking when ingredients were in short supply, cleaning with few labour-saving devices again in difficult conditions, and laundry cleaning without machines and dryers. In many working-class households men and children came home for a cooked lunch, which women were expected to prepare. In addition, transport disruption and other war hazards made getting to work tricky.

Despite the obvious need for nursery provision if mothers were to be able to work, the response by government was pitifully slow. Nurseries were always inadequate for the needs of mothers: in October 1940 there were just 14, though this had risen to 1,345 by July 1943.[77] The dramatic rise gives a sense of what could be achieved, but even so at most 25 per cent of under-fives whose mothers were war workers had a nursery place.[78] Even achieving this took a great deal of campaigning, with demonstrations such as one in Hampstead with placards demanding 'Nurseries for Kids! War Work for Mothers!'

These campaigns were backed by the TUC Women's Advisory Conference and the Labour Party Women's Sections.[79] The difficulties that many women faced, as detailed by Mass Observation, included very long waiting lists for a nursery place, locations remote from their workplaces, too short hours of opening, no provision for school-age children, dislike of anyone else looking after their child, bureaucratic attitudes of the officials they had to deal with, the fear of contagious diseases and infections, and anxiety that they would be conscripted into industry.[80]

Provision did increase, including children's 'hotels' for shift-workers in Birmingham,[81] but the reluctant and piecemeal nature with which it was provided undoubtedly made life hard for many. Women had to rely on informal arrangements and often came up against opposition to nursery provision from the authorities. It did not augur well for the postwar world, where there was no enthusiasm in government circles for maintaining the nurseries and where once again childcare became the responsibility of families and especially mothers – a responsibility still shouldered today.

Other services eased the burden on married women: food was provided outside the home through an increase in school meals, factory canteens and the British Restaurants. Time off was allowed for shopping when it became clear that women could not cope with domestic responsibilities and war work, though this was given grudgingly and was piecemeal. It certainly was not seen as setting any sort of future pattern for work. Even so the burden for working mothers was particularly hard – not least as many were effectively single mothers – as one Birmingham worker at the Tube Investments factory explained:

> 'I'm going home to do an evening's scrubbing. First I've got to do my bit of shopping on the way home. I have to queue for it, because they make no allowances for me being in the factory all day. My two little boys are in school all day. They have their dinners there, and the teacher keeps them till 6 o'clock when I call for them. But I have to get a meal ready, and there's always some washing and mending to be done every night. I never get to bed before 12.'[82]

It is hardly surprising that absenteeism among women workers was high, especially among married women. This tended to peak at weekends, when children were at home. Absence due to sickness was often attributed to boredom at work or to domestic commitments. Productivity demands in war work, which were intense, also led to many young women in particular rebelling against the factory. They would arrive late, take long cloakroom breaks and were constantly 'watching the clock', as one survey showed: 'The subject of what time it is ... by four in the afternoon has become almost an obsession.'[83]

Women workers found conditions hard and exploitative, and no less so because they were involved in war production. They also came up against a recurring problem – their rates of pay compared to those of men. While women's wages overall rose, and although they often earned far more than they would have done in peacetime occupations, their wages were still lower than their male counterparts. As in the First World War, there was growing demand for equal pay. Many male workers were ambivalent on the question, on the one hand not believing that women should earn as much as them, but on the other, wanting women to earn 'the rate for the job' as they feared women would be employed on a permanent basis to undercut men's work. This meant that the men's unions often were at the forefront of raising the demand for equal pay. In fact, the main engineering union, the AEU (Amalgamated Engineering Union) supported the demand for equal pay from the mid-1930s, although it would not admit women members until 1943.[84]

In 1943, there was a major strike at Rolls Royce, Hillington, near Glasgow over the issue, when women walked out. They were joined by the men. The strike ended with grading which gave the women a pay increase but not full equal pay.[85] In 1944 the TUC called for 'the rate for the job' and, in response to growing trade union and other pressure, the government established a Royal Commission on Equal Pay. A survey presented to the Commission conducted by the AEU found that of 1,000 women working in engineering, around two-thirds wanted to stay on after the war, and of these a third were married.[86]

By the end of the war women were in a much better position in terms of wages, but in most places this was achieved without equal pay. With trade union membership more than doubling during the war, the average weekly earnings of women in industry rose from £1 12s 6d in October 1938 to £3 3s 2d by July 1945, but the differential between men's and women's wages had only narrowed by 5 per cent. The main exception to this was women who worked on buses and trams, who were awarded equal pay by an industrial court in 1940. By 1945 they were among the top earners, with average weekly earnings of £4 1s 7d.[87] Civil defence and the armed forces remained highly unequal in terms of pay. While the war forced the issue of equal pay up the agenda, and while it had been enshrined in principle in the Treaty of Versailles, and would be in the Treaty of Rome which established the European Economic Community in 1956, it was not passed into law in Britain until the 1970s, and then was beset with a narrow definition of 'equal work', leading to numbers of strikes in the 1970s and to civil action to try to raise women's wages.

'The Whole Idea of Virginity Got Lost in the War'

The strains of war were demonstrable: the long hours, the separations, the fears of death and injury and the actual experience of it, the drabness, the blackout, all took their toll. But there was another side to the war for younger women, and that related to the opportunities for socialising, for meeting people and for sexual relations well outside the traditional roles. The conscription of women played an important part in effecting these changes. Women who joined the forces were housed in camps far from home, sometimes overseas. Those working in factories were often living miles from home too in the industrial areas. Land Army women lived in hostels or on farms. Thus geographical mobility and the ability to escape the constraints of family life opened up new horizons for these women.

The large number of service men also based in camps in Britain, especially after the arrival of the American GIs and airmen, most of whom were in the country until at least the D-day invasion of June 1944, meant there was a very vibrant social life in many areas. Many women had personal disposable income, which gave them more opportunity to go out. Cinemas, dance halls, shows and cabarets boomed. In London, the West End remained a centre of entertainment and GIs had a club in Piccadilly where they could stay after a night out.[88] The main London dance halls, like the Hammersmith Palais and the Streatham Locarno, were packed as young men and women danced to big bands. One woman described how she regularly travelled across London by tube to visit the Hammersmith Palais: 'The girls always managed to look colourful and attractive, and the servicemen of all nationalities appeared suave and handsome in their varied uniforms. We danced the night away jiving, jitter-bugging, waltzing, with a rumba and a tango thrown in.'[89]

Outside the cities, dances and other social events were organised near the bases and local women were encouraged to attend. Extensive networks of government-sponsored entertainment sprang up: concerts and plays were performed, forces entertainment was organised and there was entertainment in the factories. Workers' Playtime put on concerts and comedy shows, which were highly popular. This life was a profound change for many women.

Billie Figg, who suffered from TB in the early years of the war and could not work until 1941, describes the changes that took place and how they affected even on older married women, like her future mother-in-law:

> 'It was tremendously exciting to young women. They were mixing with men all day, there were many more chances of some romance or some nookie [sex] on the side, so it opened up behaviour quite a bit, but beyond that it changed a whole lot of things later. My husband Jack's mother must have been about 40 and she went to work in a munitions factory in Walthamstow. That meant too that there was a bit more money in the house and I think I would be right in saying that suddenly she and her husband were going out to dinner or the pub together and that probably didn't happen. Before that I don't think men and women went together to the pub very much. I certainly used to go to a pub with the girl next door during the war and a drinking club, once I got a bit better, and we'd meet soldiers. It was a terrific and much faster, more exciting life somehow. The tempo was switched up.'[90]

Women going to the pub alone was a controversial matter during the war, with Mass Observation reporting very mixed views on the subject in February 1943. It argued that women 'have not only taken over men's activities in working hours, but to a very considerable extent in leisure hours too'. Of 50 people interviewed in one London borough, a little over half saw no problem with women going into pubs, a little under half saw problems with women going into one on their own, and a few complained about young women drinking too much. Contrasting views were expressed. A landlady aged 55 in Fulham said: 'Yes the war has made a great deal of difference; I don't mind girls drinking in the bar alone or otherwise. Usually when they come in alone they don't go out alone, but who am I to criticize? My job is to sell the liquor and be pleasant to customers, not to be nosy about their comings and goings'. A 30-year-old woman said: 'All this old fashioned prudery – it's disgusting. Women are doing just as much in this war as the men. Why should they turn up their noses and look Victorian because we walk in, in trousers, and order beer. Sheer stupidity.' And a 25-year-old man said: 'I may be old-fashioned, but I don't like to see a girl drinking alone – it ain't natural to my way of thinking.'[91]

The 30-year-old's reference to women wearing trousers was significant. Women's clothes changed as much as their roles in the war years. Clothes were practical – uniforms for many women, such as the Wrens' outfits or the Land Army breeches and jumpers. Skirts were shorter, outfits made without frills or excessive decoration, shoes were thicker heeled, wedges or flats – and women wore trousers, not unheard of before the war, but now common both for work and leisure and much commented on by the older generation.

Clothing was rationed and had to be obtained with coupons, so making new garments out of old ones became part of the fashion. Women made their own jewellery, unravelled wool from old knitwear to make new jumpers and even painted seams on their legs so it looked as if they were wearing the unobtainable or extremely expensive stockings. 'Make do and mend' was the advice given by the government propaganda in the form of 'Mrs. Sew and Sew'.[92] Billie Figg, working on fashion magazines, made a smart hat from a man's old tweed overcoat.[93]

Wartime shortages and austerity meant that at one time there was talk of cosmetics being banned, but this was eventually abandoned because it was thought it would affect morale.[94] A survey at the time revealed that 90 per cent of women aged under 30 wore make-up. Cosmetics were therefore incorporated into the war spirit: Yardley ran an advertisement of a woman in uniform with the slogan 'No Surrender'. Cyclax had 'Auxiliary Red' lipstick and a foundation to suit women who wore khaki was called 'Burnt Sugar'.[95]

At the root of many of the objections to these changes in women's social, cultural and personal life was fear of the change in sex roles and the much more audacious and open role that women played in sexual behaviour. Attitudes to sex and marriage were no longer conditioned by the notion of waiting, saving oneself for the 'right man' or preserving their virginity. As Billie Figg said:

'I think the tempo and "excitement" of it all led to much more daring sexual behaviour. The whole idea of virginity got lost in the war, that's when the idea that it was of great value to you went. I'm sure that the general feeling was that too much had been attached to virginity and the idea you had to be a virgin was dropped at that time.'[96]

A male clerk wrote towards the end of the war:

'Promiscuity is no longer considered wicked, though failure to avail oneself of safeguards against either pregnancy or VD is considered to be not "comme il faut". No one seems to see any value in fidelity to one and the same partner (once the glamour has passed) and indeed it doesn't seem to have any value by our present day standards.'[97]

Another Mass Observation subject, Nina Masel, who was in the WAAF, described how:

'We're all in the same boat and we're all after the same thing. So why kid each other? And what is this thing we're all after? Obviously, a man. Preferably an officer or a sergeant pilot. I should say that 85 per cent of our conversation is about men, dances (where we meet men), 15 per cent about domestic and shop matters and a negligible proportion on other matters.'[98]

The consequences were clear: the proportion of unmarried births doubled to around 1 in 10 by the end of the war.[99] Many of these births were not to young girls but to women over 30 or married women. In Birmingham in 1944–45, one third of illegitimate children were born to married women, half of them married to servicemen from whom they were presumably temporarily parted.[100] The long periods of separation jeopardised many relationships. Divorces increased in the later war years and especially immediately following the war. The rate for 1945 was nearly double that for 1939, but that figure quadrupled in 1947, the peak year for divorces, and remained at a much higher level.[101]

There was also a massive increase in venereal diseases. The number of men coming forward for treatment doubled in the first two years of the war, and the number of women who contracted the disease continued to rise after that. While there were no regulations which penalised women as there were during the First World War, there were restrictions. A Defence Regulation of 1943 allowed for a suspected carrier to be compulsorily examined.[102]

The changes in sexual behaviour and attitudes to marriage were in part a product of extreme circumstances, and some of these changes did not outlast the war. Many women and men wanted to establish conventional families. Some women also felt that they had to go through with marriages contracted in wartime, as Penny Hicks, a socialist who became chair of Coventry Stop the War, says of her own mother:

> 'My mother lived in the East End during the Blitz and told me stories about the Second World War. What stayed with me was how betrayed she felt and how she felt she had been taken in by propaganda. Her own bedroom was bombed. She met my Dad when she was 16 and he went to war and sent her an engagement ring from Egypt. She always said that made her feel bound to him even though when he came back he was unrecognisable. I now know he suffered from post-traumatic stress syndrome all his life, culminating in suicide. My mother firmly believed that her generation had been duped and lost their youth – her own father had lost all his brothers in World War One.'[103]

There were also problems in adjusting to a disrupted family life, with fathers seeming like strangers to their children. Jenny Jones is a member of the Greater London Assembly, and, as a leading figure in the Green Party, committed to anti-war and peace causes. Born at the end of the Second World War, she describes the dislocation in her own family:

> 'My mother painted trains during the war in Brighton station. My mum was very lonely during the war, my dad was away five years and my older brother didn't know his dad when he came back. My mother saw it as five years of loss. My brother said, "Who's that man?" She talked about the camaraderie of the painting and there were actually a lot of women but a lot of men there as well and a lot of barriers seemed to come down.'[104]

It was perhaps not surprising, given the disruptions of war, that family life was encouraged after war and that some of the more conservative attitudes were reasserted, not least those about children born outside marriage, which continued to be regarded as a scandal in many working-class communities. However, the changes in divorce were more permanent, with future legislation making it easier to obtain a divorce and the numbers of those divorcing never falling to pre-war levels. Sexual freedom became more curtailed and women played a much more conventional role, but it was only a generation later that women's sexual freedom was back on the agenda.

Turning Left

Pacifists and conscientious objectors were treated less harshly than in the First World War. Those who opposed fighting in wars were often willing to play a non-combatant role, something that reflected the changing and civilian-centred nature of the war. Angela Sinclair was one of these. She experienced a great deal of danger in her work during the Blitz. Often the personal experience of women led them towards pacifism. This was true of Vera Brittain, who lost loved ones in the First World War. She describes a working-class woman pacifist giving evidence at her CO son's hearing in 1940. The woman had lost her husband during the First World War when the son was a child. Afterwards, she described how 'I suddenly began thinking: "Perhaps there's a German woman just lost her husband who feels the same about me as I felt about her". And I've been a pacifist ever since.'[105]

Angela Sinclair told a similar story:

'I've got a lovely pacifist memory from then. When the planes came over it was usually dark, I'm thinking about November or December 1940. You could hear them coming and the noise of the planes coming was very scary for people. You were waiting to know when they would stop and you would hear the first bombs. One evening I'd come out of my shelter looking to see if I could see any planes when a lovely old woman who had been in the shelter came out and said "How sad it must be to be one of those young men up there all by yourself". And that's a pretty nice thing to say in the circumstances.'[106]

The conduct of the Second World War was always highly politicised in the sense that the twists and turns of the war often had immediate political consequences. The failure of the Norwegian campaign in April 1940 led to a parliamentary vote of confidence that went against the Prime Minister Neville Chamberlain and the successful bid by Winston Churchill to succeed him. In July the publication of an attack on the old politicians and their role in appeasement caused a sensation. *The Guilty Men,* published under the pseudonym Cato, but written by three journalists including Michael Foot, was an attack on the politics and politicians who had created the conditions for war. It was published by Victor Gollancz, was refused distribution by W.H. Smith and Wymans, the two main publishing outlets, and was sold from market stalls, among other places. Within a month sales reached 200,000 copies, a sign of how bitterly resented the appeasers, especially Chamberlain and the Foreign Secretary Lord Halifax, were. Indeed after the fall of France in the summer of 1940, there was talk of Chamberlain being 'lynched'.[107]

Different class experiences of food and rationing, evacuation and war work all helped to create a more political atmosphere. In general, the role women were asked to play required so many changes in their lives and expectations that it led to a greater politicisation among some. The real political and social issues which affected people earlier in the war and which led many to campaign over issues from shelters to 'red tape' and bureaucracy evolved in the second half of the war into wider concerns about the postwar world and how a better society could be built.

In 1942, the popular magazine *Picture Post* devoted an issue to looking at a blueprint for a future Britain.[108] In the same year the Beveridge Report was published. The night before its publication, on 1 December 1942, queues formed outside the HMSO office in Kingsway. The report sold 100,000 in its first month and a total of 600,000 in full and abridged versions. Mass Observation found the next day that 92 per cent of those questioned had heard of the report and a fortnight later 88 per cent thought the government should implement it.[109] A reaction at least as much to the Depression of the 1930s as to the war, it proposed the basis of the welfare state – a benefits system based on insurance, a health service, pensions, full employment and family allowances. Beveridge talked about slaying the 'five giants': Want, Disease, Ignorance, Squalor and Idleness. It was a product of the mass struggles of the 1930s, the hegemony achieved by the Left during the war and the widespread experience of planning and state intervention from the late 1930s onwards and especially during the war.

It is a testament to the level of politicisation of people who had lived through six years of war that the report and the wider subject of a welfare state became such a hot topic. The Conservative Party's lukewarm response and their reputation as the appeasers' party led to growing dissatisfaction with them. The Commonwealth Party, which campaigned on the slogan of full implementation of the report, won a number of by-elections in the second half of the war. Women were attracted to some of the left political parties, as well as men.

The Communist Party, fully in support of the war once Russia entered it on the side of the Allies in 1941, grew in popularity through calls for a 'Second Front Now' and because of the sympathy many people felt for the Russians, especially given the sacrifices they made at Stalingrad. Anglo-Soviet Friendship Societies were set up in many areas. Stalin's war aims were to extend his influence and imperialist reach however ruthlessly, but most working people did not see it that way. Many viewed the Soviet Union as representing an alternative society.

The Communist Party was also able to give voice to many of the popular discontents which working-class and a large number of middle-class people felt. It also had links with resistance movements in occupied Europe, which were admired for their roles in fighting the Nazis. These movements consisted of young men and women who in Italy, France and Yugoslavia played decisive roles often at the highest personal sacrifice.

The new world which so many people now looked to was not just about welfare in Britain but about a more equal world. The huge numbers of refugees, the massive displacement across the world, the treatment of women, including the mass rape of German women by Russian troops,[110] the suffering of so many and the growing awareness of the genocide perpetrated against the Jews, all led to an awareness of the need for change internationally.

Angela Sinclair's work in a refugee camp led her to a direct and lifelong engagement:

'I was sent to Egypt in 1943 with a group of what would now be NGOs to look after refugees who were housed in what were now deserted military camps. The army had moved on to Italy. The camps were full of Greeks and Yugoslavs. Some were starving because they were on the islands and couldn't get supplies . . . There was nothing but sand as far as the eye could see. We were four to a tent and they were 24 to a tent. They were mostly women and children. These poor Yugoslavs had nothing to do. They wanted embroidery thread so I got permission to go to Cairo to try to find some.

'There were 6,000 refugees in the camp, but some of the Greek camps were much bigger. Basically, it was social work. The camps were run by the military – as I see it now, the rejected military. They basically hated the refugees and regarded them as a complete bore. The big difficulty was the language, so I learnt Serbo-Croat. I found a member of the committee who was educated and had read Horace, so through Latin I learnt Serbo-Croat.'[111]

The Labour Party's landslide victory in the 1945 general election reflected the radicalisation of civilians and troops alike. The attempt to construct the welfare state represented a radicalisation partly driven by women who had seen their world change and did not want the old one to return. However, the hopes of 1945 were too often not realised. Women were encouraged to return to the domestic roles they had gladly left during the war. The welfare state was a massive advance for most working people in Britain, but its gains were not always maintained, even in the early years.

Changes in attitudes to sex, divorce and other aspects of life frequently were stigmatised. People across the world did not achieve the liberation they had hoped for as their wishes and needs were subordinated to those of governments in the East and West. They also faced the threat of weapons much deadlier than those they had to endure during the war, as the people of Hiroshima and Nagasaki found in August 1945.

Yet the seeds of change had been sown by the war. The welfare state brought with it improved education, including for the first time higher education on a mass scale. The sexual mores brought about by the war led to advances in contraception and by the

1960s the contraceptive pill. Although women lost many of the 'men's jobs', they soon re-entered the workforce in clerical and white-collar jobs, in education, health and other public sector jobs.

Internationally, many of the imperial colonies saw the postwar world as the chance for independence, though they often had to fight to achieve that goal. This meant that the next battles had many of their roots in the Second World War and were a continuation of what was achieved then.

3
In the Shadow of the Bomb

'On the morning of August 6, 1945, at 8.16 and two seconds, the dream of the superweapon became reality. The first atom bomb exploded without warning over Hiroshima with the force of 12,500 tons of trotyl. A new kind of war had begun. The events of the first second of this new war unfolded like this:

'0.0 sec: The bomb was detonated at approximately 600 metres above the Shima Hospital in central Hiroshima, during the peak of the morning rush hour. The temperature at the point of detonation rose to several million degrees in a millionth part of a second.

'0.1 sec: A fireball fifteen metres in diameter with a temperature of about 300,000 degrees was formed. At the same time, neutrons and gamma rays reached the ground and caused direct radioactive injuries to living organisms.

'0.15 sec: The fireball expanded, and the blast wave expanded even more rapidly; the air was heated until it glowed.

'0.2–0.3 sec: Enormous amounts of infrared energy were produced and caused most of the direct burn injuries to people.

'1.0 sec: The fireball reached its maximum dimensions, about 200–300 metres in diameter. The blast wave, which spread the fire, advanced at the speed of sound.'[1]

The atom bomb dropped on Hiroshima on 6 August 1945 killed 100,000 instantly, nearly all of them civilians. Another 100,000 died more slowly from radiation sickness and other long-term effects of the bomb. The United States denied the effects of this bomb and the one dropped three days later on Nagasaki. They were justified by the United States and its allies on the grounds that they forced the Japanese to surrender and so saved allied lives. But the Japanese were already willing to surrender, as the United States knew.

In fact, the bombs demonstrated that the United States had a weapon possessed by no other country, which it was prepared to use whatever the consequences.[2] It also allowed the United States to try out the bombs. In effect, this was a live military test. The United States also claimed that the attack on Hiroshima did have a military target since it involved the bombing of a military base, even though the bomb was aimed at the centre of a major city with a large civilian population. At first, little information filtered out of Japan, with the US authorities denying the severity of the bomb's effects. However, an Australian journalist, Wilfred Burchett, managed to smuggle out an uncensored report, which was printed in the *London Daily Press* a month later and refuted the United States' denial:

> 'In Hiroshima, 30 days after the first atomic bomb destroyed the city and shook the world, people are still dying, mysteriously and horribly – people who were uninjured in the cataclysm – from an unknown something which I can only describe as the atomic plague.'[3]

The bomb was immediately understood to be much more destructive than anything that had been seen before. While many people in Britain felt the bombs were warranted as being the only way of ending the war in Japan, there was also a great deal of disquiet as more information became known about the devastating effect of nuclear weapons. As this understanding grew, the initial responses began to change.

Bruce Kent, former CND chairman, was a schoolboy in London. He recalled:

> 'A headline announced: "Wonder bomb destroys Jap city". I remember saying to myself, "Bloody good show, that's great, they had it coming to them. Now the war's over." It took me a very long time to think of the moral and legal significance of what had happened and to see how the arms race spun on from there.'[4]

Pat Arrowsmith, CND co-founder, then aged 15, was on holiday. She was the daughter of a West Country vicar and was a pupil at Cheltenham Ladies' College. She had recently been in trouble with the authorities there. The school had decided not to allow its pupils to leave the grounds to celebrate VE day, but Pat had other ideas:

'I remember thinking, in fact I wrote in my diaries, that I hoped that I [would] never experience the end of a world war again and I wasn't going to miss this one. So after lights out in my dormitory I went out on the town. They noticed I'd gone and a search was conducted around the house. I left a ground floor window open and left a change of clothes under a bush in the garden.

'I got on a jeep that was riding round Cheltenham but I thought that all the other women were on the game [were prostitutes] so after a while I got off. A young fellow about my own age latched himself onto me and became my escort and we wandered round. In the small hours as he delivered me back he delivered a smacking kiss on my face. He was a working-class boy.

'Suddenly a white figure appeared and the voice of my house lady said "What are you doing Pat?" and I said, "I'm just coming in Miss Garside." I was put in the sick bay. I was segregated. It was really my first experience of imprisonment and was good training for future days in Holloway as a prisoner.'[5]

This episode was just the start of a life of defiance for Pat, a Second World War child whose family had taken in refugees and who understood many of the horrors of war. She now had a sense of foreboding about the bomb:

'I was fully aware from the beginning what it would mean. It was something quite exceptional and terrible, not like the high-explosive bombs of the Second World War. I remember sitting in the kitchen on a family holiday having breakfast and seeing the newspaper.'[6]

Within a few years, Pat was to become one of the best-known campaigners against nuclear weapons. Her activism has continued for over 60 years.

The impact of these weapons was indeed different from the high-explosive bombs. There are many harrowing eye-witness reports. A worker at the Mitsubishi Electrical Machine factory in Nagasaki recalls:

'I was blown off by a blast and it became dark with a cloud of dust. It was just like night although it was a sunny day . . . We went [back] to the factory on the 12th [three days after the bombing] and it was like hell. The shelter was full of people who were burnt and it was hard to recognise who they were ... It was said that people were supposed to say "Long live the emperor" before they died, but it was not true. Many said "Mother!" before they passed away. Many people became full of maggots and died. The shelter was full of a bad smell, which made me sick.'[7]

The Cold War and Imperialism

The atomic bomb brought the war to an immediate end. The United States effectively made its own peace with Japan, excluding its allies, especially the Soviet Union, which had only just entered the war against Japan. The shape of the postwar world rapidly became apparent: the world was dominated by two superpowers, the United States and the Soviet Union, each with its own sphere of influence and armed with nuclear weapons, for the Soviet Union had developed its own bomb by 1949.

The effect of the superpowers developing nuclear weapons – not just the atom bomb but in the early 1950s the even more deadly hydrogen bomb – was to create a 'balance of terror' in which both sides were highly armed but supposedly reluctant to use them because the consequences would be the annihilation of whole cities and populations on both sides. This was known as Mutually Assured Destruction, or MAD. Within a few years, the postwar settlement had emerged as a heavily armed 'Cold War'. So the carnage of the two world wars had produced a new global politics which held the threat of an even deadlier war of annihilation.

Cold War was something of a misnomer, however, since wars broke out in a number of places, most notably Korea, and the period was marked by a dramatic increase in arms spending and the threatened use of nuclear weapons in a number of incidents.[8] It was after the Soviet Union tested its own atom bomb that the United States developed the hydrogen bomb in order to gain a decisive military advantage, and so a new arms race began.[9] This set the pattern for the 1950s, as the new imperialism of a bipolar, nuclear-armed world started to take shape. This was also a period of decolonisation, as the colonies of the European empires fought for their independence.

The arming of both camps and their allies necessitated ever greater levels of spending on weapons and the military. The United States devoted much of its resources to keeping ahead in the nuclear arms race, even though, according to Gabriel Kolko, its 'dependence on sophisticated weapons aimed at industrial and urban targets in the Soviet Union and elsewhere, as well as its conventional weaponry, could not cheaply or quickly win wars in Third World contexts, if at all'.[10] After 1950, the military budget 'became increasingly important to the health of the American economy'. A consensus developed on military spending between the main political parties, since 'although Republican conservatives strongly objected to the very notion of deficit spending, when forced to choose between fiscal prudence and the costly pretensions of being the world's anticommunist policeman, they invariably chose the latter'.[11]

By the early 1950s the world economy was booming and a return to the crises of the 1930s seemed remote. Arms spending was a major factor in preventing a recurrence of crisis and in maintaining the long boom. Economic growth from the immediate postwar period through to the early 1970s ensured rising living standards, full employment and the expansion of welfare and education.[12]

One of the major sources of military conflict in this period was the series of wars between old colonial powers, such as Britain and France, and national liberation movements. In some countries the major imperial powers did not become directly involved, but in Malaya, Kenya and especially Vietnam they were central in trying to maintain the old order. One sign of the rivalry between the superpowers was the backing often given to the liberation movements by the Soviet Union, but these were proxy wars, rather than direct confrontations between the major powers.

China too backed the liberation movements. After the revolution and rise to power of Mao Zedong in 1949, the state-controlled and centralised economy came under attack. US direct involvement in the wars in Korea and Vietnam was justified by anti-communist rhetoric. Although the Soviet Union was an ally of China, there was also rivalry between the two, and later, after the Sino-Soviet split in the early 1960s, there were separate Chinese- and Russian-backed liberation movements in Zimbabwe and Angola.

Britain came out of the Second World War severely weakened, heavily in debt to the United States and facing the prospect of being forced to grant independence to the countries that had made up the largest empire in the world. It was, however, deeply committed to high levels of military spending as a way of trying to maintain its now waning influence as a world power.

'It's Our H-Bomb!'

The postwar Labour government was determined to develop nuclear weapons despite opposition from its own party, and work on the atom bomb began secretly in 1946, with the right-leaning Foreign Minister Ernest Bevin declaring he wanted a bomb 'with the bloody Union Jack on it'.[13] By 1950 Britain had achieved this ambition and by the late 1950s the nuclear arms race was fully underway, with the British government willing to extend its use of nuclear weapons. The *Daily Express* greeted the testing of Britain's newly acquired weapon, tested in May 1957, with the headline 'It's Our H-Bomb!'[14] In the same year an agreement with the United States allowed for 60 US Thor missiles to be stationed in Britain, provided for the use of British bases to site nuclear weapons and underlined that the United States would be in control of these weapons despite their being on British soil.[15]

There was growing disquiet about these and other policies. Campaigners had been drawing attention to the dangers of nuclear weapons and opposing tests which were taking place in remote parts of the world. The testing of the first hydrogen bomb in 1954 on the Pacific island of Bikini Atoll caused widespread alarm after radiation and blast from the bomb badly affected the inhabitants of other islands and Japanese fishermen on a boat more than 50 miles away.

A small women's group in Golders Green began to sow the seeds of what would become a much larger movement. The local branch of the Women's Cooperative Guild took up the issue of radiation fall-out and its effects. From 1955, it campaigned under the leadership of Vera Leff, a communist, Agnes Simpson and Marion Clayton. They were joined by Gertrude Fishwick, a former suffragette and Labour Party member. They campaigned through local meetings, leafleting and contacts in different organisations. A survivor of Nagasaki spoke at the local branch and her graphic description of the effects of the bomb made a profound impression.

By 1955, the campaign had turned into the Local Committee for the Abolition of the H-Bomb whose inaugural meeting was chaired by a member of the engineering union. This became the Joint Local Committee for the Abolition of Nuclear Weapons by the autumn, when it attracted over 200 people to a meeting. The campaign spread, with other groups setting up across north London.[16] The Women's Cooperative Guild had a good record of campaigning on issues of peace and had a national network.

Women from a wide range of backgrounds had clearly begun to take the lead in organising against nuclear weapons.

Pat Arrowsmith was an undergraduate at Cambridge in the early 1950s, where she became involved in politics, especially campaigning against militarism and nuclear weapons: 'My first experience of speaking was for the World Government Movement which focused on picketing arms factories. We picked Bristol Siddeley because they were producing parts for H-bombs.'[17]

Events took a dramatic turn in the autumn of 1956 when British, French and Israeli forces invaded Egypt in response to President Nasser's nationalisation of the Suez Canal. Their action aroused widespread anger and the largest demonstration since the Second World War in opposition to the invasion. The Suez campaign was not supported by the United States, ended in failure and resulted in the resignation of the Prime Minister, Anthony Eden. The episode marked the end of Britain's aspiration to retain a world empire and its realisation that it could not break from the United States in any major aspect of foreign policy – a realisation that has dominated its foreign policy ever since. It also marked for many a recognition that the world was changing and that the populations of the former colonies no longer wanted to live under British rule.

At the same time, the threat of a major war involving Britain just over a decade after the end of the Second World War alerted people to how dangerous the world was. There was more information about the effects of nuclear weapons and opposition to them from influential figures. The Russell–Einstein Manifesto, produced in 1955 and signed by eminent scientists, including the two after whom it was named, famously asked, 'Shall we put an end to the human race; or shall mankind renounce war?'[18] In 1957 scientists concerned about nuclear war met at a conference in Pugwash, Canada.

One peace activist in East London, Pat Allen, summed up a growing and widespread feeling:

'Following the Korean War, the Suez crisis and the Cold War tension, there was a real fear that a major conflict could erupt at any time. As not so many years had passed since the end of World War II we all knew what another war might entail. In many towns and cities the bomb damage was still there to remind us. The great unknown was what would happen in a nuclear conflict.'[19]

1957 marked something of a turning point in the campaign against nuclear weapons in Britain. The testing of the H-bomb on Christmas Island led to the establishment of the National Committee for the Abolition of Nuclear Weapons Tests (NCANWT), which developed in part out of the north London groups. It was organised by Dr Sheila Jones and Ianthe Carswell. Soon there were more than 100 local groups.[20] In the same year a campaign to back direct action against testing – the Emergency Committee for Direct Action against Nuclear War – was formed. This campaign wanted direct action against the tests and supported a Quaker, Harold Steele, who tried to sail into the test area at Christmas Island. He did not succeed, but his attempt gained widespread publicity and helped build opposition to the tests.

Pat Arrowsmith became involved in the protests against nuclear weapons testing in remote areas but even there causing radiation sickness to those unfortunate enough to live in the vicinity: 'There were atomic tests on Christmas Island and I volunteered to be in the test areas to protest. I seriously thought we would be left in the test area to get irradiated. So we discussed over lunch what that would feel like. That is in 1957 or early '58.'[21] Pat never did go to the test areas, but her concerns were matched by those of other activists.

The committee later became the Direct Action Committee, which took the initiative for the first Aldermaston march.[22] The tests also triggered a NCANWT women's march. The women wore black sashes and over 2,000 of them marched to Trafalgar Square where more joined them. Speakers at the rally included Steele's wife, Sheila, Vera Brittain and Edith Summerskill. Peggy Duff, a member of St Pancras and Holborn Labour Party who was to play a leading role in CND, became NCANWT secretary.[23]

March, March and March Again

The Left was now stirring over the issue of nuclear weapons. The Labour Party, in opposition and traditionally the more peace-loving party, committed itself to retaining the H-bomb at its 1957 conference, to the bitter disappointment of its left wing.[24] The Labour leader, Hugh Gaitskell, was on the right of the party but the shadow Foreign Secretary, Nye Bevan, the pre-eminent figure of the Left, shocked many of his supporters by opposing a resolution calling for unilateral nuclear disarmament. Tony Benn recollected:

> 'Nye Bevan rose to speak and to the amazement of his followers on the Left he denounced the Unilateralist Resolution and said that, if passed, Britain "would go naked into the conference chamber", arguing that we had to retain our nuclear armoury in order to have any say in any future international disarmament negotiations.'

The resolution was heavily defeated through use of the union bloc vote; some weeks later Benn resigned as a frontbench spokesman on defence: 'I could not, under any circumstances, support a policy which contemplated the use of atomic weapons in war.'[25]

Many on the Left recognised that the campaign against nuclear weapons had to be taken up outside the Labour Party. A *New Statesman* article by the writer J. B. Priestley was very well received. It led to a meeting by some of the leaders of NCANWT and prominent left-wing figures at the home of Canon John Collins at St Paul's Cathedral. They included Bertrand Russell, Priestley himself, the actor Miles Malleson and the *Evening Standard* cartoonist Vicky (Victor Weisz).[26] The Campaign for Nuclear Disarmament was founded at this meeting.

NCANWT agreed to hand over its resources to the new CND, including a planned public meeting on 17 February 1958. Westminster Central Hall was packed, as were overflow rooms containing in all around 5,000 people. CND was clearly committed to unilateral nuclear disarmament.[27]

David Widgery summed up its appeal:

'CND had such emotional power because it forced people to face what they and their leaders would rather they didn't. It proved that near village greens were neat grey buildings calmly constructing atom bombs. That behind barbed wire those cheery GIs were guarding control panels where officers were poised over buttons which could explode everything. CND managed to persuade all sorts of people that they actually could hear the H-bomb's' thunder.'[28]

Pat Arrowsmith was centrally involved in campaigning against nuclear weapons and committed to direct action: 'There was also the Direct Action Committee against Nuclear War. Hugh Brock formed it and Michael Randle became involved. The committee decided to do a pilgrimage from London to Aldermaston where the atom bomb was made. That was 1958.'[29]

The first Aldermaston march took place at Easter 1958 and was organised by the Direct Action Committee, with Pat Arrowsmith as organiser. The newly formed CND was fairly lukewarm in its support, but many CND members went on the march and it was 'immediately, inextricably linked with the new-born CND in the public mind'.[30] One reason for this was CND's logo, now an instantly recognisable symbol of peace, designed by the artist and designer Gerald Holtom.

The march set the tone for the next few years of peace campaigning, a 'moving *tableau vivant* of the Left in the late fifties'.[31] Marchers chanted 'Black the bomb – black the bases'; they were joined by trade union delegations along the route. The weather was appalling, but many attended, with around 8,000 marching on the last leg to Aldermaston.[32]

The plan to march from London to Aldermaston was intended to put direct pressure on the workers there, which is why initially the route of the march was that way round. Pat Arrowsmith remembers:

> 'Later it changed to march to the centre of government from Aldermaston. There was also a peace camp at Aldermaston urging the workers there to quit. We put pickets on them and sat down at the entrance to Aldermaston. This was the first serious civil disobedience. We just sat there and refused to move for a number of hours. Eventually we did get up and go and we were threatened with arrest and so on but they didn't.'[33]

In the following years, the march was reversed, with the marchers setting out from Berkshire and arriving in London to exert maximum pressure on the government and to gather more support along the way. For the next few years the marches became a key focus for CND and the anti-nuclear movement. According to one informal survey, 40 per cent of the marchers on the 1959 march were under 21.[34]

The historian Sheila Rowbotham, a student at St Hilda's College, Oxford in the early 1960s, described the relationship of young left-wing students to CND: 'CND provided a vast umbrella – a social movement which was both political and cultural.'[35]

Women played a prominent role in organising the campaigns: 'It could attract religious pacifists, environmentalists concerned with the hazards of nuclear testing, many women previously apolitical (indeed its women leaders such as Pat Arrowsmith and Peggy Duff were a notable feature of the movement).'[36] Duff played a key role as a CND worker in the early years. CND also attracted prominent women such as the writers Iris Murdoch,

Jacquetta Hawkes and Rose Macaulay, and the actresses Peggy Ashcroft, Mary Ure and Constance Cummings.[37] The movement grew, organising ever larger marches and meetings, and taking the arguments for unilateral disarmament back to the Labour Party, especially with the help of the Transport and General Workers' Union general secretary, Frank Cousins, who fought hard for unilateralism.[38]

Many CND members and supporters were extremely militant and were drawn to forms of direct action. The Labour Party's 1960 conference held in Scarborough was met by a CND demonstration and that week the conference adopted a pro-CND resolution, reversing its previous position. Again the union bloc vote, cast by Cousins for the TGWU, was decisive, but the split within Labour over the issue continued, with Gaitskell vowing to 'fight, fight and fight again' to reverse the policy.[39]

In the months that followed, the campaign against nuclear weapons took a more militant turn over the question of direct action, which appealed to many CND members but about which its leadership was more hesitant. This led Bertrand Russell to set up the Committee of 100, which was committed to defying the law. Its members included Vanessa Redgrave, Lindsay Anderson, Philip Toynbee, Shelagh Delaney, John Osborne and John Braine.[40] Its first demonstration was a Ministry of Defence sit-down of 4,000 people. In the summer of 1961 it held a protest in Trafalgar Square for which permission was denied. On 17 September, 6,000 demonstrators occupied the square until nearly midnight. As their numbers dwindled police vans moved in and a total of 1,314 people were arrested – the largest mass arrest in English history. The 89-year-old Russell had already been imprisoned days before for incitement to riot.[41]

There was some tension between those who favoured direct action and the more mainstream CND supporters.[42] Pat Arrowsmith felt differently. She remembers how

'The whole Committee of 100 was imprisoned at one point. It . . . effectively replaced the Direct Action Committee . . . I was unusual in not seeing a contradiction between CND and the Committee of 100. I didn't have much time for conflict between the two. There was a case for a large organisation which campaigned and a case for another campaign to take Non Violent Direct Action (NVDA). Violent Direct Action was never seriously contemplated.'[43]

The Committee of 100 was especially concerned with campaigning at Holy Loch. This was the site of the US Polaris nuclear missiles, which the British government had allowed to be stationed in Scotland from 1960. David Widgery describes a demonstration at Holy Loch 'with Scots unilateralist workers thumping it out with much less restrained police, while Pat Arrowsmith's kayak bobbed between the parked nuclear submarines'.[44]

Pat Arrowsmith recollects:

'Simultaneously, there was a mass arrest at Aldermaston and up in Scotland at Holy Loch which was [organised by] the Committee of 100. I went to Holy Loch and got imprisoned up there a couple of times. The second time for a couple of months. I was adopted by Amnesty as a political prisoner. I've been a political prisoner 11 times. That doesn't include all the times in custody. The longest was 18 months and two more were for 6 months.'[45]

The youth of the movement and the number of women involved was not in doubt. Chanie Rosenberg, a socialist, was on the first march as part of a small Trotskyist group, the Socialist Review Group, within the Labour Party: 'We were involved in the movement. I went to Aldermaston on the first one and walked 18 miles. I couldn't walk the last few miles because my legs gave in. I walked most of the way back over four days. When the march was due to take place it involved us completely. The political organisations took their people.' She remembers, 'I was always aware, for instance, on that first Aldermaston march there were very few women sleeping over, but on the marches themselves there were lots of women. Then, you didn't sleep where there were men.'[46]

The contrast between the women marching to Aldermaston and the narrow conventions which governed so many women's lives summed up the social changes underway. Underpinning the involvement of women and young people were social, cultural and political developments that were transforming postwar Britain. Society was now committed to full-time education for all up to the age of at least 15 and with this came the opening up of higher education for a new generation. Young men and women from lower middle-class or working-class backgrounds could now go to university; they were usually the first members of their families to do so. This in turn opened up the opportunity to enter professional occupations, something denied to previous generations. These developments had a particular impact on young women, freed from the immediate confines of home and family, and therefore able to challenge some of the ideas about women's role in society and their right to independence. Sheila Rowbotham describes how:

> 'My generation in the sixties was living through big social changes: the expansion of higher education, the opening of new employment opportunities, the increase in consumption and the growth of the media. These were combining to alter the boundaries between public and personal aspects of life.'[47]

Simultaneously, a general liberalisation on a political and cultural level was in train. This had a profound impact on women and created a change of consciousness. Women's horizons expanded, with the chance to free themselves from the narrow constraints of the family by moving away from home, to begin to consider what it meant to be a woman and contemplate issues of politics and social change.

Increasing numbers of women went to university – something which almost inevitably made their lives very different from those of their mothers. Higher education led to women entering more professional roles. They were part of the development of a wider student body which had the time and space to develop political and social ideas. There was growing political and artistic concern over the Cold War.

This new generation of men and women was exposed to novel ideas at university. They also had the time and leisure, as a group of students funded to attend higher education, to think about wider issues, among them questions of war and peace. In the background there was a cumulative concern about war. Middle-aged people had lived through two world wars and now they faced the threat of nuclear annihilation. While previous generations might have accepted the necessity of war, experience of battlefield slaughter, civilian bombing and ever-more fearful weapons helped to create anti-war sentiment.

There was also a revolution among writers, film-makers, actors and artists who expressed discontent with the status quo. Throughout the second half of the 1950s they produced work which expressed the reality of society beneath the often banal culture which reflected establishment views. Playwrights and novelists such as Arnold Wesker, Bernard Kops and John Osborne wrote about working-class life and about opposition to the old values of empire, public school and duty. Shelagh Delaney, Joan Littlewood and Doris Lessing were among the women writers and directors who articulated a new and much more trenchant critique of society. Film directors such as Lindsay Anderson and Tony Richardson brought a new sense of realism to the cinema. These artists were able to articulate the fear of extinction which now gripped many people.

Rae Street was seven when the war ended and remembers news of the Holocaust, but cannot remember any specific news about the bomb at the time. However she was affected by it as she grew up:

'It wasn't until I was a student in Manchester that I became aware of the movement against nuclear weapons. I sympathised completely but never thought I could join the march to Aldermaston as everyone seemed to be way above me in status – there in the press pictures was the march led by the Earl Russell and Canon Collins. As a student, I was constantly worried about money as my family were extremely hard up. I had to plan to raise my fare from Manchester to Leeds, so London was out of the question.'[48]

Like many working-class women, she did not think that central involvement in the movement was for her for she lacked the confidence to take action which seemed to be beyond her experience:

'But in 1960 I saw the film "Hiroshima, Mon Amour"; this had a huge effect on me. I even wondered how people could have children. I felt I could never bring myself to do that with the risk of such suffering. (Now I have three grown up children and four grandchildren.) But, again, I lacked confidence to join any group. Then I began to speak out locally on environmental issues and I suppose you could say I found my voice. I joined CND in the late '70s and have been campaigning against weapons of mass destruction and war ever since.'[49]

War Again?

The momentum of the movement did not develop through concerns about the bomb and nuclear testing alone – the world had come close to a major war during the Suez crisis in 1956. In the early 1960s a number of events raised the spectre of war again. The United States and the Soviet Union both resumed nuclear testing, and this led to a number of protests. The building of the Berlin Wall in August 1961 led to greater international tension and talk of nuclear war. The abortive US-backed invasion of Cuba fuelled fears of wider war.

At around this time women's involvement in the movement increased, with the CND Women's Group becoming very active.[50]

Jane Shallice went to Bristol University in 1961. She came from a highly political left-wing family in Manchester. Her father was a Marxist who 'religiously' attended the Aldermaston marches. Her mother had been in a student anti-war group while at university in the 1930s and the family was interested in peace issues: 'When I went to Bristol I joined the Labour Club. I did a lot of work around the international solidarity movements and around CND, and I went to Aldermaston in the early 1960s. It was primarily international politics I was interested in.'[51]

Perhaps the threat of nuclear war was at its starkest during the Cuban missile crisis in 1962. After the invasion failed, the United States made plans for an economic blockade and further invasion. During the summer the Soviet Union began to install missiles both to challenge US weapons domination elsewhere and to protect

Cuba. When the United States found out, it considered airstrikes on the missiles, but this plan was not pursued.

In October the United States imposed a naval blockade. Tensions increased and both countries put their armed forces on nuclear alert. The UN Secretary General U Thant intervened in an attempt to persuade them to back down. Eventually the Soviet Union withdrew the missiles on the secret promise that US missiles would be withdrawn from Turkey and in exchange for a pledge that the United States would not invade Cuba. The game of global 'chicken' played by the two leaders, John F. Kennedy and Nikita Khrushchev, was over.[52]

The Cuban missile crisis brought the world to the brink of nuclear war. Terrified people believed that the two giant nuclear-armed camps could be at war within days, and the fact that war was only narrowly averted was little comfort to them. Jackie Mulhallen is now a campaigner in Norfolk. She was born during the war near Plymouth, a major Navy port almost destroyed by bombing:

> 'I was from a naval family and supposed that "defence" was important in preventing war. My father didn't believe in war, quite the reverse in fact. He said only people who hadn't had to fight one believed in them. My generation thought that the third world war was inevitable, and I can remember two occasions when I thought it was about to break out; when I was 11 in 1952 there was a news announcement that there would be a third world war, and 10 years later there was the Cuban missiles crisis.'[53]

Sheila Rowbotham bought a book at Blackwell's in Oxford while thinking 'this could be the last book I ever read'. She then phoned her mother to warn her of the imminent danger.[54] Similar phone calls were no doubt being made around the country.

Jane Shallice was arrested for sitting down and blocking the street on a demonstration: 'We had a demo over the Cuba crisis. It was mainly students and people from the Trades Council in Bristol. We walked through the shopping centre and the vitriol was huge. People were yelling "go back to Russia". The police arrested us and held us for a few hours.'[55]

The crisis gave a further impetus to anti-war sentiment. The 1963 Aldermaston march was very large, but it began to reveal tensions within CND itself and with the Committee of 100 over direct action and impatience over the methods CND used. Just before the march, 'Spies for Peace' issued a document showing that there was a secret Regional Seat of Government near Reading on the route of the march. Peggy Duff tried, but failed, to stop about 1,000 marchers who broke away to occupy the secret location by telling them to carry on for lunch. 'Defiantly, we turned off to the left, down a path which led into the woods. Fancy her thinking we could be dissuaded by our stomachs!' recalled Sheila Rowbotham.[56]

More widely, debates within the movement were changing. The years of stultifying Tory rule were drawing to a close and there was the prospect of a Labour government for the first time in 13 years. Expectations began to turn to Labour dealing with nuclear weapons. In addition, CND tactics, which had once seemed radical, now appeared tame to a generation of young and increasingly politicised activists.[57]

Paradoxically, the end of the Cuban missile crisis brought a change in attitude to the threat of nuclear war. After the two powers withdrew, it seemed as though there was more chance of political solutions. Jackie Mulhallen tells of how 'In the early '60s, I was even for a bit in a sort of reserve organisation which my father commanded. [It] trained women equally to be able to command small boats, and that was really because I wanted to go to sea, but the ostensible reason was a sort of civil defence one.' While she felt that this might be necessary given the real threats of war, 'In the mid-'60s, because war hadn't resulted over the Cuban missiles, however, I felt that there could be diplomatic solutions.'[58]

There were also moves by the superpowers to limit testing. A Partial Test Ban Treaty was signed by the United States, the Soviet Union and Britain in 1963. This banned all nuclear weapons testing in the atmosphere and helped to make the Cold War appear less threatening. However, France did not sign and China tested its first atom bomb the following year.[59]

The world had gone to the brink in 1962. The relief felt that there were now steps which might prevent something similar happening was palpable. This had a dampening effect on CND, since the sense of urgency which had led to its creation was no longer there. Thus CND came to the end of its first phase as a mass movement, as the concerns of especially the new generation of radicalised young people moved on to campaigning on a range of alternative issues. The campaign had articulated much of what a New Left felt was wrong with a society whose prosperity was premised on the cone of a bomb. But the Left's agenda was changing, and for the first time in several years the movement against nuclear weapons was no longer a top priority.

In 1964 Labour came to power, when a military conflict in Vietnam was gripping the attention of those who wanted to campaign against war. The activists often transferred their allegiance to new forms of campaigning and new causes around which to organise.

CND and the various movements against nuclear weapons played a major role in politicising women who were beginning to grapple with a society that was changing rapidly and for whom war and peace were among the most important issues confronting them. Some women were of course already politicised, coming from Labour or Communist Party backgrounds and with experience of campaigning on other issues. Others, especially married women with children, sympathised with the movement but were not involved until later. Angela Sinclair came back after some years working abroad with her husband:

> 'When I came back to England I was very much at sea. CND had already started so I didn't go on any of the big early marches. I went to a meeting in the town hall about pensioners. I decided to start a charity about getting them their rights. Then I joined all the political things that went with it. The Greater London Pensioners' Association, the National Pensioners' Association, I went on all the marches and I went to Aldermaston, Greenham Common'.[60]

Jane Shallice's mother, a peace campaigner since the 1930s, did not go on the Aldermaston marches, but did attend local events.[61]

But even for women like her, CND had a very powerful effect, politicising the end of a relatively conservative decade and making nuclear weapons a national topic. It appealed to younger women who might not have joined one of the established parties and who were not necessarily members of trade unions.

Sheila Rowbotham recalls going to her family home in Leeds and wearing her CND badge with pride as something which marked her out as somehow different and perhaps slightly dangerous.[62] The peace movement provided an entry into politics which opened up women's horizons and from which they took energy and imagination into different campaigns.

It is hard to imagine the campaign against nuclear weapons in this period without the beginnings of a student movement, the signs of a youth culture and the wider horizons for women, especially through education. Opposition to the Vietnam war centred on young people and students.

Women were still more on the periphery of the movements than they are today, but in CND women could find a place in grassroots, activist campaigning. This had a major effect on wider society. In this it marked the first modern protest movement, whose consequences would continue to be felt 50 years later.

4
Vietnam and the Liberation Decade

> I smell something burning, hope it's just my brains
> They're only dropping peppermints and daisy-chains
> So stuff my nose with garlic
> Coat my eyes with butter
> Fill my ears with silver
> Stick my legs in plaster
> Tell me lies about Vietnam
>
> Adrian Mitchell, 'To Whom it May Concern'

At the beginning of the 1960s, the war in Vietnam seemed no more than the distant rumble of a long-running national liberation conflict, barely making an impact outside the immediate region. By the end of the 1960s it was a major conflagration with the direct involvement of US troops and had shaped the anti-war consciousness of a whole generation.

It started as a colonial war, with the Vietnamese fighting the French, who had claimed Vietnam as part of their empire since the late nineteenth century. A succession of national movements fought against the French, the most successful being the Viet Minh, founded in 1941. The Japanese occupied Vietnam during the Second World War and so the Viet Minh were partly funded by Japan's enemies, the United States and the Chinese nationalists.

After Japan surrendered in 1945, the Vietnamese nationalist leader Ho Chi Minh declared independence in the northern city of Hanoi. But Vietnam was returned to the French. The war between France and Viet Minh nationalists ended in defeat for France at the battle of Dien Bien Phu in 1954. Peace negotiations led to the partition of the country into North and South Vietnam, with the North run by the communists and the South by governments closely allied to the United States.[1]

In 1960 President Kennedy sent the first US troops to Vietnam to help the South Vietnamese government contain 'communist insurgency'. But the conflict continued and escalated, with Kennedy's successor, Lyndon Johnson, sending more and more troops. Eventually 500,000 American troops were deployed there. In 1965 the United States began sustained bombing of Vietnam.

The war was in effect a proxy war between the Cold War superpowers. But it was also an attempt by US imperialism to stop Third World revolution from spreading, as it saw its interests threatened by liberation and anti-colonial movements underway in Africa and Asia.

The North Vietnamese communists were a real threat: they were a popular nationalist movement committed to radical social reform, especially land reform. That is why the insurgency was well supported and why the United States believed that if elections were held in the South, Ho Chi Minh would win 80 per cent of the vote. That explains why the United States backed the dictatorship in the South and why so many young people around the world came to see the war as immoral. Vietnam symbolised everything that was wrong with the world: imperialism, poverty, injustice, inequality and war. The Vietnamese – victims who fought back – were inspirational.

The guerrilla insurgency in the South, organised by the Viet Cong, was met by a ground war which attempted to defeat the communists but failed, despite overwhelming might and firepower. The ground war in the South was brutal enough, but the North was subjected to an aerial bombing campaign. The bombing was unprecedented in its horror – more tonnage was dropped than in the whole of the Second World War.

The movement against the war initially was small, but by 1967 large demonstrations were taking place in the United States – around 300,000 attended one in New York in April that year – and protests elsewhere. In October 1967 the marches went to Washington and 150,000 marched on the Pentagon, the nerve centre of the US war machine.[2] In Britain, anti-nuclear sentiment channelled by CND fed into more general opposition to war. This had already surfaced in 1956 with mass protests against

British involvement in Suez, and there was increasing agitation against colonialism and empire. These different strands came together a few years later in opposition to the war in Vietnam. The international solidarity movement also had a profound effect on the other social movements of the 1960s, not least on the emergent women's liberation movement.

The Labour governments headed by Harold Wilson (1964–70) did not involve Britain directly in the war by sending troops, which Labour recognised would be highly unpopular. However, Wilson did not openly criticise the war or Johnson's policies as the bombing escalated through the mid-1960s. A pretext for war was created with the Gulf of Tonkin incident in 1964, when the North Vietnamese were alleged to have attacked US ships, an accusation now known to have been false. Congress passed a resolution allowing the president to order military operations in South East Asia without declaring war.[3]

B-52s began a sustained bombing campaign of the North in February 1965. Within a few weeks 'Operation Rolling Thunder' was launched, aimed at the systematic destruction of North Vietnam.[4] US troops poured in: by late 1965 there were 184,000 in Vietnam 'assisting' 570,000 South Vietnamese troops, against 100,000 National Liberation Front and 50,000 North Vietnamese troops.[5]

Labour's Left became increasingly disillusioned with Wilson's policy over Vietnam. While still in opposition he had opposed any escalation of the war, but despite his talk of a 'special relationship' with Johnson, any reservations he might have expressed were ignored or brushed aside and his public stance was one of obsequious support for US policy.

Wilson travelled to Washington in December 1964, where he stressed his support for Johnson's policy. He tried to arrange a meeting with Johnson to stop the bombing in February 1965, but it was made clear that this was Johnson's decision alone. Wilson capitulated, telling the House of Commons in April 1965 that this was a fight of freedom against communism: 'We have made absolutely plain our support for the American stand against Communist infiltration in South Vietnam.'[6]

Solidarity and the New Left

The fact that Britain did not send troops did little to pacify the Left. A New Left had begun to form following the Russian invasion of Hungary in 1956 and the disillusionment with communism which set in as a result. Radicalised by the anti-nuclear movement and with a strong grassroots orientation which appealed particularly to young people, Vietnam was one of the key campaigns around which it now began to mobilise.

The women who became politicised through CND now saw in the Vietnam war the symbol of everything destructive caused by militarism. The bombing campaign and ground war were only a part of it. The United States used a chemical defoliant ('Agent Orange'), which destroyed trees and crops, and not only caused food shortages but also was terribly damaging to health. Whole areas were turned into wastelands and many Vietnamese became refugees. A full half of the peasants in South Vietnam were living in refugee camps.[7] As the war went on there were reports of atrocities, the most notorious being the My Lai massacre in March 1968.

All of these features of the war combined to increase opposition to it, especially among young people and students. Jane Shallice came to London in 1964 after graduating from Bristol University. She maintained her political involvement and when the Vietnam Solidarity Campaign was formed in 1966 she joined it. She remembers that in February 1966 Richard Gott stood against Labour in a by-election in Hull on a platform against the Vietnam war. In the same year Jane helped to form the innovative left-wing theatre group CAST along with Claire and Roland Muldoon and Red Saunders. Their first play, *John D. Muggins is Dead*, was about a soldier.[8]

Sheila Rowbotham was at the founding meeting of the Vietnam Solidarity Campaign in the summer of 1966, a consequence of growing militancy and radicalisation on the issue:

'I was the delegate from Hackney Young Socialists to a new Trotskyist-inspired organisation, the Vietnam Solidarity Committee [*sic*], formed to campaign for victory to the Vietcong rather than peace. Our first demonstration attracted only a few hundred people, but VSC was to become the main force in the anti-war movement as the mood changed.'[9]

Campaigning spread across the country and more and more people were mobilised. Chris Harman was a member of the International Socialists and attended VSC meetings, where he and other IS comrades argued for a demonstration under the slogan 'Victory to the NLF'. This much larger demonstration took place in October 1967 in London in solidarity with the NLF and on the day after the Washington march to the Pentagon. Harman says: 'The size of the turnout amazed the organisers. About 20,000 people assembled in Trafalgar Square. The police too were amazed. The demonstrators took over the whole road as they marched to the US embassy in Grosvenor Square.'[10] Sheila Rowbotham recalls being 'exhilarated by the size of the march, a great gathering of everyone I had ever known plus thousands more besides'.[11]

Jackie Mulhallen, growing up in the years after the Second World War, always felt a sense of foreboding about war: 'My generation thought that the third world war was inevitable.' She continues:

> 'I hated the racist and imperialist attitudes which led to the Vietnam war. In 1967 I began to work my way round the world starting in Canada, where I met intelligent, thoughtful, gentle Americans who had gone to live there to avoid being sent to Vietnam.
>
> 'The following year, in Australia, I went to a meeting where Simon Townsend spoke, a conscientious objector who had been tortured by the Australian military. I joined the anti-Vietnam demo in Sydney. As I travelled overland back to England, I went to Cambodia but was unable to go to Laos because Americans were fighting there secretly, so I was only too aware that the Americans would bomb Cambodia, it was no surprise to me. I also went to Afghanistan on this journey. Nearly everyone I knew was opposed to war and we taught each other about it through conversation, we didn't have [the] Internet. When the Vietnam war ended, we knew we had helped defeat the USA.'[12]

For young people in general, but for women especially, the 1960s were changing attitudes and consciousness. If the Vietnam war symbolised much that they felt was wrong with the world, it was not the only issue which affected and influenced them.

The Birth of Women's Liberation

The 1960s women's movement had its gestation in the civil rights movement and in the anti-war movement and its aftermath. There had been campaigns for women's equality before that. Indeed, in the United States there is some evidence that working-class women used the confidence they gained from their wartime role in industry to campaign to demand equality in the unions two decades before individual concerns of middle-class women began to surface.[13] However, much of the radical impetus for social change expressed by women in the unions was purged from US society by the anti-communist McCarthyite witch-hunts which dominated American society in the early 1950s. So when new movements sprang up a decade later, they had to learn a new politics.

The movement against the Vietnam war had a direct link to the founding of the women's liberation movement. The anti-war movement in turn had its roots in the campaign for civil rights in America's Deep South, which politicised a new generation.

Women were heavily involved in the movement for civil rights in the South in the early 1960s and many of them expanded this protest politics to opposing the Vietnam war later in the decade. Civil rights had become a major issue in American politics after the Second World War. The movement against racism and black oppression dominated the 1960s. Its best-known leader was Martin Luther King, famous internationally for his powerful speeches and his commitment to desegregation.

The civil rights and black movements became intertwined with the war. The campaign to win the right to vote, to end segregation and to achieve full social and political rights for Southern blacks attracted both Southern white women and women from the North who travelled to the South to help campaign and organise to win these rights.

By the early 1960s many Northern students considered it not enough to campaign on their campuses but moved to the segregated states to take action to achieve their aims. They helped to register blacks to vote and organised campaigns, including direct action, to draw attention to segregation. They encountered bitter opposition from racists, the police and authorities in the South and often faced real personal danger. Some were killed. They showed immense courage and dedication. Usually organised through the Student Non-violent Coordinating Committee (SNCC), these young men and women went on to build the anti-war movement and the women's movement.

The students' politics were egalitarian and one of their most popular slogans was 'Let the People Decide'. They were known as 'red diaper' babies for many came from communist or other left-wing families who had suffered under the McCarthy witch-hunts of the 1950s. But whereas the Old Left of the 1940s and earlier had a strong formal commitment to equality and would try to ensure that public figures in the movement included women, the New Left espoused different politics. McCarthyism had severed many of the connections with the Old Left and the students had much less understanding of issues such as oppression.

Some of the women who went South reflected later on what it meant to them. Lise Vogel, a feminist writer, was a 'red diaper' baby whose parents' concerns as she was growing up were 'money and McCarthyism'.[14] She recollected the time she spent in Mississippi as central to her experience: 'I got far more out of being in Mississippi than I was ever able to give back.' Arrested twice and spending twelve days in jail, 'In the end I knew that I had participated in history, that what we did made a difference, and that I had been tried and not found wanting.'[15]

Mimi Feingold had attended May Day marches since childhood and when she went to college in 1959 she got involved in campaigning against nuclear weapons. She welcomed the direct action of the civil rights movement: 'Something was happening . . . after the fifties when everything was dead . . . I wanted to run South straight away . . . On the other hand, I was scared to death.'[16]

Kathie Amatniek at first refused to go out of fear:

'I thought it would have been absolutely certain death to go to Mississippi. And a friend of mine, a black guy who was also a student at Harvard . . . I didn't want him to go. I begged him. I was sure he would be killed, because my vision of Mississippi was Richard Wright, *Uncle Tom's Cabin*, where everybody just got slaughtered, and I just felt it was certain death.'

She changed her mind when the friend returned, invigorated and excited by campaigning in the South.[17]

While women became politicised as a result of going to the South, they also encountered many difficulties on a personal as well as an organisational level. As Sara Evans commented in *Personal Politics*: 'The presence of white women inevitably heightened the sexual tension that runs as a constant current through racist culture. For Southern women this tension was a key to their incipient feminism, but it also became a divisive and explosive force within the civil rights movement itself.' As she observed, 'Interracial sex was the most potent social taboo in the South.'[18] It became a feature of many women's lives in the South, but caused tension, including between black and white women. These relationships were not necessarily free or egalitarian.

By the mid-1960s there was growing unease among some women about the male leadership of SNCC. Women's role in the civil rights movement tended to be secondary, even though they had a broad range of talent and ability. Women carried out the traditional administrative and caring roles expected of them, while the men filled the more public roles of writing and speaking. In shared houses, it was usually taken for granted that the women activists would do the housework.

As early as 1964 some women in SNCC wrote a paper cataloguing inequality in the movement. An SNCC Position Paper (*Women in the Movement*) was written anonymously by Mary King and Casey Hayden. They were apprehensive about the response it would receive. They catalogued grievances, such as women being consigned to clerical work, excluded from decision-making and being referred to as 'girls' while men were called 'people'. They drew repeated parallels between men's treatment of women and whites' treatment of blacks and talked of an 'assumption of male superiority'.[19]

While the paper was largely ignored, the response by one leading black member, Stokely Carmichael, became notorious. In replying to the paper's title he said, 'The only position for women in SNCC is prone.'[20] This was bad enough, but changes in the nature of the movement created more tensions.

The focus of anti-racist activism shifted from the South to the black ghettoes of the North, fuelled by the riots in Harlem and Watts and the emergence of black nationalism and Black Power. The movement against the Vietnam war was also growing. At its centre were Students for a Democratic Society (SDS), which campaigned on a range of issues to do with race and war, but whose analysis of oppression did not extend to women. The leadership of the student movement was liberal but male-dominated and heavily influenced by personal experience rather than theory as a guide to action.

For the women in the movement there was another difficulty. The US involvement in Vietnam was deploying ever greater numbers of troops and this meant that young men were being drafted or conscripted to fight. As large numbers of usually working-class and often black men were called up, the movement against the Vietnam war increasingly involved opposition to the draft. Demonstrators burned their draft cards, went into hiding and sometimes moved to Canada or Sweden to avoid being sent to the war. Women could only watch on the side-lines as it was only men who were drafted; they tended to be marginalised in the movement with their role auxiliary rather than at the centre of campaigning. This was highlighted by the slogan 'Girls Say Yes to Guys Who Say No', which summed up the situation for women in the movement – they were playing a subordinate and comforting role rather than a full and equal political one. The tensions were set to explode.

That began in 1967. An SDS conference saw women organising a 'Women's Liberation Workshop'. Drawing directly on the Vietnam experience, this equated women's oppression with colonial oppression: 'Women are in a colonial relationship to men and we recognise ourselves as part of the Third World.'[21]

It took a further leap forward at the National Conference on New Politics convention in Chicago in August 1967. A women's caucus was initially denied time to move a resolution to the whole conference but was then added to the end of the agenda. But the women standing at microphones were ignored. Then, when a male speaker was called to talk on 'The forgotten American, the American Indian' women rushed to the front. The chair patted one of them on the head saying, 'Cool down, little girl, we have more important things to talk about than women's problems'. The woman in question was the radical feminist Shulamith Firestone.[22]

The tone of many men on the New Left ranged from the patronising and condescending to the abusive and sexist. *New Left Notes* followed up the SDS conference with a cartoon of a woman wearing earrings, a polka-dot mini-dress and matching knickers holding a sign saying 'We want our rights and we want them now'. As Sara Evans comments, 'SDS had blown its last chance'.[23]

After the NCNP conference, women felt alienated from a process which had highlighted racism and black oppression but ignored women's issues. Firestone and Jo Freeman called a meeting to discuss these problems and this began the process of creating a women's liberation movement. Its paper 'To the Women of the Left' marked that beginning.

Not all men behaved oppressively; some supported the demands of women. In 1969, women protested at being expected to carry out the housekeeping tasks in a student occupation in New York's Columbia University and were supported by many men.[24] Individual men were sometimes supportive of women's liberation, but a number of factors within the movement tended to prevent women from coming into the leadership. The sexist response especially of men in the leadership of the movement only made it harder.

By the 1960s women's liberation's time had come. Women were able to play a role in politics unknown to previous generations. They came up against the contradictions of women's roles in society repeatedly. They also saw women playing a role in liberation movements as fighters and campaigners, which broke down many of the stereotypes about their supposed passivity. Vietnamese women fought bravely, as did the Palestinians like Leila Khaled.

The women who founded women's liberation deliberately took the name from the liberation movements they supported in other parts of the world, just as the nineteenth-century movement for women's emancipation took its name from the movement to free the slaves. They were part of a brave and principled generation which wanted to change the world. But they found themselves in a situation of great hurt and bitterness when those supposedly closest to them politically and often in personal relationships with them were also insensitive to their oppression and sometimes deeply hostile to it.

In the United States it was this individual experience, as much as the social and economic changes which women faced, that propelled them in a certain direction. It coloured the nature of the women's liberation movement which now developed. The failings of the internal workings of the movements led directly to the women's liberation movement. But while many women rejected the male domination of the movements, they neither rejected the movements entirely nor forgot what had politicised them. So at the same time women's liberation and feminism were connected with the anti-war movement, and Vietnam remained fundamental to the 1960s generation.

An early collection of writings from women's liberation in the United States makes this explicit. An excerpt from testimony about the My Lai massacre is followed by the comment:

'How can this happen? It happens because we have learned that the Vietnamese are not *real* people . . . We have developed a language and an ideology to rationalise genocide.

'What does the Vietnamese war have to do with women's liberation? Everything! Women in the movement here are talking about the essential rights of people to live full and meaningful lives, demanding an end to the way women, throughout history, have been objectified and dehumanised.

How then can we not recognise these same claims are being made not only by the oppressed in our own country, but by those oppressed *by this country* abroad?'[25]

By the seminal year of 1968 women's liberation organisation was becoming a reality across the United States. It was driven by a sense that women needed to organise themselves and that the attempts at compromise and cooperation with men in the anti-war, black and student movements had failed. It was also powered by some of the most dramatic events which pushed the movements forward.

The war changed qualitatively in early 1968 when the Tet Offensive gave the first indication that the North Vietnamese were able to defeat the mighty US war machine. The May student uprisings in France, followed by a general strike of workers there, created a new sense of what was possible. On the other hand, the Prague Spring was broken by Russian tanks that summer; Martin Luther King was assassinated; and American cities rioted and burned in rage.

All that year mass demonstrations against the war continued in the United States, Britain and Germany. For many young women this became a potent mix which fuelled their demands for liberation. Lise Vogel was part of a women's liberation group which met every Friday in Boston from 1968. She always attended 'no matter how exhausted I felt'. For her, 'A powerful longing for freedom and community flooded through these first moments of women's liberation'.[26]

The British Movement

In 1968 Jane Shallice joined the International Marxist Group, one of the left Trotskyist groups which grew out of the ferment of student and anti-war protest. She was influenced by a range of politics:

'None of us were theoretically sophisticated but we set up Sunday lunches and invited people to talk about Freud and Trotsky. Politically I was becoming more sophisticated. The black liberation struggle in the US was really energising, also the national liberation movements.'

She admired the Argentinian revolutionary Che Guevara, killed in 1967 in the Bolivian jungle, who had become an icon for much of the Left. 'I got very Guevarist at times – it was immensely attractive. Wrong but attractive.'[27]

Sheila Rowbotham watched the Tet Offensive on a flickering television in London. 'There is nothing as powerful as an example and the Vietnamese resistance sent a sense of possibility flashing out over the airwaves all around the globe. If the Vietnamese could take on the mightiest power in the world, what about us?'[28] She threw herself into campaigning against the war, organising a Victory to the Vietcong jumble sale at her house in Hackney, covering parking meters with stickers advertising an anti-war demonstration, dropping an anti-war banner from a bridge at the Oxford and Cambridge boat race, and mobilising for the first mass protest against the war in March 1968. For her, the suffering of the Vietnamese people, together with the mass international protests against the war, was the motivation: 'Vietnam was to be my generation's Spain and the suffering of the people became imprinted in our psyches.'[29]

While the movement never reached the heights it did in some other countries, there were two very important demonstrations, in March and October 1968. On 17 March, fighting broke out in Grosvenor Square between demonstrators and police. The demonstration was much larger than previous demonstrations and made national headlines because the police violence was unusual at that time. The marchers chanted 'Ho, Ho, Ho Chi Minh' and 'Victory to the NLF', slogans which marked a new militancy, in contrast to the call simply for peace. Now the demonstrators were clearly identifying with 'the enemy' of US (and by extension British) imperialism. The fighting and attempts to break through police lines too represented a new anger on the streets.[30]

'Its ethos contrasted with CND's "We the good people bearing witness" style. We were more angry than good and far less passive than was customary on British CND demonstrations, pushing against the police lines, arms linked at Grosvenor Square,' was how Sheila Rowbotham described it. The mounted police attacked with truncheons. The next day newspapers featured a photograph of a young woman being carried off by police, her skirt pulled up to reveal her underwear, and a policeman raising his hand. It carried the headline 'Spanked'.[31]

The police violence came as a shock to the demonstrators. One woman describes being kicked on the shins by a policeman: 'I couldn't believe an English policeman had deliberately kicked a girl so much smaller than him, so obviously helplessly caught in the situation.' She watched newsreel of the demonstration on the television that night and vowed 'never to go on a march again without wearing boots, jeans, and being prepared to defend myself'.[32]

The mobilisation over Vietnam continued throughout 1968, with organisers determined to stage a mass demonstration in the autumn. The war was only one issue in that remarkable year. The student movement and general strike in France in May 1968 had a profoundly radicalising effect internationally.

The movement was increasingly countered with state and right wing violence, however. Grosvenor Square was only a small part of it. In April the assassination of Martin Luther King was followed by the shooting of the German student leader, Rudi Dutschke, by a right-winger, which again brought British activists onto the streets. Students fought with riot police in the streets of Paris. In August the world was shocked by news from the United States, as police attacked demonstrators outside the Republican Party convention in Chicago. Around the same time, Russian tanks moved into Czechoslovakia to crush the Prague Spring.

The movement internationally was making some advances. Perhaps most important was President Johnson's decision not to stand for re-election in 1968. Anti-war and egalitarian opinion was strengthening, but it was also polarising. Many young activists decided to commit to socialist organisation, as Jane Shallice had done. The need to organise against a whole system of war, racism and exploitation gripped many students and young ex-students and workers. But at the same time, there was right-wing reaction, such as the London dockers' support for Enoch Powell MP after he delivered his notorious 'rivers of blood' racist speech in April 1968 and growing tensions over black and Asian immigration. In the United States the most militant black activists who espoused Black Power were assassinated by the police or FBI in the years following 1968.

The 27 October demonstration against the war was one of the largest seen in Britain, numbering 100,000. Demonstrators were very young, mobilising the growing Left which was cutting its teeth on a range of international and domestic issues. They were also very militant, although the organisers had made the decision not to return to the US embassy in Grosvenor Square, but to march from the Embankment to Hyde Park.

While the route and the decision not to go to the embassy were bitterly contested, and while some 2,000 left the main march to go to Grosvenor Square, most of the Left agreed, recognising that their aim was to broaden the movement as far as possible in order to put pressure on the government. While the press, politicians and small numbers on the Left focused on the breakaway demonstration in Grosvenor Square, the real significance of the march was to bring a mass demonstration together over an international issue. A letter to *The Times* from Roger Protz, a member of the International Socialists, made this clear:

'Here was the real threat to the system – the fact that such an enormous body of people could accept the aims of the organisers, could link arms and march that distance without being deterred by disrupters, uniformed or otherwise. Here is the force that is going to make the link between the demonstration and the growing struggle of the industrial workers. When that link is forged, we hope we will not disappoint you with our revolutionary potential.'[33]

One of the new shoots of industrial struggle was the strike of the Ford women machinists for equal pay. It was the first of many strikes on this issue over the next few years and had a symbolism for many activists, especially women, who were turning their attention to issues to do with women's liberation. While the situation in Britain was very different from that in the

United States, a number of similar concerns began to surface. One of these was the fact that men dominated the movement while women often played a subordinate role. Many of the speakers at meetings and demonstrations, and those involved in much of the central debate, were men. The movement in Britain was much closer to the traditional Left and the trade unions, and there did not seem to be as many of the extreme examples of sexism which so divided the US student movement in particular. But women were still only beginning to find their way in education and work. There was a much greater tendency in the 1950s and 1960s to see women primarily as wives and mothers. Women who played a prominent role in politics were relatively few and they were often either single or, if married, without children.

The opening up of sexual attitudes and relationships which was such a feature of the 1960s could be double-edged. More open display of sexual images did not necessarily challenge sexual stereotypes. More open relationships were not necessarily equal relationships. Sheila Rowbotham recalls being angry at a joking suggestion that the radical left magazine *Black Dwarf* should carry pin-ups of women.[34]

By 1969 the impact of the writings and ideas of women's liberation from the United States was being felt in Britain. A number of women's groups were formed, brought together successfully at the Oxford conference in 1970, and marked the beginning of the women's movement in Britain.[35] This was never a mass movement, however, and did not succeed in breaking out of a relatively small circle of mainly professional women. An interview with members of one London group by a student for *Shrew* magazine in 1972 gives a snapshot of this. Of seven women she talked to, only one was under 25 and four were over 30. Three had been born in North America and four in Britain. All were from middle-class backgrounds.[36] A recollection of the Tufnell Park group describes its composition:

'They were predominantly American and in their mid-twenties. Some of them had been active in Camden Vietnam Solidarity Campaign. Most of them had husbands who were very deeply involved in revolutionary politics.

Many of them too had had small children and felt very isolated both as housewives and as foreigners.'[37]

Two factors stand out: the high level of involvement of American women living in London and the fact that most women had prior political experience of the movements and the Left before they came to women's liberation.

While the American movements had all been mass movements, and therefore the women's movement in the United States also became a mass social phenomenon, this was not true in Britain. Only the anti-war movement could be described as a mass movement and its activity declined markedly after 1968.

The war ground on until 1975, but there was very little mobilisation in its final years. The bombing of Cambodia and Laos, which began in 1970, brought with it a new wave of protests, but not on the same scale. In the United States four students were shot dead by the National Guard at Kent State University for protesting at the bombing. This brought mass protests there, but had a much smaller response in Britain.

The women's movement remained relatively small, though it was influential. But women's organising was often outside this, in Left groups, trade unions or other campaigns. Jane Shallice recalls how she became heavily involved in trade union work in the early 1970s. The politics of the 1960s now informed the way in which young workers began to organise.

Successive women's liberation conferences became more fractious and divided, with increasing tension between those who defined themselves as Left, Marxist or socialist feminists, and radical feminists who wanted completely separate organisation from men. This was reflected in the changes in women's movement campaigning, which moved away from activity round trade unions and equal pay towards issues such as domestic violence and rape. In Britain, as in the United States, feminism sometimes led to a breach with men and mixed movements.

The Vietnam war ended in 1975. US embassy staff in Saigon had to be airlifted from the roof of the building as Vietcong fighters swarmed through the rooms below. The indignity of the final defeat was cheered around the world as a superpower was humbled. It was a seminal moment. The historian Eric Hobsbawm described how 'Since Goliath had been felled by the slingshot of David, there had not been such a debacle.'[38] It created the Vietnam syndrome whereby the United States found it increasingly difficult to intervene directly in other countries. This only changed fundamentally with the collapse of the Soviet Union and the end of the Cold War.

Gabriel Kolko wrote that the Vietnam war was 'the quintessential conflict in the long history of warfare in our century, one in which the social, economic, and organisational dimensions of wars increasingly overshadowed the purely military to become decisive in determining their outcomes.' He outlined the future choices for US imperialism: 'It might fight to a stalemate, as in Korea, or lose, as in Vietnam, but the victories it coveted by force of arms were now far beyond its ability to attain.'[39]

That was why the world's mightiest power had been defeated by forces quite different from the conventional enemy of another major power. It had been brought down by the heroism of the Vietnamese. One in ten Vietnamese were casualties, with 1.5 million people dead in the catastrophic war and another three million wounded. 60,000 US soldiers also lost their lives.[40] But the United States had also been defeated by movements at home and elsewhere. Soldiers, anti-war protestors and anti-racism activists had played key roles in defeating their own government.

That the tensions inside the movements also gave rise to the women's movement had contradictory effects. It created a layer of women who began to articulate demands about equality which had an important impact on wider society. This coincided, in Britain, with a rise of trade union militancy, which saw many women workers taking strike action for the first time. It also coincided with a raft of legislation on social issues from abortion to equal pay and divorce, which improved the position of women. However, as the 1970s went on, the dominant strands of feminism became more obviously detached from socialism and the Left. Women's liberation was defined by activists as meaning autonomous organisation, separate from men, and this led many away from joint campaigning and organising, and withdrawal from membership of Left groups.[41] Its theorists developed critiques of the Left as a justification for this break. These critiques came against a background of decline within the movements and a weakening of the trade union struggle in the second half of the 1970s. These two elements became mutually reinforcing.

When a new movement developed over issues of war and peace in the early 1980s, its most celebrated and iconic component embraced these separatist ideas.

5
From Greenham to the Gulf

'The only alternative to nuclear deterrence is surrender or capitulation.'
Margaret Thatcher

The US government was forced out of Vietnam in humiliation and defeat, routed by the bravery and determination of the Vietnamese people, and by mass opposition among its own civilians and military. This had a profound impact on the military reach of the greatest superpower. It was effectively prevented from intervening directly in wars elsewhere. This outcome – the Vietnam Syndrome – was important for the United States and was only fully overcome at the end of the Cold War when it began a series of invasions and wars in the Middle East. Before this, in the second half of the 1970s, the United States shifted its strategic aims and turned its attention to developing weaponry and arms which could give it a decisive advantage over its Cold War adversary, the Soviet Union. One example was the proposal to develop a neutron bomb, designed to kill people while leaving infrastructure intact. Opposition to this new weapon was understandably overwhelming, especially in Europe, and the plan was abandoned. But by the end of the 1970s a new threat had emerged: the deployment of Pershing and cruise missiles which would be sited across Europe.

This phase of the Cold War was also a reaction to the long recession of 1973–92. It involved an increase in arms spending in response to growing competition or tensions between states in a period of economic crisis.

Opposition to cruise missiles spread very quickly. The missiles were intermediate-range and ground-launched. They were missiles for 'theatre nuclear war' – a supposedly limited nuclear war – which would be played out in Europe. The fear generated by cruise missiles lay in the fact that they seemed to overturn the 'balance of terror', which many believed had made nuclear war unlikely. Mutually Assured Destruction meant that the two superpowers could not start a war without destroying themselves, such was the scale of their nuclear arsenals. Now the possibility of using tactical nuclear weapons made a 'limited' nuclear war more likely. In the proposed theatre of war – Europe – this generated a new movement of people horrified at the prospect.

In 1979 the Labour Prime Minister James Callaghan agreed that cruise missiles could be sited in Britain. He did so without consulting Parliament. The West German Chancellor Helmut Schmidt followed suit. The announcement that the missiles would be in Britain by 1983 was made after a NATO summit in Brussels in December 1979, by which time Margaret Thatcher was prime minister. This was the trigger for the start of a movement that would produce some of the biggest demonstrations in Britain since the Second World War and the birth of a mass movement across Europe.

The missiles were to be sited at two locations in England: at the bases at Greenham Common in Berkshire (quite close to Aldermaston) from 1983, and later at Molesworth in Cambridgeshire. As well as the new submarine-launched Pershings, which would replace existing missiles, there would be 464 cruise missiles across Europe: 160 in Britain, 112 in Italy, 96 in West Germany, and 48 each in Belgium and the Netherlands.[1] The British government also announced in 1980 that it was to buy the Trident nuclear submarine system to replace Polaris – the target of many demonstrations at Holy Loch.

Suddenly, after some years of decline when anti-war activity had focused more on Vietnam than on nuclear weapons, CND rebounded as a mass organisation. At the same time, another organisation was formed, headed by the eminent Marxist historian E. P. Thompson. It covered some of the same ground as CND, but explicitly addressed the potential for protest and mobilisation Europe wide. European Nuclear Disarmament (END) did not build a membership organisation, which might have led to competition with CND. Even so, some in CND were wary about

END, which they saw as engaging in politics in Eastern Europe. Thompson himself described it as 'a resource centre serving the British peace movement, and in close association with CND'.[2]

END was the outcome of an appeal launched by Thompson and the Bertrand Russell Peace Foundation in April 1980. This directed its message not just to Western Europe but to the Eastern Bloc, since all these countries would find themselves in the centre of any theatre of nuclear war, however supposedly limited its scope. It wanted a nuclear-free Europe and called on the people of Europe to demand disarmament. It was not only opposed to cruise and Pershing, but also called on the Soviet Union to stop producing its SS20 missiles.

Thompson was author of the pamphlet *Protest and Survive*. Its name derived from the government's civil defence plans, contained in a government booklet called *Protect and Survive*. These plans were widely ridiculed as providing no serious strategy in the event of a nuclear war, its advice including hiding under the stairs for 14 days. It had a similar impact to an earlier US government campaign which had urged those threatened by nuclear war to 'duck and cover'.

Protest and Survive, published by CND and the Bertrand Russell Peace Foundation, was a bestseller and its title became the effective slogan of the movement. While CND remained much more of a campaigning organisation, END, and Thompson in particular, helped to raise awareness about the missiles.

One woman, a CND executive member from Brighton, described the effect of the

'wonderful pamphlet . . . throwing up the whole question of missiles and the need for a nuclear-free Europe. The *outrage* that followed! We were so busy, we organised a petition . . . and had 2,000 people on this great march up the high street of Lewes . . . The same thing was done in Chichester for West Sussex on the same day. And this happened all over the country.'[3]

CND grew throughout 1980. Local anti-missiles groups were springing up everywhere and they tended to gravitate to CND. In 1980 a number of demonstrations showed the strength of feeling against cruise. The Protest and Survive demonstration in Trafalgar Square on 26 October of that year was estimated at 80,000.

The following months saw many more protests, including a trans-Pennine CND march at Easter 1981, where up to 10,000 mainly young people crossed from Bradford to Manchester over four days.[4] In autumn 1981 the peace movement reached a crescendo with huge protests across Europe and at least a quarter of a million in London's Hyde Park.

The new movement in Britain involved veterans from the 1950s and early 1960s but also very many new campaigners. The radicalisation over Vietnam, and then over wider social and political questions, had continued throughout the 1970s, when Britain saw waves of strike action matched only by Italy in the early 1970s, and women's liberation and gay liberation grew. Student, anti-racist, anti-fascist and other radical movements sprang up and helped to create a sizeable Left.

The second half of the decade saw a reversal of some of these gains, with agreement between the Labour government and the unions to hold down wages in a period of recession and series of cuts in public spending starting in 1976 at the insistence of the International Monetary Fund. A series of defeats internationally, including the Portuguese revolution of 1974–75 and the successful military coup against the left reformist government in Chile in 1973, further weakened working-class confidence amid industrial defeats and retreat.

Two factors impacted especially on the peace movement against the missiles. The first was the growing radicalisation inside the Labour Party. The Callaghan Labour government lost to the Conservatives in the spring of 1979 having presided over several grim years as working-class living standards went down, street fascism grew and the labour movement became more sectional, divided and weaker.

The response within the Labour Party to its defeat was that many activists moved to the Left and demanded a change in policy. This reaction crystallised in the campaign for democratic change to make the party more accountable, which in turn led to the campaign to elect the left-winger and former Cabinet minister Tony Benn as deputy leader of the party.

Many of those first radicalised in the 1960s now joined the Labour Party. Among the range of issues which galvanised the Left was the question of the missiles and nuclear disarmament and this once again became a major debate within the party. At the party conference in the autumn of 1980 a position was passed in support of unilateral nuclear disarmament.

The second, and related, factor was the direction in which the women's movement and feminism was going. By the late 1970s there were often sharp divisions between socialist feminists and radical or separatist feminists. The movement had effectively split, with the 1978 National Women's Liberation Conference in Birmingham conducted in an atmosphere of such acrimony that it was the last one to be organised in Britain. Many socialist feminist women now joined Labour and were often active in CND. Separatist feminists rejected this path, although they campaigned around peace. Once again the issue of women and war was closely connected.

The women's liberation magazine *Spare Rib* carried an interview with Benn in its 100th issue, in which he confirmed his support for socialist feminism within the Labour Party.[5] Joan Ruddock, a campaigner from Reading, became a leading spokeswoman for the movement and chair of CND in 1981. She later became a Labour MP.

More women were going into higher education and beginning to benefit from some of the changes introduced in the 1960s, with more job opportunities, financial independence and a keener sense of their role in politics. The movements of the 1960s and 1970s had politicised many young people. This radicalisation continued into the early Thatcher years.

Kate Hudson, who later became chair of CND, was highly politicised and focused on the missiles as one of her key campaigning issues:

'I had two phases of involvement with the peace movement, the first in the early 1980s, which I guess is a common experience for people of my age. I left university in 1980, the height of Thatcherism. I'd just joined the Communist Party in the late 1970s, but I think the big movements that were going in the early '80s probably shaped me as much: the anti-apartheid struggle and CND, the big campaign against cruise missiles.

'We all shared an extraordinary fear that we were going to be blown up and there was going to be a nuclear holocaust. Those films at the time – like *When the Wind Blows* and *Threads* – were so devastating. Like hundreds of thousands of other people, I became involved then and went on the big demonstrations.'[6]

One feature of the new movement against missiles was the emergence of peace camps outside US bases. The specific oppression of women was highlighted by the emergence of the peace camp at Greenham Common in 1981, which changed the whole emphasis of campaigning against the missiles.

The Greenham Common Movement

Ann Pettitt was living in rural Wales with her partner and two young children when she first became concerned about cruise missiles. She came from a political background – her father was a Communist Party member and her French mother had experienced war and occupation as a teenager: 'My parents were not like those of my friends.'[7] She had taught in London but became disillusioned with city life and opted for self-sufficiency in the country. But she found that the threat of war followed her to the most remote rural corners and felt compelled to do something about it.

She started organising against the missiles in 1980. She was one of the many who read *Protest and Survive* and was energised by its arguments. In between milking the cow and bringing up toddlers, in early 1981 she planned a women's march from Cardiff to the Greenham Common base to protest at the siting of the missiles there.[8]

Ann and three other women planned and organised, gradually winning more women to a commitment to march. She contacted peace campaigners along the route to ask them to provide food and shelter. Some were sceptical. One man who was phoned wanted to know who was really behind it: 'This march thing, is too big to be just ordinary women, like you say you are, just doing it.' Ann replied that they were Women for Life on Earth.[9]

One of the women who joined them was Helen John. She was living in Powys, having left London to escape pollution. She then learnt that the government was planning to bury nuclear waste in the area and so joined a campaign to stop this. It led her to join Ann Pettitt's march and she 'grew more committed as we walked'.[10]

The march set off in August 1981, arriving at Greenham in early September. Helen John describes what happened next:

'We arrived at the base, having decided to take a leaf from the Suffragettes, and four of us chained ourselves onto the front fence. On the evening of 5 September 1981 the American Base Commander looked at us with disdain and told us we could stay there as long as we liked. I decided to accept his kind offer and his words changed the whole course of my life.'[11]

That was literally true in Helen's case, for she stayed at the camp from then on. The women had to brave all sorts of hardship and separation from their families to set up the camp. They were not particularly high profile in the movement, and Pettitt and other Greenham women decided to march from Newbury to join the mass CND demonstration in Hyde Park in October 1981, where she was given a speaking slot. Support for the camp snowballed after that.

The women adopted the tactic of blockading the base to protest at the building of silos to house the missiles. This continued throughout 1982, and they were subject to evictions, prosecution and imprisonment. Lynne Jones documents how women were served with eviction orders, had to go to court, refused to comply and were sent to prison.[12]

But the camp kept going, attracting more publicity and support. The women decided to hold a demonstration of women surrounding the whole of the vast base. Around 30,000 women and a good number of men travelled from across Britain on 12 December 1982 to 'embrace the base'. Many placed mementos on the perimeter fence. The demonstration attracted worldwide publicity against the siting of cruise missiles, which were due to arrive the following year.

Greenham became a mass movement. Angela Sinclair, a campaigner since the Second World War, was one of the many thousands who went there:

> 'There was this wire and I had a pair of secateurs in my car. I went round snipping all the wire. One of my big regrets [was] when I went to Greenham. It's called Greenham Common, so I went onto the common and a policeman stopped me and I said, "I want to walk on the common." He didn't know what to say so he let me pass. So then I got to the Americans and I couldn't get past them. I didn't dare persist because I didn't know what the law was. Some people went to prison. I think if I'd persisted I'd have got them out a couple of years earlier.'[13]

Kate Hudson was also inspired by Greenham:

> 'In 1982 I went to Greenham to the women's camp. I strongly identified as a feminist at that time. I didn't really understand the military issues but it was just something again that everyone felt they should do to survive. The peace movement was so big at the time because it was a survivalist thing. Protest and survive, the slogan, really meant something. The message was a very strong one. When there were 35,000 surrounding it, I just remember getting up in the dark, getting dressed in the dark, standing around this fence, and then going home when it was dark. It was a good atmosphere though.'[14]

Rae Street felt that it helped her political confidence and development. She played a more central role in the movement, travelled and did things she had never expected to do:

> 'I have many recollections of the '80s. One of the most vivid – as with so many women – was the extra confidence and motivation that the Greenham peace women gave me.
>
> 'It was through them, in particular Gwyn Kirk [who co-authored *Greenham Women Everywhere*] that I experienced some of the most important times of my life as a peace activist and anti-nuclear campaigner. The Greenham women had resolved to take the US government to court for breaking international law by deploying cruise missiles in Europe. For this campaign they need funds and awareness-raising inside the US. Gwyn

heard me speak in Manchester at a women's conference and asked if I would go on a lecture tour in the US. So, with some trepidation, I did.

'I toured the Mid-West, giving, I think, in all 25 talks in two weeks. I travelled north from St Louis to Milwaukee. I just loved every minute. Not only had I found my voice, but you see, folks listened, be they in schools, colleges, women's groups. No one recognised my accent as 'inferior'; they actually liked it. I couldn't believe it. All my life until that point I had been dogged by people who found my Leeds accent "broad" and even "common". Equally, I got satisfaction from bringing folks who were not very "political" (this was especially true of the Mid-West) a different view from Europe on war, weapons and militarism.

'I did three more tours after that and met innumerable friends and peace activists with whom I am still in touch.

'In those years, too, I took over from Bill Moyer, a US writer, Quaker and supporter of non-violent direct action, the People-to-People Network linking peace campaigners in the UK and North America. I think we did useful work in raising awareness, mainly in the UK, of resistance movements in the US. But there is still a huge deficit in general knowledge of a "different America".'[15]

Greenham caught the imagination and symbolised the changing role of women in society. Chanie Rosenberg recalls: 'My niece, Beeban Kidron, made a film [*Carry Greenham Home*] about it. She won a film competition with that film. She was the only woman in her class. There was tremendous support for Greenham from women and men.'[16]

Women were taking direct action at least in part on the basis of being women. Their action would be echoed just two years later when miners' wives and families formed Women against Pit Closures during the year-long miners' strike. In that sense, Greenham changed politics and brought women's issues to the fore. It also influenced future generations and activists. Kate Connelly, growing up in Cambridge, remembers:

'I have always been opposed to war because it is incompatible with freedom and equality, and because ordinary people are always the ones to suffer the most. When I was in my early teens I did participate in a demonstration outside Lakenheath where the American military were keeping very dangerous weapons. (I think they were nuclear, but I cannot really remember now.)'[17]

Many activists became involved in later campaigns, and women in Stop the War often had connections with Greenham. Jackie Mulhallen thinks that women's involvement in organising for peace was influenced by women's liberation:

> 'The feminist movement may have had something to do with it. That was not the case with me. But I know women ten years or more my junior who were feminists and who became involved in the anti-war movement, such as my co-organiser in Kings Lynn Stop the War who was a former Greenham Common woman.'[18]

The camp continued after the missiles were sited in 1983. The women were repeatedly harassed, were taken to court, were opposed by many local residents and endured bitterly cold and wet weather. Some were jailed and suffered further hardship for their cause. They were regarded by many as inspirational and looking back 30 years on, it is clear that their legacy was a permanent one.

However, there were many political differences over the camp and what it should represent. Kate Hudson explained how it 'helped shape the political culture round feminism at the time, that was the form of feminism, round Greenham. It was separate from socialism then and was more of a radical feminist trend which was very influential in the peace movement.'[19] Greenham was supported by women and men across the socialist and peace movements. Tony Benn backed the camp and many Labour Party members were strongly supportive. But the politics expressed there often made people uneasy.

Jane Shallice, heavily involved in developing anti-racist teaching policies, felt that being a union activist raised questions of race and class as well as of gender. For her, the way Greenham was projected was too narrow, even though 'it probably did attract women who would not have gone to a mixed demo':

> 'I'm a socialist and would never call myself a feminist because I believe socialism should embrace all of these. At Greenham I thought that gender

became the framework of everything. That made it more difficult to work with the Greenham women. I went on the big demos, but that was all.'[20]

Kate Hudson approached the campaign as separate from some of her other political activity. She thought that radical feminism and pacifism 'were very much interlinked and didn't really impinge that much on my party political life. My involvement [with Greenham] wasn't through my party branch. Some of the CP's theoretical arguments on women would have gone over my head.'[21]

The theoretical arguments over feminism could be outlined at Greenham. One was about the role of men. The initial march organised by Ann Pettitt was conceived as women-only, with support welcomed from men at each stage and stop of the march, although a couple of men were allowed to tag along and initially joined the camp. Quite soon this changed and it became women-only.

The justification for this was mixed. The women's movement had from its outset stressed the right and, in the view of the majority, necessity of women organising separately from men in order to achieve a non-oppressive environment. Part of the motivation for the camp was that it encouraged and empowered women, building their confidence as campaigners and organisers. However, there were other motivations, including the idea that missiles were representative not just of military values but specifically of male values. A popular slogan was 'Take the Toys from the Boys', suggesting that men were responsible for wars and weapons and that 'female' values were different. Non-violence was equated with the female and violence with the male. The idea was very problematic for many who supported the camp but who came from socialist feminist and Left backgrounds. They did not see the issue in gender terms, pointing to women such as the Prime Minister, Margaret Thatcher, who was as belligerent as any man about the missiles. She had also just led a bloody and jingoistic war in the Falklands/Malvinas in 1982. The sinking of the Argentinian ship *General Belgrano* as it was sailing away from the conflict zone under Thatcher's orders was one of Nicola Pratt's earliest political memories:

'I don't remember when I became conscious of questions of war and peace. I do remember the woman who challenged Margaret Thatcher on live TV about the sinking of the *Belgrano*. I remember her voice as a lone anti-war voice against the jingoism of the mainstream media. But I was too young to do much about it.'[22]

Most socialist feminists saw issues of war and peace more in terms of a competitive economic system which depended on militarism and war, and tended to reject the notion that gender was the key division.

A related disagreement stressed women's caring and nurturing roles, which, it was claimed, made them more inclined to support peace than war. Some socialist women felt that this overemphasised the traditional stereotypes which they had spent the previous decade and a half trying to escape. This view also underestimated the many men on the Left and in the peace movement who rejected so-called masculine values.

Radical or separatist feminism could sometimes take the form of hostility to men. Jane Dennett (Rowley), who lived at the camp, described how her teenage son was treated when he visited her:

'The things radical feminists said to him were *dreadful*. "Have you come to get your bottle filled?" "Why don't you leave your mother alone?" "It's because of *your* sex that we're in this situation" . . . The hatred was *terrible*. It was almost as obscene as the weapons. How *can* women hate men so much?'[23]

The conviction that, because they gave birth, women necessarily would be committed to peace was very strong. Tamar Swade, a founder of 'Babies against the Bomb', explained in an article written in the early 1980s that she was more committed to peace after having a child: 'I am responsible for its existence – and no amount of word-juggling can get away from this. It is my responsibility and my urgent desire to ensure its survival.'[24]

Some of the politics in the camp moved very far from traditional Left organising towards a more mystical analysis, which talked about the goddess and stressed women's role as witches, dragons or weavers, weaving webs around the base. The word 'spinster', a term often used condescendingly to denote an unmarried woman, was reclaimed, stressing women's important spinning and weaving role.[25] There was also an argument about who had the right to decide – was Greenham the property of the wider movement or were only the women involved in camping allowed to make the decisions?[26]

The mass nature of the movement waned, probably in large part due to the increasingly inward-looking nature of the politics, although the camp continued. Commitment to the camp was high, with women having to leave home and family to make their political point. But while passive support was strong, few felt able personally or politically to make the commitment.

Its main legacy includes women-only peace activity and the permanent part that peace camps now play in the movement. Greenham reinforced a strong emphasis on direct action. Women like Helen John and Lindis Percy represent this tradition today. Kate Hudson points to the women's support groups in the miners' strike in 1984–85 and believes:

> 'The women's peace camps were part of the impact of '70s feminism definitely, from my point of view. Then there was the argument about women's sections and black sections [inside the Labour Party]. I think I'm shaped by feminism as much as by my communism. I've had arguments with younger women about how they were relating to men in recent years. I'm totally shaped by '70s feminism.'[27]

For Helen John, still active in organising peace camps: 'Greenham is a memorable victory of the thousands of women who lived there for years and the women and men of Cruisewatch who covered the roads all over the country, never allowing the weapons to be moved in secret.'[28]

Welcome to the New World Order

The economic and political architecture established at the end of the Second World War was long-lived, so long that it seemed to many that it would last forever. But it did not. Economic and military competition between the United States and Soviet Union was financially draining to both sides but more so to the Soviet Union, with an economy only half the size of its rival's.

The missiles race of the early 1980s was aimed in part at weakening the Soviet Union economically. It was forced to allocate a very high percentage of its wealth to arms rather than to its own citizens. The war in Afghanistan exacerbated the problem and the Soviet withdrawal in defeat was followed by economic and political crisis.

The revolutions of 1989 in Eastern Europe ushered in the collapse of the second superpower and Eastern Bloc. They were expected to bring with them a 'peace dividend' and the end of the nuclear arms race. But this was a convulsive change in politics and one that gave rise to a new era of wars, with very different characteristics from previous ones.

Now that the United States was the only superpower it felt able to engage in wars of intervention, first in Iraq in 1990–91 and then throughout the 1990s in the former Yugoslavia, which broke up under the pressure of economic and social crisis. The ethnic tensions which surfaced led to a series of wars, culminating in the NATO bombing of Serbia and Kosovo in 1999.

Humanitarian intervention was expressly given as a reason for the West's role in the various Balkan wars and to some extent for the first Iraq war. Nevertheless, these wars triggered anti-war mobilisations, sometimes on a considerable scale and often led by women, but not to mass movements the size of some previous campaigns.

The international relations of the post-Cold War world were soon tested in the Middle East, when Iraq's invasion of Kuwait in 1990 was met by full-scale war, with the United States mustering a massive force to drive the Iraqis out. President Saddam Hussein had been an ally of the West when he was waging war against Iran in the 1980s but that changed once the war was won. His incursion into Kuwait, which he believed had been given tacit support by April Glaspie, US ambassador to Iraq, was his pretext.

An anti-war movement was set up by CND activists. Carol Turner formed the Committee to Stop War in the Gulf, which included a number of CND figures, among them Bruce Kent and Marjorie Thompson, as well as trade union, Left and peace campaign representatives. A long-time peace campaigner, Carol began organising when still a teenager in the 1960s. She was involved in CND and Labour CND throughout the 1980s and became national secretary to the Committee to Stop War in the Gulf (1990–91). She was later national coordinator of the Committee for Peace in the Balkans (1993–2005), and coordinator of the cross-party Iraq Liaison Group (2002–5). The Committee organised a number of demonstrations against the war.

Anti-war feeling was modest compared with more recent wars but the bombing of retreating Iraqis at the end of the war on the Basra Road caused revulsion at the vast numbers killed. It was called to a halt by President Bush Sr. because he feared a popular backlash.

Nicola Pratt became involved in anti-war campaigning tin this period:

'When I moved away from home to university [in Salford], this was in the autumn of 1990 and coincided with the build-up to the first war on Iraq. At the time, I was also affiliated with the Revolutionary Communist Party. I remember that mobilising against the build-up to war was an important part of the RCP's activities during this period and it was also something that I personally felt deeply about. I have a strong memory of watching the first air strikes against Iraq on British TV and feeling very sad about the inevitable loss of life. Later that day I attended a rally in Manchester that was organised by a coalition of groups.'[29]

The impact of the war was to alter the balance of forces in the Middle East. Bush had turned against a US ally, whom they had backed in the 1980s and the United Nations now imposed sanctions and a no-fly zone on Iraq, which were to contain the seeds of future wars.

Kate Hudson became involved in peace campaigning again in the 1990s because she could see the direction international politics was taking. During the first Gulf War she was involved in general politics: 'In the last years of the Communist Party I was London district secretary from 1989 to 1991 as a young woman . . . [I] was able to operate in a less woman-friendly environment and I was determined that there was no obstacle to doing anything.'

The Gulf War and its aftermath left a sense of disquiet and foreboding among many in the Left and the peace movement. This was prescient and reflected an accurate perception of the situation. The United States could go on the offensive more aggressively than at any time since the Vietnam war and there was little that opponents could do about it, other than mobilise on the streets and try to raise awareness. This is what attracted Kate Hudson to peace campaigning again:

'After the cruise campaign ended people thought weapons were no longer an issue. In the mid- to late '90s I became concerned about NATO expansion, missile defence and the war in Yugoslavia. It wasn't that I thought that the end of the Cold War meant an era of peace and reconciliation, but the fact that it was so quickly clear it was the reverse of that propelled me into activity, so I thought I would join CND.

'I went along to London region and there was a long-running crisis in the London region. People were at loggerheads. At the AGM I was asked by the existing chair to stand as chair and was elected without opposition. I was accepted by both sides and things went more smoothly. That was in 1999, then the following year I was nominated for a vice-chair position nationally. London region is relatively Left in CND terms and was often in conflict with the national leadership and they put me forward. I got the highest vote for vice-chairs and then two years later in 2003 I became chair.'[30]

Other women developed an interest in issues around the Middle East. Nicola Pratt became involved in solidarity work with Palestine:

'Maybe a year after the first Iraq war ended I drifted away from the RCP and at the time I wasn't drawn into any other particular groups or movements, although I had strong links with the Palestinian Students Society on campus. I have recollections of the wars in the former Yugoslavia but I didn't feel that this was something around which I should become active. I was much more motivated by the notions of Western imperialist interventions in the Middle East. This was probably a result of my exposure to Marxism-Leninism as well as learning Arabic at university.

'During the 1990s, I attended a couple of events in London to protest against the sanctions on Iraq and I also undertook a 'sanctions-busting' act by sending a parcel to Iraq (which, of course, was returned undelivered). After I finished my degree, I went to live in Egypt for a few years and there was no opportunity for activism there (this was the 1990s). But living in Egypt made me feel even more connected to the Arab world on a personal level and made later wars feel even more personal.'[31]

War Returns to Europe

The decade was marked by new threats of war. Although no one could have predicted the way in which the War on Terror would begin, the build-up to war was unmistakeable in the 1990s. Arguably, the war can be seen as the continuation of a series of wars dating from the first Gulf War through the Balkans wars and the Kosovo bombing in 1999, to the present wars and conflicts in the Middle East and South Asia.

The economic system of neoliberal global capital which has spread throughout the world, leading to privatisation, free market policies and deteriorating working conditions, has been accompanied in the West by the growing threat of military power against any regime which chooses not to comply. The United States' decline as a great power economically, and the rise of rivals such as China, have only increased its tendency to resort to military solutions.[32]

So the 1990s was marked by a series of wars involving tacit or open involvement by the Western powers in two crucial regions: the Middle East and the Balkans. The background to these wars was the need for the West to deal with instabilities and uncertainties following the collapse of the Eastern Bloc and for it to reassert its control in regions in which it had strategic and economic interests. These interests included control of resources, crucially oil from the Middle East. They also included the geopolitics of the region. The Balkans have long been a hub of conflict, situated as they are on the border of Europe and Asia. They were also the site of exit for a new gas pipeline from the Caspian Sea.[33] Control of the

Middle East and its oilfields has been central to US policy since the Second World War.

When conflict erupted in the Balkans, therefore, various powers intervened. Throughout the 1990s wars accompanied the break-up of the former Yugoslavia, which can be seen as the most extreme example of collapse in the Eastern Bloc at the time. The country came under increasing economic crisis from the mid-1980s onwards, accumulating huge debts to the West and coming under attack from the International Monetary Fund, which imposed stringent measures leading to food rationing, unemployment and wage cuts. Workers struck and demonstrated in protest. The crisis brought national tensions to the surface in a country which had been largely free of them since the Second World War.

Slobodan Milošević used Serbian nationalist rhetoric against other nationalities to bolster his support.[34] In 1991 these tensions came to a head and the bureaucracies of the various Yugoslav republics abandoned the centralised state and went their own way. The United States and various European powers supported one side or another, trying to broker various deals and backing this with military intervention. Austria and Germany encouraged the richest states, Slovenia and Croatia, to declare independence. The British government backed independence for Croatia in return for opt-outs to the EU Maastricht Treaty.

The drive to separation led to war, mainly between Croatia and Serbia. Bosnia, with a large Muslim population, seceded in 1992, leading to a war involving Croatia and Serbia, both of which had large ethnic populations there too. Years of ethnic cleansing, massacre and killing involving different ethnic minority populations followed.

The Western powers intervened increasingly on the side of Croatia. The NATO bombing of Serb troops in Bosnia in 1995 effectively ended that phase of the war and was followed by the Dayton Agreement, which was supposed to bring peace. Tensions between Serbs and ethnic Albanians in the majority Albanian Serb province of Kosovo led to unsuccessful peace talks in Rambouillet, France in early 1999. The failure of these talks led to war.[35]

The Balkan wars marked the inauguration of the doctrine of humanitarian intervention which was to become the hallmark of wars in the Middle East. The Kosovo intervention was presented as saving Kosovans from nationalist oppression. This war marked the start of Tony Blair's career as a warmonger. His enthusiasm for the war knew no bounds and his hawkishness exceeded President Clinton's, as he desperately searched for a European leadership role for Britain and thought he had found it in military adventures.[36]

Blair expressed the view behind the 'new wars' in a keynote speech in Chicago during the Kosovo war in 1999:

> 'We are all internationalists now, whether we like it or not. We cannot refuse to participate in global markets if we want to prosper. We cannot ignore new political ideas in other countries if we want to innovate. We cannot turn our backs on conflicts and the violation of human rights within other countries if we want still to be secure.'

He continued by announcing a new doctrine by which he thought wars and international conflict should be governed:

> 'Today the impulse towards interdependence is immeasurably greater. We are witnessing the beginnings of a new doctrine of international community. By this I mean the explicit recognition that today more than ever before we are mutually dependent, that national interest is to a significant extent governed by international collaboration and that we need a clear and coherent debate as to the direction this doctrine takes us in each field of international endeavour. Just as within domestic politics, the notion of community – the belief that partnership and cooperation are essential to advance self-interest – is coming into its own; so it needs to find its own international echo. Global financial markets, the global environment, and global security and disarmament issues: none of these can be solved without intense international co-operation.'[37]

Blair and Clinton both seized on the new wars with enthusiasm. They justified them as being waged by a generation of post-Second World War politicians who would go to war to protect moral and civilised values rather than to grab land or power. In reality, they were waged for the same sordid and self-serving reasons as most previous wars.

Another development took place around this time: NATO, historically the military wing of the United States and Western Europe, now began to incorporate states of the former Warsaw Pact. Just before the war broke out in Kosovo, in March 1999, Poland, Hungary and the Czech Republic were admitted as NATO members. In April 1999 five former Soviet Union states attended NATO's anniversary celebrations in Washington and formed a pro-Western federation, GUUAM (Georgia, Ukraine, Uzbekistan, Azerbaijan and Moldova).

Western military organisation now extended to the borders of the Balkan states. The Kosovo bombing had as its aim asserting strategic control there, while minimising the influence of Russia in its former sphere of influence.[38] The broken Balkans states were to be brought under Western control, partly through military alliance and economic investment, and partly through direct semi-colonial rule, a situation that continues to this day in Bosnia and Kosovo.

I called a meeting to protest at the imminent bombing of Kosovo in the spring of 1999. It struck me very forcefully that they were about to bomb a European city for the first time since 1945. Two hundred people, including a number of prominent campaigners and journalists, attended. I then became part of the Committee for Peace in the Balkans, which usually met in Parliament and was strongly supported by Alice Mahon, Labour MP for Halifax. This committee held protests, several national demonstrations and many public meetings, some of which were debates. In Coventry Tariq Ali and I debated with the Labour MP Denis McShane, a proponent of 'humanitarian intervention'.

The relative popularity of the government, and the fact that it was a Labour government, made opposition to war harder to build. Many people who might have naturally been anti-war and who might have opposed the Vietnam war or nuclear weapons now supported the need for war.

The media played a particularly pernicious role, though there were exceptions. A *Times* journalist, Eve-Ann Prentice, described how she discovered that cluster bombs were being used by NATO in the bombing of Nis, in south-east Serbia:

> 'These are bombs that, when they explode, they have a whole lot of bomblets in them and these are full of fragments of hot metal and nails ... it's just like the effect of submachine guns spraying all over the place. Everywhere there were dead and dying people who'd been buying in the marketplace. It was pretty gruesome. I counted 33 bodies. Other journalists saw loads more in the hospital.'[39]

She and her colleagues forced NATO to admit to the use of cluster bombs. But most reporting stressed the government's view and its supposedly humanitarian role. This made campaigning more difficult, but also forced those who opposed the war to look beyond these questions to the relations between the major powers, at why the post-Cold War world was riddled with tension and at the connections between the globalised neoliberal economy and the drive to war.

While the wars did not result in the mass protests which have become much more common over the past decade, they created awareness among a minority. By the late 1990s, a new movement for social justice began to emerge. Those affected by neoliberal economic systems – ranging from trade unionists to eco-warriors to the indigenous peoples of Latin America – began to protest at their effect.

The huge demonstrations against the World Trade Organisation in Seattle in November 1999 highlighted how widespread these movements were. Activists met at the World Social Forums and European Social Forums. Peace and anti-war campaigning fitted into that, as did opposition to the arms trade. Women played a very big part in the protests, and feminist ideas were to the fore. They also protested at the numerous gatherings of world leaders in opulent venues where they discussed plans to extend this unequal economic system even further. One of the largest of these protests was in Genoa in July 2001, where a summit of the Group of Eight leaders was taking place. While large parts of the port city were sealed off to prevent protests, riot police repeatedly attacked demonstrators, killing a young man, Carlo Guiliani, and assaulting many more.[40]

As the fighting continued in the streets, unprecedented levels of security kept the politicians away from the protestors. The world leaders met in palaces and stayed on luxury ships anchored in the harbour. Helicopters circled overhead and the security services seemed very concerned about a possible attack from the sky. Only two months later we found out why.

6
A Mass Movement is Born

'I reminded them and their families that the war in Iraq is really about peace.'
George Bush, after visiting soldiers wounded in Iraq in 2003

Helen John was maintaining her solitary peace camp outside the Menwith Hill US spy base in the North Yorkshire countryside on the afternoon of 11 September 2001:

'The news of the attack on the Twin Towers was brought to me by two Ministry of Defence police officers, who came to ask what I thought this meant. I answered that in my opinion the US Treasury doors would now spring open, the funding currently restricted by Congress from the Bush regime would be granted, and the US's Star Wars, resource wars for oil, minerals, land and water would commence.'[1]

Helen's reaction was based on years of experience of peace campaigning, dating back to Greenham Common. Salma Yaqoob, a young Muslim professional in Birmingham, had no previous experience of anti-war campaigning: 'Like countless others whose lives are caught up in the cauldron of the War on Terror, my life would never be the same again after the events of 9/11.'[2] Salma described the fear that many Muslims, particularly women wearing the hijab, felt at the wave of hostility that they encountered: 'Some of my female friends were abused and attacked. I was spat on as I walked with my three-year-old son in busy Birmingham city centre.'[3]

The events following 9/11 threw women like Helen and Salma into a new anti-war movement. Like many they reacted to the approach of the Prime Minister, Tony Blair:

> 'We've offered President Bush and the American people our solidarity, our profound sympathy, and our prayers...this is not a battle between the United States of America and terrorism, but between the free and democratic world and terrorism. We therefore here in Britain stand shoulder to shoulder with our American friends in this hour of tragedy, and we like them will not rest until this evil is driven from our world.'[4]

Blair's words, uttered outside Downing Street hours after the attacks on New York and Washington, set the tone for his performance for the next six years of his premiership. He never wavered in his support for Bush and in his enthusiasm for war, especially the war in Iraq. It lost him one million votes in the 2005 general election and his unswerving support for Israel's war in Lebanon would cost him his job.

The events of 9/11 ensured that the first decade of the twenty-first century was dominated by US-led wars. Blair's policies meant that Britain remained the closest and most uncritical US ally. Yet there was opposition from the outset. This was weakest in the United States, which now experienced a groundswell of patriotism and revulsion at the attacks. These tended to isolate the anti-war voices. But in Britain the horror at what had taken place and at the deaths of nearly 3,000 people produced a contradictory response.

There were many who believed that war was justified to avenge the attack on the United States. This was the view of most of the media and nearly all politicians. But there was another response, which questioned whether 9/11 had been made more likely by the foreign policies of the United States and its allies. Some also argued that the terrible events of that day would lead to wars which would in all likelihood worsen the lives of millions, mainly in Afghanistan and Iraq. The horror of the 9/11 attacks was matched by fear that the reaction of Bush and his allies would prove to be a much greater threat.

Jane Shallice was on holiday in Greece that day, staying in a house without a television or radio. She went to a taverna where everyone was gazing at what she thought was a film on the TV. Her Greek friend asked someone what had happened, and was told, 'Maybe the Americans will understand what it means to attack someone.'[5] Views like this received little coverage in the media.

One immediate effect of the attack was to suspend much of ordinary politics. Carol Turner was on her way to the TUC annual congress in Brighton to help launch a

'labour movement initiative in response to the United States' announcement of 22 August that it would unilaterally withdraw from the Anti-Ballistic Missiles Treaty – the cornerstone of nuclear arms control for three decades – and had given the go-ahead for a missile testing site in Alaska which would be part of its so-called national missile defence (NMD) programme. The planned fringe meeting to launch this initiative never took place. The TUC was abandoned after the attack on the Twin Towers.'[6]

Rania Khan, now an independent Tower Hamlets councillor, was living with her family in East London:

'My personal memories are one of shock and horror. I remember seeing people standing in the streets looking through the windows of TV shops as the images of the Twin Towers with smoke bellowing out of them were being screened live. After the shock subsided and the news coverage shifted to Muslim fundamentalism I became scared. I knew instinctively Muslims were going to be subject of a backlash and that this one atrocious incidence would damage the decades of positive race relations in our country and worldwide. I became frightened and knew that we as a Muslim community needed to speak out against 9/11. That is when I decided to wear my hijab, believing that I could promote my religion in a positive light and not those extremists who claim to represent [it] and those who were given all the airtime in our media channels.'[7]

The all-embracing nature of Bush's war was immediately apparent. There was talk of waging war on Afghanistan if the Taliban government refused to hand over Osama bin Laden, the alleged perpetrator. But it was also evident that the real target was not war-ridden, impoverished Afghanistan, which posed no real threat to any Western state, but Saddam Hussein's Iraq. On the day after the attacks, the US government started to claim links between them and the Iraqi regime and to talk about a future attack on Iraq. Prior to 9/11, the Bush administration had been trying to find ways of escalating its confrontation with Saddam Hussein, following a decade of war and sanctions.

This marked a continuation of the policy embarked on a decade and more earlier. The wars carried out in the 1990s had not brought greater stability but continued conflict, and while the 1999 Kosovo war had decisively defeated Serbia and led to the eventual overthrow of Slobodan Milošević, the situation in the Middle East was much less satisfactory to the United States and its allies. Its policy in the region was creating unrest. Osama bin Laden expressly stated his grievances over 9/11 as continuing sanctions against Iraq, the plight of the Palestinians under Israeli occupation and the presence of US troops in Saudi Arabia.

At the same time, the United States and its regional allies were facing opposition. US troops were defeated in Mogadishu in 1993, Saddam Hussein was contained but still in power ten years after his defeat in the first Gulf War, the second Intifada had shown the resilience of the Palestinians and the Iranian Islamic republic was still in place. The War on Terror launched by George Bush after 9/11 was an attempt to deal once and for all not only with the Taliban but with Saddam Hussein too, installing pro-Western governments in Afghanistan and Iraq and asserting strategic control throughout the region.

The War on Terror has had a reach greater than any wars since 1945, and in its wake has come death, displacement and destabi-lisation throughout the Middle East and South Asia. Despite its stated aim, the war has done nothing to reduce terrorism; on the contrary it has led to a new wave of terrorist attacks from London to Mumbai and Toulouse. Even key figures in British Intelligence recognise that attacks such as the London bombing in July 2005 stem from grievances connected to the wars.[8] A vicious circle has evolved, where wars which began ostensibly to end terrorism have helped to fuel it.

Islamophobia and attacks on civil liberties are at the heart of the War on Terror. Racism against Muslims has increased. Surveillance of mosques and of Muslim students in universities is common, and the media and politicians equate Muslims with extremists and terrorists. From the very beginning, torture and imprisonment without trial went hand in hand with the war, from Abu Ghraib in Iraq to Guantánamo Bay. The United States and Britain in particular have enacted ever more restrictive anti-terror legislation which is increasingly targeted at young Muslims.

The Stop the War Coalition

While the media and government consensus was to back Bush's actions unequivocally, there was much dissent from numerous sources. While responses to the attacks invoked great sympathy for those killed and their friends and families, there was from the beginning an articulate minority questioning what the response should be. In Britain, opposition to the war ranged from large sections of the Muslim community, itself predominantly drawn from South Asia, to peace campaigners with a long record of opposing wars and some on the socialist Left, although some prominent left-wingers supported the war. But the movement went much wider than that to include some on the traditional Right who did not see war as ending the problems of terrorism; trade unionists, some of whom came out very strongly against the war; and members of the growing anti-capitalist or anti-globalisation movement.

This minority came together in the weeks and months after the attacks, convinced that the response should not be another war. A new anti-war movement was therefore born. These different streams helped to create an anti-war movement on a larger scale than had ever been seen before. It became an international phenomenon, with millions marching across the world on 15 February 2003 to try to stop the coming war with Iraq. One of the strongest and most enduring sections of this movement was in Britain.

The Stop the War Coalition was an ad hoc body organised at short notice by socialists and activists who had worked together in various campaigns and in the anti-capitalist movement. They rapidly drew up a series of arguments to combat the drive to war by the Blair government and the overwhelming majority of the media.

I helped to organise a meeting entitled 'Stop the War Before it Starts' held ten days after the attacks. The large hall at Friends Meeting House, the main Quaker meeting hall in London, which could seat over 1,200, was booked with some trepidation on the part of the organisers, and the Stop the War Coalition held its first meeting at the end of September 2001. The response was overwhelming. Over 2,000 people attended, filling the main hall, an upstairs overflow hall and leaving 500 people to be addressed by various speakers outside. Even then, some were turned away.

The meeting was addressed by speakers such as the political activist Tariq Ali and Jeremy Corbyn MP; it attracted many of the Left, seasoned peace campaigners from CND and Greenham (Helen John was one of the speakers), but also many young people and especially a large number of people from the Muslim community. The following week an organising committee, called to plan the campaign in more detail, attracted 500.

Both meetings were diverse, with large numbers of Muslims who, although sometimes active in raising money and aid for Bosnia, Chechnya and Palestine, were more often new to this type of Left or peace campaign politics. The enthusiasm of the meetings trickled down to local organisation, not just in London but across the country.

Jane Shallice became involved from the start: 'When the meeting was called I was so delighted. I just knew I had to find a way of helping and participating. The way it was formed and run was on a level I don't think any other united front has been . . . It opened up a lot of creativity in people.'[9]

The anti-war movement had a remarkable political impact. It mobilised the largest protests on any issue ever seen in towns and cities across Britain. It was highly diverse in terms of age, race, gender and nationality. It was essentially a grassroots movement, organised on a shoestring financially, never dependent on big donations and democratically structured through local groups and affiliates with a national steering committee elected at conferences.

One of the Coalition's most remarkable features was the involvement of women in organising and leading the movement. From the beginning it had many women at its heart: the present author chaired the first meeting and was subsequently elected convenor at the Coalition's first conference. Helen John spoke at the first meeting, along with Liz Davies from the Socialist Alliance. A long-time socialist and NUT activist, Jane Shallice became treasurer. Shaheeda Vawda, a young Muslim from South Africa, helped to found Just Peace, a Muslim anti-war group within Stop the War. Yvonne Ridley, a journalist, captured by the Taliban in Afghanistan in the autumn of 2001, spoke at the first demonstration against the war.

Although relations with CND were not particularly close to begin with, they became so later, especially after the CND leadership changed in 2003 and Kate Hudson became chair. Carol Turner from Labour CND was closely involved from 2002. In Birmingham the chair of Stop the War was Salma Yaqoob, a Muslim not previously involved in politics who was horrified at the racism against Muslims in the days after 9/11. Especially noticeable were the number of Muslim women involved, refuting stereotypes which suggest that their culture and religion place them in a passive or submissive role.

Women in the movement developed both a practical and ideological leadership. They learnt the skills of organising meetings, stewarding demonstrations, writing leaflets and articles, and speaking at meetings and on platforms at demonstrations. They also learnt about visiting mosques, trade union branches, schools and colleges to explain the case against war. Most people were not familiar with the facts about Afghanistan and had to learn very quickly. Some argued that war was part of an imperialist project, not just an attack on Muslims but part of a series of wars.

The involvement of women at this stage came from broadly two different sources. There were the long-time Left and peace activists, radicalised by events ranging from the Vietnam war and civil rights in the 1960s, the working-class struggle and movements of the 1970s to the Greenham Common movement in the 1980s. Many would describe themselves as feminists and some would accept the idea that women rather than men were more likely to campaign for peace. Some were pacifists, but many were not. Some were socialists or Marxists. Their various backgrounds brought a wealth of experience of politics, campaigning and direct action that was invaluable. They were brought up by parents who lived through the Second World War so were affected by their views and memories. Kate Hudson was among these and deeply influenced by her father's politics and experience:

> 'My father was from a mining community and his father was a NUM activist/lay official in the union, Labour of course because it was County Durham. My father was more left-wing than that. He used to read *Labour Monthly*, the Palme Dutt edited magazine in the late 1930s. He fought in Burma during the Second World War and that made him a very strong anti-imperialist. He was on leave in Calcutta when there was the great famine and this consolidated his anti-imperialism.'[10]

Others had direct experience of war and this led to their opposition to it. Dahabo Isse, now living in London, is from Somalia and has been at the forefront of campaigning against the wars in her country, helping Somalis in Britain over a range of issues and campaigning more widely about war. She describes the impact of war on her:

> 'I was first upset by the war in Palestine in that many innocent people, mainly women and children, were killed. I experienced the war in Somalia in which I myself was injured and some people wanted to kill me. That left a fracture on my skull and also continuing headaches. I have seen women and children die in front of my eyes, and many were facing starvation, displaced and on the brink of death. I decided to volunteer my time and knowledge to help those affected by the Somali war.'[11]

Yvonne Ridley, a journalist who entered Afghanistan in disguise after 9/11 and was captured by the Taliban, tells how war broke out literally over her head:

> 'On the night of 7 October 2001 I was held in a prison in Kabul and got a bird's eye view of the war launching and unfolding. The US and UK dropped more than 50 cruise missiles on the capital and you can hear them explode and feel their tremors and roars from 20 miles away. For the first time in my life I realised bombs don't discriminate between civilian and military, man, woman, child. There was nowhere to run and nowhere to hide for

anyone. It was, for me, a truly terrifying experience and I promised myself if I ever got out alive I would tell as many people as I could and would join an anti-war movement if I could find one. Little did I know that the Stop the War coalition had just been born.'[12]

Capture by the Taliban and being there during the war was a life-changing event for Yvonne, altering her views on many issues, including religion:

'It was a terrifying experience and one which I genuinely did not think I would survive. I had bought into all of the propaganda that I had been arrested by the most evil, brutal regime in the world and they hated women. I genuinely thought they would torture and kill me. It was only when they released me that I was able to reflect on the experience and realise they had been demonised by recognition. It also made me realise what I'd long suspected. Governments will tell you anything to manufacture fear of others and try and get their populations to hate people because you can't drop bombs on nice people.'[13]

The younger generation of women tended to have a different set of experiences. They came into politics against a background of globalisation. They had known greater opportunities for women, especially in education and work. On the other hand, they were part of a generation which experienced high levels of uncertainty about their futures. Some had participated in major social movements and demonstrations, such as the mass demonstrations against the World Trade Organisation in Seattle in December 1999, or the anti-G8 protests in Genoa in July 2001, which led to a growing radicalisation around anti-globalisation and anti-capitalist movements.

Young women felt that they faced an uncertain future and now saw the threat of globalisation and war as a new challenge. At the same time, they saw themselves as fully the equals of men. They were often highly educated and regarded it as normal that women should go to university and equip themselves for a career on the same terms as men. Whereas a generation earlier they might have joined a political party – and some did now – many saw the 'movements' as a political home, at least in the short term.

Tansy Hoskins was a student at the London School of Economics in 2001 and explains how she got involved:

'I wasn't at the founding meeting of the Stop the War Coalition but quickly became aware that something big was happening when there was a buzz on my university campus. I had been wanting to do something that expressed how I was feeling since 9/11 so I went along to one of the planning meetings and was impressed at the size of it and how eager to do something people were.

'We held big meetings on campus with speakers like Tariq Ali. Our STW group was keen to have women on the platforms and so I ended up chairing quite a few of the public meetings. We also passed lots of anti-war motions at our weekly Union General Meeting, held die-ins, did banner drops, stopped George Robertson, the Defence Minister, from coming to campus and held a protest when Blair's spin doctor and the architect of the 'dodgy dossier' Alistair Campbell came to the LSE.

'I had some very forthright and outspoken women in my university group, particularly Americans, who were always pushing for more involvement and leadership from women.'[14]

Kate Connelly was at school when she became politically active:

'The War on Terror did change my understanding of war and why it is important that it is resisted. In 2001 I identified myself as a pacifist. I had been brought up a Catholic but later became a member of the Society of Friends [Quakers] because their interpretation of Christianity made peace a fundamental principle. The War on Terror was so unlike the template of wars I had in my mind – for example, the First World War – in that there was such a glaring inequality between the might of American power and the Afghan people, who were amongst the poorest in the world. This, and learning about what had been happening in Palestine since 1948, forced me to confront the violence of resistance movements and I felt that there was a fundamental difference between the violence of imperialism and the violence of resistance. I was not religious and now I knew that I could no longer remain a Quaker because I was no longer a pacifist.'[15]

Young Muslim women were part of this generation and therefore subject to the same influences. But they also faced Islamophobia, an insidious form of racism which mushroomed as a result of the war. This experience gave their political activism an added edge. Muslim women were especially active in the anti-war movement, and in this process challenged stereotypes of their role. They had to overcome the usual problems of passivity and lack of confidence about performing political tasks which often undermine women. They also faced a degree of racial prejudice about their role, and they sometimes encountered problems within their own community or family because of their decisions to speak out and organise, which some elders and Islamists believed was not appropriate for women. Those problems were not always overcome, but where they were it was in the course of organising and campaigning that these women found a new role and a voice.

By the time the 'Coalition of the Willing' launched its war on Afghanistan in October 2001, the nascent Stop the War Coalition was established in many places. Its slogans were simple. To the main aim of 'Stop the War' were added the defence of civil liberties and opposition to any racist backlash, agreed at the 500-strong organising meeting.[16] The Coalition attracted broad support from its inception and groups were set up around the country. Thousands of people became involved – many for the first time – in political campaigning against the war.

The scale of the movement took many people, including the participants, by surprise because the mainstream mantra was that the war must be supported and that any other course was to give support to the terrorists. The rejection of these arguments by large numbers of people who were also prepared to campaign against the war demonstrated both a lack of trust in what the government and media were saying and a high level of knowledge about the issues involved.

The activists were young and old. Hundreds of meetings were held, petitions signed, coaches booked and debates conducted up and down the country. Penny Hicks describes how the movement came together in Coventry:

'I convened and chaired the first meeting in response to 9/11 in Coventry. Bringing the widest possible range of people together – I remember the tension, shock and fear in the meeting as well as anger. A Labour councillor, a Communist Party member and I visited the Mayor of Coventry – an ex-GMB shop steward at British Gas I had worked with when I was a Unison steward at British Gas – and secured the mayor's suite at the Council House for regular Stop the War meetings. The movement was vibrant and exciting and a complete shock to me.'[17]

Kate Hudson found herself in at the deep end of organising from the start:

'I became vice-chair of CND four days after 9/11, so I was rocketed into this extraordinary and remarkable situation. I found the inner resources to do this in my forties, something I wouldn't have been able to do ten years earlier. Women in their forties and fifties are ready to take on anything. In the earlier years there are more obstacles or hang-ups. It was as if everything I'd learnt came together.'[18]

Carmel Brown, a socialist journalist and radio producer in Merseyside, began to organise a meeting after the London one:

'I heard there were 3,000 people at a meeting in London and was asked could we get a big meeting in Liverpool, using some of my skills to do it differently from how things were usually done. I'd never organised one before. I did it the only way I knew how. I had lots of media contacts. I booked a hotel. I talked to all the union people; my own union (the NUJ) and the Prison Officers Association, gave me £100 each which paid for the room. It wasn't the most dynamic platform but it attracted capacity, about 300, so we knew we were onto a good thing.'[19]

Nicola Pratt had recently returned from living in Egypt:

'I . . . started working at the University of Birmingham. This was late summer 2001 and I remember being at my desk when the Twin Towers were hit. It was all people were talking about for the next week or so. When Stop the War Coalition was founded to oppose the US war on Afghanistan, I began attending meetings on campus.'[20]

Salma Yaqoob in Birmingham became an activist and chair of Stop the War. She was central to campaigning in the city and over the next few years helped mobilise many thousands for demonstrations, large public meetings and activities:

'From the outset there was an effort to build the biggest and most diverse anti-war movement in which Muslims could play a central and visible role. I was approached and supported to stand as chair and act as the public face of the Coalition in the city. Other Muslims also took up leading roles.

'My life changed as I began speaking in public and trying to encourage other people to also make a stand against the war. It entailed going into churches, mosques, temples, universities, trades council meetings and community centres, organising demonstrations and public meetings, as well as speaking to the media.'[21]

The mass involvement of Muslims followed a decisive act of solidarity at the first major demonstration. This turned out 80,000–100,000 people on 18 November 2001 – far more than many observers expected. A number of Muslims involved in Stop the War felt that the demonstration would be weakened if Muslims stayed away because it was during Ramadan and they would not be able to break their fast easily, which was due to take place at around 4.30 in the afternoon. It was agreed to mark the breaking of the fast on the stage with a prayer from an imam.

The Muslims organised to get dates and water, as well as the imam, so that every Muslim who wanted to would be able to attend the demonstration. The event was announced across mosques in London. The breaking of the fast as dusk fell in Trafalgar Square was a very moving moment, especially as non-Muslims were offered dates and water as well. It was a demonstration of solidarity which meant that Muslims were more likely to feel at home in the organisation. Salma Yaqoob wrote:

'One of the most striking memories for me was from one of the early demonstrations which took place during the month of Ramadan when Muslims fast till dusk. Watching thousands of Muslims and non-Muslims joining together in Trafalgar Square in the breaking of the fast, sharing food and water, all united against war and oppression, but diverse in colour, race, cultures and faiths, gave a glimpse of what another world could look like.'[22]

It was an historic first for an anti-war movement to achieve this degree of political unity across very diverse communities and this proved crucial to the growth of the movement.

Shahed Saleem, one of the founders of Just Peace, a Muslim organisation set up at the first STW organising meeting, described its importance on hearing the prayer in a 'packed and silent Trafalgar Square to resound in the heart of empire, so inscribing another line in the post-colonial history of Britain'.[23]

The Road to Iraq

The first phase of the war in Afghanistan was relatively short. The overthrow of the Taliban government took only two months and there was some feeling in the movement that this would mark the end of campaigning round the War on Terror. The movement continued but at a lower level, with smaller demonstrations in early 2002. However, it became increasingly clear that Bush's real target was Iraq and that he would not be satisfied until the United States and its allies had brought down Saddam Hussein.

When Tony Blair visited Bush's ranch in Crawford, Texas in April 2002 war was already in the air. Bush told the ITN reporter Trevor McDonald, 'I made up my mind that Saddam has to go'.[24] It was on this visit that Blair committed himself to war – a firm commitment he did not share with most of his colleagues, let alone the British public. 'Crawford was the turning point for Blair. That weekend he and [David] Manning [Blair's foreign policy adviser] concluded nothing would stand in the way of Bush and his mission. The question was not *if* there was going to be a war, but on what terms it would be fought.'[25]

The drums of war became louder as the year progressed. A meeting held in July 2002 in Downing Street to discuss the situation made this clear when it was eventually leaked in the run-up to the 2005 general election. The head of MI6, Sir Richard Dearlove, reported back from a meeting in Washington that 'Military action was now seen as inevitable. Bush wanted to remove Saddam Hussein, through military action, justified by the conjunction of terrorism and WMD [weapons of mass destruction]. But the intelligence and facts were being fixed around the policy.'[26]

The Labour MP for Halifax, Alice Mahon, put down an Early Day Motion in Parliament in April 2002 opposing military action in Iraq. It won substantial parliamentary support, including a majority of backbench Labour MPs. She set up a Parliament-based Iraq Liaison Group in April 2002 to campaign within Parliament and outside against war on Iraq. Carol Turner was coordinator and later became part of Stop the War.[27]

Over the summer of 2002 it was impossible to ignore the signs pointing to war. In September Blair's government published a dossier claiming that Iraq had developed weapons of mass destruction which, according to British Intelligence, could strike British bases in Cyprus in 45 minutes. These claims were greeted by the anti-war movement with scepticism and the Saturday following their publication saw the largest demonstration so far against war in Iraq. It also saw the largest mobilisation of Muslims in the anti-war movement to that point.

The situation in Palestine had been deteriorating badly, partly as a result of the changed politics created by the War on Terror, and in May 2002 there was a mass, almost exclusively Muslim, demonstration organised by the Muslim Association of Britain in protest at the massacre in Jenin refugee camp in April of that year. When there was a clash between another MAB-organised Palestine demonstration and a 'Don't Attack Iraq' demonstration organised by the Stop the War Coalition, it was decided to build one mass demonstration round two slogans. This was a highly controversial but very important step in bringing the Muslim community into the heart of the anti-war movement, rather than the different strands effectively having their own movements. Some of the more difficult issues, such as the lack of women speakers proposed by MAB, were resolved over time, and women speakers and organisers became much more prominent.[28]

The September 2002 demonstration was a turning point. It mobilised 350,000–400,000 people and was probably the most diverse demonstration ever seen in Britain. Meetings were held up and down the country. Penny Hicks 'chaired Coventry's largest public meeting in decades [about 500 people] . . . It was the first political group in the city not dominated by one political party – a genuine coalition. Some on the Left found this a problem and became ambivalent about being involved but it was its strength.'[29]

Jackie Mulhallen, living in a relatively isolated part of Norfolk, describes her involvement:

'I went on the September 2002 Stop the War demo with my husband but wanted to do more. Although he is not a Quaker himself, he was brought up in Quaker circles and still has contacts with them, so it was through the King's Lynn Friends that we met the CND organiser with whom we set up King's Lynn Stop the War. We arranged our first meeting in January 2003 and there were 50–60 very angry people in a town of only 35,000 – the room was too small. A lot of good political arguments were made. We booked two coaches, including a group from Wisbech, for the February 15 demo and one for the demo immediately following the outbreak of war.'[30]

In the aftermath of the September demonstration it became clear that the movement was growing rapidly. At this stage CND began to work more closely with Stop the War. There were tensions between some of the CND leadership and the newly formed Stop the War in its early years, with some in CND adopting an arm's length approach to the new movement. However, before 15 February CND's then chair Carol Naughton had asked to be part of mobilising over the war. CND therefore joined Stop the War and the Muslim Association of Britain in building the largest demonstration ever in British history. This helped bring the traditional peace movement more centrally into the new movement.

Kate Hudson was always in favour of this and understood that it would benefit both movements. This led her to challenge for the position of chair in 2003:

'The reason I stood for chair was to ensure that CND played a full and positive role in the anti-war movement and I wasn't convinced the existing chair fully understood the importance of that approach. In one way it was very important I stood. I wanted to be able to give expression to the majority viewpoint, which was in no doubt that CND has to be involved in anti-war activity. The leadership wasn't fully seized of the issue and I was determined to do that in a political way. I wanted to enable the majority politics to hold sway.'[31]

The closer relationship with CND endured much longer than the immediate issue.

Between October and December 2002 there were thousands of local events as well as national marches: direct action, included the blocking of roads, an occupation at the London School of Economics, banner drops on the main roads into cities. Halloween night was also the scene of demonstrations round the country. Tansy Hoskins remembers:

> 'For me the time when I most felt like we were going to actually stop the war was at the Halloween evening demo before the war [in October 2002], we got loads of people to come out from LSE and marched through London to join groups from other universities, the demo seemed to get bigger and bigger and we took over all the streets until we reached Parliament Square and took that over as well. Now I can see that it was "just another demo" but for me at the time it just seemed so big and so united that I couldn't see how we couldn't do whatever we wanted.'[32]

Carmel Brown attended a Halloween demonstration in Liverpool, which stopped the traffic in the city centre:

> 'One of the first demos was the Halloween protest in 2002, and I said it's Halloween, can't we do pumpkins with "no war" on and have a photo. I went on the Liverpool demo with my pumpkins and lots of people were there and chained themselves to a bus. The "not fairness" of the whole thing appeals to women generally.'[33]

Between that September and the outbreak of war in March, local demonstrations, die-ins and protests took place everywhere. Thousands turned out in towns and cities. These were often extremely large mobilisations, as Rae Street, long-time CND member and peace campaigner, remembers of the one organised in Greater Manchester:

> 'The main square in front of the Town Hall was filled to capacity – the largest demonstration Manchester had ever seen. I spoke on that platform where I was particularly concerned to raise the question of nuclear weapons. We knew by then that Saddam Hussein did not have a nuclear weapons

capability. That issue, and the lies and misleading information given by Tony Blair, his ministers and the media, rumbles on to this day.'[34]

School Students Rising

One unanticipated source of support came from school students, who organised two major coordinated strike days and many other protests and strikes. Young women often led these walkouts, reflecting the change in their position in education and increased political awareness. Kate Connelly describes her experience in her first year at a sixth form college:

'As the issue of the war grew increasingly prominent a group of us joined School Students Against the War and attended its meetings in London where we were asked what we would do to protest in the build-up to the attack on Iraq. My friend announced that, like all the other schools we had heard from, we would walk out. This national strike of school students was called partly in solidarity with action we knew that school students in America were planning to take.

'We went back to college with a pledge to walk out and we told everyone that we would only walk out if we got over 200 names, to avoid victimisations or people losing confidence about whether others would join them on the day. The day before the proposed strike we achieved over 200 names, got up early and stood on the gates in a sort of picket line and argued with people not to go in. Hundreds of students stayed out, we held an impromptu mass meeting and voted to march into town.

'No one listened to the police who told us that this would not be allowed, and even after they arrested three of us – including me – everyone continued to march. They held a sit-down protest outside the police station and, when it was clear that we were not going to be released any time soon, they did march off into town, held a rally in the Market Square where students took turns to address the audience, and then invaded Kings College bar before marching on parts of the town – the main shopping centre locked all its doors.'

Sinead Kirwan was also in the sixth form in London. Her group held meetings, including a debate with a representative from the US embassy. She was central to the walkouts:

'I think I got a banner and hung it outside the school and talked to people as they were going in and lots of people were doing things independently in other places. At 11 o'clock we'd arranged for everyone to walk out and everyone did. A couple of teachers actually did come down to keep an eye on us when we all walked out. I remember being quite shocked that one of the teachers who we thought was left-wing was actually threatening to expel people for leaving school. Other teachers were quite supportive. I remember trying to get people down to central London, a mixture of eleven year olds and older. We directed people to the tube station. That was the day war broke out. It was quite quiet at first, but then more and more people kept turning up and we sat in the road.'[35]

In Camden and other London schools the students frequently found themselves ending up in Parliament Square demonstrating, including on the day war broke out.[36] The students often faced discipline from the schools and were sometimes physically prevented from leaving the school building.

Henna Malik, from School Students against the War which coordinated the events, said of the strike on the day war broke out: 'We really did believe we could put some sense into this mad government . . . There was a lot of police violence. I used to have a little bit of faith in the police . . . but I saw them punching a boy right in front of me.'[37]

Working-class and Asian school strikers were often badly treated by the authorities. One campaigner in East London recalled hundreds leaving St Paul's School by breaking out of the school grounds. Sometimes they scaled the fences to march against the war.[38]

In Birmingham, Joanne Stevenson helped organise a mass campaign by 'going underground'. Believing that the school authorities would lock the students in if they registered for school, she arranged for the strikers to meet in town with other schools. When the school found they hadn't arrived, they locked in all the younger pupils. Those who managed to escape left through the fire exits, but some were caught on CCTV and later punished.[39] School students used mobile phones and texting to communicate –

a forerunner of the school student demonstrations of 2010. They called for a mass strike on Day X, when war broke out.

The school students' mass strike affected hundreds of schools. Kate Connelly describes it:

> 'In the morning lots of us turned up to college but we did not bother with lessons. It was to spread the message of the strike. We painted banners in the quad, decorated the college trees with peace signs and chalked around bodies on the ground to symbolise the Iraqi dead. We held a lunchtime rally and marched out. We blockaded one of the main junctions in Cambridge for hours that afternoon.'[40]

In Newham (a working-class, multi-ethnic borough in East London) students disrupted lessons or walked out in every secondary school and even some primaries. Police responded by 'kettling' them and then photographing them individually. But they could not stop the protests, which included spontaneous marches round all the main streets resulting in massive disruption to traffic.[41]

15 February 2003: The Largest British Demonstration Ever

Strength of feeling over the war allowed the movement to develop such momentum that a vast number of people not only agreed with what the anti-war activists were saying, but were also convinced that their own participation would make a difference. Many demonstrations may have the tacit support of many more people than those who actually go on them. However, on this occasion people believed that their presence on the streets could actually stop the war. One of the continuing issues over the legacy of Iraq remains the sense of injustice that many in the movement still feel over the failure of the government and politicians to acknowledge such a level of mobilisation.

The war also raised questions about democracy. In the weeks before 15 February the Blair government tried to impose a strategy of tension against the anti-war movement. Tanks and soldiers were stationed at Heathrow airport because of an alleged terrorist threat. (Just after the demonstration the 'threat' evaporated and the tanks withdrew.) The aim was to deter those who were planning to protest because of an undefined threat.

Then the government made a remarkable tactical error: only a week before the demonstration, the minister responsible, Tessa Jowell, declared that the march would not be able to hold its rally in London's Hyde Park, because of fears that so many people would 'damage the grass'. When a range of people, including the former Labour leader Michael Foot, announced their intention of marching to the park and if necessary forcing their way in, the government was forced to back down, but not before many people, outraged at this denial of free speech, had committed themselves to turning up for the march.

Another factor in building the march was the role the *Daily Mirror* played. The paper helped campaign for the demonstration and even produced its own placards. Having a major national newspaper on side took the anti-war message to a much wider audience than traditional Left or pacifist publications had and it helped counter the bias of the BBC in particular.

The day of demonstrations around the world – 15 February – just weeks before the Iraq war broke out, was one of superlatives. It was the largest coordinated day of demonstrations ever, the largest demonstration ever in British history and the most diverse demonstration ever. In Britain, an estimated two million marched, while another 100,000 besieged Blair at the Scottish Labour Party conference in Glasgow. Up and down the country hundreds of protests were held by those who could not make it to London or Glasgow.[42] The demonstration was by a slight majority female and was relatively young.[43]

Everyone has their own memories of that day: cities where the coach operators simply ran out of coaches; Preston where demonstrators were brought to London in taxis when all other transport was fully booked; people left standing on pavements; the hours spent at the Embankment as the giant march, starting from two different points, slowly made its way through central London, so that there were still people at the starting point when the front of the march arrived in Hyde Park; the fires lit in the park as darkness fell; the eerie silence in Park Lane on Saturday night, except for the occasional departing coach of tired demonstrators.[44]

Carmel Brown, who was responsible for much of the press work and liaising with the many celebrities who attended, remembers one incident which convinced her of the importance of the different elements of the campaign:

> 'On February 15 Tony Benn was being mobbed and I linked arms with him and we were walking arm in arm and there were masses of stewards, teenage women in hijabs, and they parted and let us both through and then made a circle round him. It was all a great learning curve.'[45]

She also remembers looking out from the stage in Hyde Park at people as far as the eye could see: 'I don't think there can have been a bigger high than standing on the stage on February 15th and just looking down the field and thinking, "My God what did we do? We got this so right." It wasn't just that: there was a tide of feeling.'[46]

Tansy Hoskins recollects:

> 'My main memories of February 15 are the Make Love Not War event that we held at LSE the night before the demo, the large turnout that we had at LSE on the day itself, Chris Bambery's speech where he said that the only excuse for missing February 15 was if you were dead and that even if you were dead we would dig you up and take you there anyway, the fact that Ms Dynamite sang at the demo and the fact that unlike most other demos I didn't see a single person I knew which was how I knew it was a colossal demo.'[47]

The political impact of the demonstrations was immense, creating huge problems for the government. Such were the fears about public opinion in Britain that US Defense Secretary Donald Rumsfeld offered a reduced backseat role for Britain which would not involve the direct deployment of British troops. This caused consternation in Whitehall, and Blair made clear he was going to continue his warmongering.[48] He spent the next month trying to win over sufficient Labour MPs to carry a vote in the House of Commons – something he eventually achieved with the support of the Conservative opposition.

However, the demonstrations had shown the power of mobilisation. One journalist's assessment put it like this: 'the fracturing of the Western alliance over Iraq and the huge antiwar demonstrations around the world this weekend are reminders that there may still be two superpowers on the planet: the United States and world public opinion.' The article, entitled 'A New Power on the Streets', continued:

'In his campaign to disarm Iraq, by war if necessary, President Bush appears to be eyeball to eyeball with a tenacious new adversary: millions of people who flooded the streets of New York and dozens of other world cities to say they are against war based on the evidence at hand ... The fresh outpouring of antiwar sentiment may not be enough to dissuade Mr. Bush or his advisers from their resolute preparations for war. But the sheer number of protesters offers a potent message that any rush to war may have political consequences for nations that support Mr. Bush's march into the Tigris and Euphrates valleys.'[49]

Many trade unionists and non-union workers walked out, held meetings and protested in a variety of ways. Two train drivers, members of ASLEF, refused to move goods that could be used for the war. Their action made the headlines. Hundreds of workplaces were affected by walkouts on the day the war began. Many towns and cities saw militant protests, including the blocking of motorways and other roads. Activists in Dover helped to blockade the road to the ferry port.[50] Virtually none of these protests was reported in the national media.

The mobilisations were on an unprecedented scale. They triggered direct action, including industrial action. The refusal of Blair to listen was one of the worst political betrayals in British history, for which Iraqis and British people are still paying. However, Blair is also paying a price – although not on the scale he should. He has been hounded because of the war and has never been able to overcome its legacy. In the face of such intransigence, only one factor would have forced Blair to retreat; industrial action sufficient to paralyse the country. Despite the courage of many individuals in trying and sometimes succeeding in achieving such action, it remained at a low level and relatively isolated. A decade later we have still not seen such mass action even over domestic issues such as the welfare spending cuts. This only underlines the difficulty of winning such action and the scale of feeling which produced even the levels that it did.

Despite smaller mobilisations following the war and occupation in Iraq, the movement has continued. When George Bush came to Britain in November 2003, 350,000 people blocked central London making it the largest weekday demonstration in British history, then against Tony Blair at the Labour conference in Manchester in 2006, repeatedly over Iraq, and again as the war worsened there, over Afghanistan. The Stop the War movement also mobilised against the war in Lebanon in 2006 and over the Israeli bombing of Gaza in 2009, linking these issues with the wider War on Terror.

The involvement of women (and children) was noticeable, with many, including Muslim women, fundraising, organising vigils and protests, and speaking. The movement was large, encompassing wide sections of the Left and the traditional peace movement. One of its unique features was the wave of occupations in solidarity with Gaza which took place in over 30 universities. Many of the students were too young to have protested over Iraq and saw this as their cause. Women, including Muslim women from Palestinian and South Asian backgrounds, were instrumental in this series of protests, many of which won substantial demands.

Military Families Speak Out

One of the most remarkable effects of the anti-war movement was the involvement of the families of a number of soldiers who had died in Iraq or Afghanistan. This was unprecedented in British history and showed the changing approaches to war and the impact on families. In previous wars, the dead were buried on or near the battlefield. Their families mourned them from a distance and were expected to accept their loss without complaint or too much inquiry into why they died. Few British soldiers died in Afghanistan between 2001 and 2003. It seemed like a war free from human cost – at least from the British point of view. That changed as the war continued. But before that there was Iraq.

It was not the loss of life that made Iraq so different. It was the fact that the war was contested and built on a tissue of lies which gave impetus to the families' bitterness at losing their husbands, sons and brothers. As the war dragged on, meeting much greater resistance than expected, and the number of western soldiers killed rose, it became ever more apparent that there were no weapons of mass destruction. Parents felt that their sons had died for a lie, and that this was a war of aggression, not defence. Reg Keys, whose military policeman son was killed in an attack on a police station near Basra a couple of months into the war, protested single-handedly by climbing a lamppost outside the Labour Party conference in Brighton. He became an active campaigner, eventually standing against Blair in the 2005 general election and making an excoriating speech which Blair was forced to listen to. Other fathers included Graham Knight, whose son was killed in Afghanistan, and Peter Brierley, whose son had also been killed. All became part of Military Families against the War, which organised delegations and protests.

But it was a mother who caught the mood of anger and who campaigned tirelessly against Blair. Rose Gentle is a working-class woman from Pollock, Glasgow who lost her only son, Gordon, when he was killed by a roadside bomb in Basra in June 2004. She, her husband George and her younger daughter Maxine became regulars at demonstrations and protests over the war. On one occasion, Rose went to Downing Street with Stop the War activists and managed to force her way in to meet the Deputy Prime Minister, John Prescott. Rose explains:

> 'To be honest, I was like most of the families that lost a loved one. When we were told that we could be hit with weapons of mass destruction we didn't think we were lied to by our country. But the more Tony Blair talked about it and kept changing his mind as to how we went in to Iraq, then we had to question it and then we knew. Gordon was killed and let down very badly by Blair and the rest of his puppets in government.'

Rose decided that she would continue campaigning: 'I had to speak out. I promised Gordon when I got him home in his coffin that I would fight to know the truth as to why we lost him and why we went to war.' She was amazed at some of the things that she did: speaking at public meetings and demonstrations, helping to organise a peace camp outside Downing Street, organising protests at the Cenotaph, appearing on television and radio, and hounding Blair: 'I never ever saw myself standing up and talking in front of 100,000 people or even taking the government to court or even camping outside Downing Street.'[51]

On the day that Blair left office in May 2007 Rose insisted on being in Downing Street and as he spent the last few minutes before leaving his official residence, her voice rang out denouncing him as a liar and a murderer. To the very last, standing on a window sill opposite No. 10, she grabbed the attention of the world's press.[52] When Blair was summoned to the Chilcot Inquiry, which was investigating Britain's role in the Iraq war, Rose was there to protest.

Joan Humphreys is from Dundee. Her grandson, Kevin Elliott, was killed in Afghanistan in August 2009. Joan had been involved in anti-war protest before, going on the 15 February demonstration at the Scottish Labour Party conference in Glasgow and then on subsequent marches:

'After Kevin's death I was staying with my son in Newhaven and I saw the Labour Party Conference was on in Brighton. I went down at about 8 am on Sunday with a placard I had made that said: "Private Kevin Elliott 24 years old was killed in Afghanistan on 31st Aug 2009 WHY?" Whilst doing that the police were particularly nasty. A female police officer was very helpful and announced to all the other police who had been harassing me that I was there with permission and kept coming back to check on me. She told me there was an anti-war demo meeting near Brighton Pier. So I went to join them. When I arrived somebody from Glasgow recognised me and introduced me to a tall, grey-haired man . . . who introduced me to Lindsey [German]. I was made to feel very welcome. When we started marching and chatting Joan (my daughter) joined us. Lindsey asked me to speak but I said no. I was too raw at the time.

'Lindsey kept in contact with me and I eventually agreed to speak in Trafalgar Square in November 2009. On December 21 I again travelled to London to take a petition to Downing Street . . . I really don't remember who was there and I was taken for a meal and taken to my overnight bus. It was snowing heavily. Whitehall was amazing. I went to No. 1 Parliament Street to be interviewed by the press. I think this was before the petition was delivered. Paul Hanes has always been there!

'I remember little of Christmas 2009 and Hogmanay 2010.'[53]

The success of the families in raising anti-war issues was very important in developing a deeper consciousness on the issue. The army and the Right have used a number of the techniques and approaches pioneered by the Military Families against the War. They have provided support mechanisms for bereaved families and have tried to disentangle the question of support for soldiers from support for war. They are forced to adopt this approach because the wars remain so unpopular. Part of the credit for this lies with women like Rose Gentle and Joan Humphreys. Rose Gentle says:

'Would I do it all again? Yes, for one we have heard a lot of lies that have came out from the Iraq inquiry that has proved Tony Blair misled this country into war and he is partly responsible for my boy being killed.

'Now it has made me a stronger person and I will stand up and say what is on my mind and will not back away from anyone in government.'[54]

Women to the Front

That thousands of women were central to 15 February and to the movement before and since is hardly in doubt. On the march itself, 46 per cent were men and 54 per cent women. Around 16 per cent were under 24, with 15 per cent having reached higher secondary education. Of all marchers 67 per cent were university-educated and nearly half were from largely public sector professions such as education and health. A fifth of the marchers were students.[55]

Those regarded as having the highest 'protest potential' – who when questioned were most opposed to war under any circumstances – were more concentrated among the under-forties, more likely to have a degree, more likely to be left-wing and more likely to be women.[56] Clearly, the role of education in encouraging people to protest is crucial.[57] The increasing role of young women in protests has long been noted, reflecting the radicalisation of the 1960s movements and the rise of feminism. In 1979 one study noted that:

> 'Overall, men are more ready than women to be mobilized, but young women have an impressive political potency that, unlike the even handed versatility shown by men, is pointed sharply in the direction of protest methods. Indeed, this evidence dispels any wonder that may linger about the success of the feminist politics now snapping at the flanks of conventional party systems.'[58]

While early studies relating to gender generally concluded that women were less likely to participate and less likely to vote or take part in politics, more recent studies have found that things have changed and sometimes been reversed.[59] According to one American study, women have voted at higher rates than men in every presidential election since 1980. The gender gap has widened slightly with each election.[60]

The changes in women's lives since the 1970s would seem to be a large part of the explanation. As many women now enter higher education as men. They are likely to work in 'caring' professions. The radicalisation of young women in social movements has had an impact on their awareness of different issues. Perhaps most importantly, some have a greater sense of themselves as social actors, people in public life, rather than as passive recipients of politics. All these factors helped to make women central to mobilising in 2003.

Another reason for the involvement of women in the anti-war movement is the breadth of the movement itself. Stop the War from the beginning took up issues of civil liberties and Islamophobia and so was always more than a single-issue campaign, even though the issues are closely related. Many women found a role campaigning round these issues as part of the wider anti-war movement. In addition, Palestine was quickly linked to the anti-war message and also helped mobilise women, some of whom had been campaigning to raise money or aid for the Palestinians before the war began.

The grassroots nature of the campaign meant there was little in the way of structure, never more than two small offices in which paid employees and volunteers worked together, and with no funding apart from voluntary donations. The local groups came together on the basis of affiliated organisations and activists. They were open to anyone and created a pool of volunteers who undertook the work of leafleting, booking coaches, protesting and speaking. This made them particularly accessible to women, who might be less familiar with more formal structures.

Protest Politics of the Twenty-First Century

The anti-war movement has its place in a very twenty-first-century protest revival. It is part of a long arc which stretches from the Seattle protests in 1999 through the anti-capitalist and anti-globalisation movements, to the Occupy movement which erupted in October 2011. The links between them have been at times considerable: 15 February 2003 was chosen as a world day of protests at the European Social Forum in Florence in November 2002.[61]

While the anti-war movement's focus was the prevention of attacks on Afghanistan and Iraq and the campaign against those wars when they started, it has always had a much wider remit. The scope of the War on Terror is wide, not just geographically but also politically. It impacts on civil liberties, Islamophobia, dictatorship in the Middle East, Israel and its role in the region, government accountability, the legality of war, the right of protest and many other issues. Hence it has become a movement not just of protest, but for protest. It became an opposition force to the government, rather than a single-issue campaign.

But there were other factors at work. One was the changing pattern of politics. There has been a marked decline in many of the more established Western democracies in the involvement in conventional and party politics. Recent decades have seen fewer people voting, joining political parties and generally engaging in the political process. This is particularly the case among young people, who are far less likely to vote than their parents' generation. According to one survey, by the late 1990s internationally 55 per cent of under-25s voted compared with 88 per cent of people in late middle-age.[62]

Concurrently, there was a rise in the numbers involved in other forms of political expression and protest in Western Europe between 1959 and 1990, especially among the young and educated.[63] The movements have led to different forms of political expression and protest and in many cases to a greater engagement, not least among young women.

Young people are not suffering from apathy, as is so often claimed by conventional politicians who fail to engage with them; if anything, more people are active in the new social movements. This is part of a long-term trend.

While political involvement and engagement were fairly high in the years immediately following the Second World War, protest politics and direct action were an important part of peace and anti-war movement politics in the 1950s and 1960s, with the emergence of CND and the movement against the Vietnam war. The rise of protest continued to 1979. In the 30 years since, there has been an accelerated decline in conventional politics, with a corresponding rise of different forms of direct protest.

As Pippa Norris puts it: 'The proportion of citizens engaged in protest politics has risen, and risen dramatically, during the late twentieth century.'[64] In Britain, West Germany, the Netherlands, Austria, the United States, Italy, Switzerland and Finland between the 1970s and the 1990s,

> 'The proportion of citizens who had signed a petition . . . doubled from 32 per cent to 60 per cent; the proportion who had attended a demonstration escalated from 7 per cent to 19 per cent; and the proportion participating in a consumer boycott tripled from 5 per cent to 15 per cent. Participation in unofficial strikes and in occupations remains confined to only a limited minority, but even here there is evidence of growing numbers.'[65]

By the mid-1990s, the 'most popular protest activities across all countries were signing a petition (28 per cent of all citizens), attending a demonstration (16 per cent), and joining a consumer boycott (9 per cent)'.[66]

Demonstrations have become a part of everyday life and people are more likely to turn to this kind of action, rather than electoral politics, to achieve their aims.

> 'An alternative perspective suggests that the image of demonstrators as disaffected radicals reflects popular stereotypes common in the framing of social movements during the 1960s but is no longer relevant to the contemporary world, because the demonstration population has gradually "normalized" over the years to become mainstream, heterogeneous, and conventional in both attitudes and social characteristics.'[67]

While all these trends in political participation show a decline in support or confidence in the established political channels, they tell only part of the story. This comes against the background of a long-term decline in traditional party organisation. Socialist or Labour parties, which a generation ago would have been the home for many wanting to protest, have largely been stripped of activists. Their policies now tend to support the status quo – perhaps most acutely demonstrated by Tony Blair's enthusiasm for the War on Terror.

Since the breakdown of the long postwar economic boom, the crisis of the system has taken an increasingly generalised form. Parliamentary democracy and mainstream politics have become less relevant and less representative. The neoliberal counter-offensive of the past decades has weakened labour and trade union organisation. These factors have led to a greater radicalisation, generalisation and resort to street protest on the part of those who want to effect change.

The large-scale nature of the problems, from war to economics to climate change, necessitate a wider and more political approach from many activists. However, it would be a mistake to regard participation in movements, demonstrating and the other forms of action as an alternative to more traditional politics. There are many signs that those who protest are also involved or interested in politics in other fields. An early study showed that people willing to protest in CND against nuclear weapons were more likely to engage in conventional forms of political activism, not less.[68] Similarly, a study of the 15 February 2003 demonstrations internationally revealed that many of those who protested were more likely to have voted than not in the previous election. In England, 9 per cent of those questioned said they did not take part in the previous election for political reasons; 77 per cent voted in the previous election, while the national turnout was 59 per cent. In Scotland the figures were 5 per cent, 86 per cent and 58 per cent respectively. The demonstrators were therefore much more likely to have voted than the general population.[69]

But the overwhelming majority of the demonstrators were not active members of a political party (5 per cent in Scotland, 8 per cent in England). Even when active, passive and former members of parties were added together, only 30 per cent of demonstrators in both England and Scotland fell into any of these categories.[70] This suggests a high level of political awareness but much less enthusiasm for organised party politics. When it came to participation in earlier protests, these included 46 per cent who had been on a previous peace demonstration, 26 per cent who had been on an anti-racism demonstration, 27 per cent on one over social issues and 12 per cent on one about global justice. Eight per cent had been on one over women's rights.[71]

The relation between party politics and the 15 February mobilisation soon became clear. In Britain, the Labour Party, the only governing Left party in Europe to support the war, lost one million votes in the 2005 general election. Four of the top ten swings away from Labour were achieved by the anti-war Respect Party. In East London George Galloway won the safe Labour seat of Bethnal Green and Bow on an anti-war platform.

In countries with right-wing governments they lost support to social democratic parties in the elections following the invasion of Iraq.[72] In Britain there were big swings away from Labour (although not to the other major party, which was also pro-war).[73] The war on Iraq created a crisis for the Labour Party, one that is still unresolved, with a decline of membership reinforcing the shift from traditional politics to social movements. The challenge to established politics continues from the wider social movements, of which anti-war campaigning is now an established part.

The role of the internet, emails, texting, Twitter, Facebook and other forms of media has played a role in the new movements. But only some of the new media existed at the time of the 15 February demonstrations. There is relatively little film of the events beyond the main newsgathering organisations, whereas if it occurred now it would be filmed and photographed by tens of thousands of people.

Twitter and Facebook have helped plan and organise demonstrations in recent years, and have played an important role.[74] School students used it to gain national reach in a way that they could not possibly have done in a previous era, when their contacts would have been restricted to who they could meet face to face. But any technology is secondary to how people are actually mobilised, because any mobilisation relies on real individuals, committed to organising and prepared to use any means at their disposal. Angela Davis, the US black communist campaigner for more than 40 years, wrote recently of the photographic images of the My Lai massacre in Vietnam and its galvanising effect on the movement across the world. Similar points could be made in relation to Iraq about 'Shock and Awe' or the torture of prisoners in Abu Ghraib. However, Davis argues that:

'The photographs did not organize the movement – it was organized by committed women and men who were enraged and engaged, not only at the point of mobilization, but in other areas of their lives as well. Their engagement created the context for the reception of those photographs. Their engagement produced the meaning that was attached to those photographs.'[75]

The anti-war movement was the creation of tens of thousands of individuals who used and continue to use the newest methods at their disposal to get their message across. They succeeded in mobilising the largest numbers of demonstrators ever seen on one day – the majority of them women.

7
War, Liberation and Muslim Women

'We will not abandon you, we will stand with you always . . . [it is] essential
that women's rights and women's opportunities are not sacrificed or trampled
in the reconciliation process.'
   US Secretary of State Hillary Clinton to Afghan women officials in 2010[1]

Where would the War on Terror be without its repeated appeals for
women's liberation? The implication that the forces of US military
and US economic power are the thin line between salvation and
desperation for millions of women is repeated to justify continued
war and the threat of future wars. It is the final refuge of those
who can no longer explain or justify a war which has lasted
longer than the First and Second World Wars put together and
which is not achieving its stated aim of making Western countries
safer for their citizens or bringing stability and democracy to the
people of Afghanistan. It requires ignoring the lived reality of
women in the country – which is in many ways no improvement
on the situation before the war – let alone the fact that the
Western-backed government does not differ fundamentally in its
attitude to women from the Taliban. It justifies continued war and
occupation simply by warning of something worse for women if
the troops are withdrawn.

Women's rights have always been at the heart of the War on
Terror. They were used from the very beginning to convince some
who might otherwise have been sceptical that it was justified.
The wars are seen as acceptable to some feminists, liberals and
socialists because they appear to promote a higher sense of
morality. The wars may cause death and destruction and they
may be supported by some people with whom the Left has nothing
historically in common, but their end – the emancipation of

women from seemingly archaic forms of patriarchal oppression – surely justify the means.

The thesis that the world faces a clash of civilisations, between modernity and backwardness, between secular values and Islam, is the starting point for such views. In the words of Samuel Huntingdon, 'While at the macro or global level of world politics the primary clash of civilisations is between the West and the rest, at the micro or local level it is between Islam and the others.'[2] Conflicts between imperial powers and the developing world are cast in terms of the absolute superiority of the Western political and economic system and its values, with Muslims the most violent, irrational and hate-consumed of the rest.

These ideas are not new. They have their roots in centuries of colonialism which portrayed the colonised as in need of protection from the more extreme or brutal aspects of their culture. Imperial and colonial ideology had to justify its actions by pointing to the need for Western civilisation on the one hand and the need to overcome divisions within the countries they colonised on the other.

Since then biological racism has been superseded by cultural racism, which stresses religious and ethnic divisions. Such beliefs have been given new force by a particular narrative about 9/11. This ignores any political reasons for the attacks, but casts its perpetrators as uniquely evil, driven by a notion of Islam which justifies suicide bombing and which so hates Western values that it is prepared to launch an attack of such horror. If Afghan women are seen as powerless and in need of protection, the enemies of the United States are seen as the opposite. Near the top of the tree of villains, the late Osama bin Laden, the Taliban and al Qaeda are seen as effectively holding Afghans to ransom. The task of any 'civilised' country, therefore, is to rescue these hostages from the fearsome fanatics and install them in a democracy modelled on that of the Western powers who are presented as in every way superior.

To fit into this model women have to be portrayed as weak, helpless and dominated by their husbands and fathers, rather than as independent women who act of their own free will. The clash of civilisations means that Westerners can bring enlightenment to women who would otherwise be incapable of liberating themselves. Some feminists echo these views. They highlight issues such as female genital circumcision, forced marriage and honour killing, even though these practices are neither representative of most Muslims, nor confined to those who follow Islam. Concentrating on these issues as though these were the main ones facing Muslims in Europe can lead to political difficulties. Liz Fekete argues that for this reason, even some feminists and gay rights activists are backing calls for immigration controls against Muslim immigrants. She points to

> 'a generalised suspicion of Muslims, who are characterised as holding on to an alien culture that, in its opposition to homosexuality and gender equality, threatens core European values. Strict monocultural policies, besides, are seen as a necessary corrective to the multicultural policies of the Left that, in the name of cultural diversity, have turned a blind eye to patriarchal customs such as polygamy, clitoridectomy, forced marriages and honour killings.'[3]

According to this view, all Muslim cultures oppress women, and Muslim women are unable to challenge their oppression. It has echoes both of a pre-feminist view of women as passive victims rather than the subjects of their own history and of the colonial mindset which believed that the task of empire was to bring to its subjects the civilising effects of a superior culture. This has been true to a degree of all the wars since 2001. While Afghanistan was occupied supposedly to end women's suffering under the Taliban regime, the war in Iraq was justified both by the false allegation that Saddam Hussein possessed weapons of mass destruction and the more general charge that he was a dictator responsible for atrocities against the Iraqi people. The bombing of Libya in 2011 was supposedly to avert a predicted massacre of the people of Benghazi. All were carried out in the name of humanitarian intervention. War was no longer about imperial power, aggression or geographical expansion, but about protecting the victims of dictatorship or oppression. This ideology has been reinforced by governments and international agencies that have adopted the need to protect citizens as a specific factor overriding limitations on military intervention.

In 2005 the United Nations adopted the responsibility to protect principle, following the International Commission on Intervention and State Sovereignty's 2001 report, which stated that when states fail to protect their own citizens or deliberately terrorise them, 'the principle of non-intervention yields to the international responsibility to protect'.[4] This underlined the theory and practice used in 1999 and 2001 and extended justification for future wars on humanitarian grounds. In linking war and humanitarian intervention, feminist and liberal ideas were absorbed into the justification for war. The ideology of the neo-conservatives was adapted to become a crusade for women's rights. The US bomber was now an agent of women's liberation.

Much effort was put into promoting the idea that the war would free women in Afghanistan from generations of oppression, allowing them access to education and liberating them from oppressive social customs, such as wearing the burqa. Laura Bush used one of her husband's weekly radio broadcasts to make the case for going to war to protect women. Accusing the then Afghan government in the strongest terms, she said: 'Only the terrorists and the Taliban forbid education to women. Only the terrorists and the Taliban threaten to pull out women's fingernails for wearing nail polish.'[5] Cherie Booth, wife of the British Prime Minister, made similar calls and held a Downing Street event with women Cabinet ministers to publicise how the war would help women. A Downing Street spokesman talked of 'people . . . executed in football stadiums in front of cheering crowds . . . girls have had to be educated in secret'.[6] Feminism was an integral part of the post-9/11 narrative: that the people who had committed such attacks 'hated' Western culture; that the war represented a 'clash of civilisations'; and that a benchmark of Western civilisation was women's rights.

Feminists in the United States were co-opted into support for the war on grounds which one writer has described as 'beyond cynical'.[7] Bush was able to use a powerful set of networks of feminists to underline support for the war in the wake of 9/11 and to use traditionally non-militarist opinion to support his wars. Eleanor Smeal, leader of the Feminist Majority organisation, met a group of US generals and was impressed to hear of advances for women in the US military.[8]

In a development beyond satire, successive International Women's Days saw the Bush family claiming credit for liberating women. In 2002 Laura Bush declared that the war was helping to rebuild lives, while in 2004 her husband boasted in a White House speech to mark International Women's Week that the wars in Iraq and Afghanistan meant that 'for 25 million women and girls, liberation has a special significance. Some of these girls are attending school for the first time. Some of the women are preparing to vote in free elections for the very first time.'[9] As Hester Eisenstein points out:

> 'Ironically, the very success of the women's movement in the United States was now being used by the very people who fought against it to sell capitalism around the world. If terrorism was the overriding threat, and if Islamic fundamentalism was the core of the terrorist network, and if the suppression of women was crucial to Islamic fundamentalism, then logically the emancipation of women became a keystone of the US ideological framework for the War on Terror.'[10]

Blair's narrative about the 'international community' asserted that Western imperialism was the embodiment of democracy, human rights and civilised values, while those opposing the collective will of the 'community' were representatives of backwardness and brutality who detested modernity, launching attacks like 9/11 because they hated Western values or were jealous of 'our way of life'.

Selling the war to feminists relied on two false assumptions. The first was that those justifying the war were doing it to help women who could not help themselves. According to this view, the war was not a major military attack by the richest and most heavily armed country against one of the poorest, but a liberal crusade for women's rights, greater democracy and the establishment of Western values in a benighted and backward land. It never seemed to occur to those promoting these ideas that there might be feminists and others in Afghanistan who were already fighting against oppression and who bitterly rejected imperialism and the hangover from a colonial system when Britain had tried to rule the country directly.[11]

That the war was accepted by so many feminists speaks to the deep divisions which feminism now experienced. The radical movement of the 1960s always contained within it different wings. Some saw women's advances as finding a place for women within society: more women politicians, wider job prospects, greater access to education. They tended not to consider these questions in a wider social context and so ignored or avoided questions such as those concerned with race and class. This led to greater divisions among women and men. Their accommodation with the system also led then to accept the need for military intervention, especially when it was couched in egalitarian terms.

Any attempt to put an alternative point of view which spoke up for such women and opposed the war was widely attacked. When a group of prominent feminists, including Jane Fonda and Alice Walker, issued a statement opposing war and supporting Afghan women, and stressing that many US feminists opposed the war,[12] they were sharply criticised by the media and government representatives.

The second false claim was that countries like the United States and Britain were beacons of women's equality. Many feminists opposed the war in Afghanistan for a range of reasons; some did so at least in part because it was hard to take Bush or the neo-cons seriously when they claimed to support women's liberation. These were the same people who tried to deny abortion and contraception rights to women, enthused about traditional family values and rejected any sexuality that did not conform to the ideal of married monogamy. To these social conservatives the limited freedoms achieved by women in the West had already taken things too far. They were hardly in a position to tell Afghan women how to improve their lives.

It was also clear that the exacting standards demanded of countries such as Afghanistan did not extend to the unelected monarchs and dictators of the Middle East who did the West's bidding. Bush and Blair turned a blind eye to the absence of equality for women in Saudi Arabia, while pushing it up the list of war aims to justify bombing Afghanistan.

Those with whom the West formed alliances over the war also had appalling records. Even in 2001, organisations such as Amnesty International made it clear that the Western allies in Afghanistan, the Northern Alliance, had a record on human rights and women's rights abuses similar to the Taliban's. In testimony to a US government subcommittee it said:

> 'Unfortunately, conditions under [the] Northern Alliance are not much better. The United Nations and several countries recognise the Northern Alliance as the government of Afghanistan. During their rule in Kabul from 1992 to 1996, the Northern Alliance was responsible for numerous human rights abuses against Afghan civilians. Violations were widespread and included rape, extrajudicial executions and torture, as well as long-term detention of prisoners of conscience. In 1996, the Northern Alliance lost Kabul to the Taliban and subsequently lost most of their territories to the Taliban. Although the abuses by the Northern Alliance continued, the reports of such abuses have declined in recent months. This may be the result of the Northern Alliance controlling limited territory. Such abuses could easily increase as the armed conflict spreads.'[13]

None of this made any difference to the euphoria that greeted the overthrow of the Taliban. The burqa has become the symbol of Afghan women's oppression and conversely the abandonment of the garment is seen as a totem of liberation. As one writer commented, 'Burqas and veils have come to embody the ultimate in gendered persecution. Bikinis equal freedom; sex is emancipation.'[14] In the United States there was more coverage on the burqa issue than on education or women's rights.[15] One Afghan woman campaigner illustrated the US feminist obsession with the burqa, saying that after the fall of the Taliban women from Eleanor Smeal's Feminist Majority bought lots of burqas which they took back to the United States and 'cut the parts that covers the face to raise money. We were offended and objected. They responded by refusing to include us on their platforms.'[16]

This politics was counterproductive. Feminists in imperialist nations aimed to end one form of oppression – women being forced to wear the burqa – by allying themselves with their government which was bombing women and children in the name of liberation. It is hardly surprising that Afghan women's resentment grew.

Following the overthrow of the Taliban, *Business Week* titled its front cover 'Liberation' above the picture of an unveiled Afghan woman. It gushed:

> 'The scenes of joy in the streets of Kabul evoke nothing less than the images of Paris liberated from the Nazis. Women taking to the streets to bask in the Afghan sun, free at last to show their faces. Children gathering to fly kites, a once-forbidden pastime. Old people dancing to music, banned for years . . . The warm embrace by ordinary people of the freedom to do ordinary things is a major victory for Western humanist values.'[17]

But Kabul was not Paris 1944. Instead the war has dragged on for another eleven years and has worsened. War did not bring liberation.

Humanitarian Intervention: Who Has Benefited?

So what is the record more than a decade later? The Afghan war, thought by some to be effectively over by December 2001, has intensified since 2006. The war in Iraq is widely regarded as a catastrophe leaving in its wake multiple problems. The most recent intervention of the Western powers, in Libya in 2011, has left at least 30,000 dead. There are constant threats of future Western intervention, most notably Syria and Iran. This does not include wars connected with the War on Terror: Israel's attack on Lebanon in 2006 and its weeks-long bombing of Gaza in 2008–9; the destructive Western-backed interventions in Somalia by Ethiopia and Kenya; the drone attacks on Yemen.

Dahabo Isse describes how the Western powers' failure over Somalia affected her: 'They refused to assist after Somali rebellions ousted a dictator president. The War on Terror benefited many warlords who got sympathy from Western powers to kill their own people by justifying that they were fighting with terrorists. The War on Terror makes the world more dangerous to live now.' She spells out the practical effect of the war on women's lives:

> 'Many become single mothers and had to look after many small children. Women become destitute and lose all their property. Women become [the] breadwinners as they lose their husbands. Women become refugees in an alien country [where] everything is different from their original indigenous homeland.'[18]

The 2008 UN Development Report ranked Afghanistan as one of the least developed countries in the world. It showed that life expectancy had fallen since 2003 to 43.1 years; the infant mortality rate had risen from 2001 and stood at 135 per 1,000 births; more than six million Afghans did not meet their daily food requirements; less than a third of the population had access to clean water; and 100,000 children were disabled or physically afflicted by the war.[19]

Afghanistan remains one of the poorest countries in the world. Women and children bear the brunt of much of the war, suffering death, injury and displacement as refugees. The devastation alone would be bad enough but there is a mass of evidence that the situation of women has not improved with regime change. Women still do not get access to education in many parts of Afghanistan. They still wear the burqa. They are still subject to forced marriage, rape and domestic violence. A poll in June 2011 of women's rights professionals in the country assessed Afghanistan as the most dangerous place in the world for women to live, worse even than the Congo. Violence, poverty and poor healthcare were given as the main reasons.[20] This is the reality facing Afghan women. It is in contrast to the constitutional position, which supposedly enshrines women's equality in law and which allows for a quota of women in the Afghan Parliament. But this is more of a nominal than a real commitment to women's rights, owing more to external politics than to internal change.

In this situation, questions of how to dress are not necessarily the most important ones facing women. Elaheh Rostami Povey interviewed Alama, in her book *Afghan Women*, who said:

'They keep talking about freeing us from *chaddari* [the burqa]. The reality is that *chaddari* is not our problem; the problem is lack of security, lack of employment, lack of education and health. If we have these, then we can sort out the *chaddari* issue, some women may continue to wear it and others make take it off or wear other forms of Islamic cover such as in rural areas.'[21]

Perhaps the most eloquent witness to this situation is the former Afghan MP Malalai Joya. A young woman who has stood up for women and equality, who has travelled the world campaigning against the war, and who has endured danger and persecution to do so, Malalai is unequivocal in her opposition to the war and occupation. Her reason is straightforward: the Western powers replaced the oppressive Taliban with the equally oppressive Northern Alliance, and the presence of troops and occupation makes it harder for those Afghans who want democratic change and equality to achieve it. In *Raising My Voice* she describes the Western narrative about the occupation as 'a lie, dust in the eyes of the world'.

'I am the youngest Member of the Afghan Parliament, but I have been banished from my seat and threatened with death because I speak the truth about the warlords and criminals in the puppet government of Hamid Karzai.'[22]

She continues:

'We are caught between two enemies – the Taliban on one side and the US/ NATO forces and their warlord friends on the other. And the dark-minded forces in our country are gaining power with every Coalition air strike that kills civilians, with every corrupt government official who grows fat on bribes and thievery, and with every criminal who escapes justice.'[23]

Her demands are to end the war, send real humanitarian aid, put an end to the rule of the warlords and withdraw all foreign troops.[24]

Other voices echo these concerns, associating social problems with the war. Mitra Qayoom, a young Afghan woman living in London, talked to Khorshid Noori and Masooma Rahim from the women's organisation Afghan Women Skills Development

Centre (AWSDC), whom she met while visiting Kabul in summer 2012. They made their position on the war clear:

> 'We don't want to be hugged by Hillary Clinton, given fake promises and then be forgotten. We don't want them to just come here and take reports but then do nothing about it. They [the United States and NATO] don't care about the Afghan women or people. They are here for our resources. They started this mess and they can stop it by leaving.'

Asked why domestic violence and street harassment have increased, they replied:

> 'Because of a lack of education and poverty, which are consequences of this and the previous wars. Men are not educated and they are not aware of women's rights. Poverty has made boys/men resort to quitting school and start work at a young age. We are not talking about jobs in offices; we are talking about setting up a stall on a street corner and selling vegetables. Most days these men don't make much and this leads to stress and frustration, which then comes out on the wife at home. Also a large number of Afghans, both men and women, suffer from mental health as a result of many years of war and this again contributes to domestic violence.
>
> 'There are no laws that forbid men from beating women or harassing them on the streets. There are laws that we have been trying to get passed by the parliament for three years now, which for example, punishes men for seven years for slapping a woman. The problems we are facing is that these laws stop when they reach the parliament and are not being signed off to be implemented. And knowing who the powerful men in the parliament are makes sense of why this is so.
>
> 'After the 2014 withdrawal [of Western troops] the Taliban will try to take control again. The West could have stopped this and still can, but they don't want to. They don't want Afghanistan to be peaceful. If they really wanted to bring peace and stability they would have done this and achieved it a long time ago, but they don't want to because then the Afghans and their own people in the West would ask them to leave.'

Mitra also noticed how much security had increased around the US embassy and the city centre compared to a year earlier. She was told:

'It is to create tension and fear in order to make people believe they are not safe and need Western support for their security. The latest attacks in Kabul are all drama created by the US to make the world think the Afghan people need them here to bring peace and stability, and that our own people are not capable to achieve this without their help.'[25]

The objective problems of insecurity, poverty and lack of development have to be added to the religious and social structures in Afghanistan which place women in a subordinate position and which result in women's lives being home-centred, without education and subjected to family-enforced codes of morality. The incidence of rape, forced marriage, child marriage and domestic violence remains high.

These structures have been reinforced by the war. Under attack from foreign invaders, Islamic traditionalism becomes an expression of resistance. However, many NGOs and women's organisations oppose the withdrawal of occupying troops because they fear that it will endanger the position of women further. This statement from a Canadian Women's Organisation is typical:

'We are staunch supporters of a strong international effort in Afghanistan that seeks to secure basic human rights and peace, with coordination and increased strategic intervention on diplomatic, development, and military fronts. We oppose any positions that would ultimately lead to more bloodshed and civil or regional war in Afghanistan, such as a premature withdrawal of international forces; or to an Afghan state that fails to uphold the basic rights of women and girls.'[26]

Louise Hancock, co-author of an Oxfam report published in 2011 on women in Afghanistan, argued:

'Afghan women tell me that they do not feel that they can count on any of the main players in peace efforts to safeguard their rights. They want a place at the table so that they can protect their hard-won gains. The greater stake women have in a peace process the more likely they are to support and promote reconciliation within their families and communities, which is essential for lasting peace.'[27]

Yet the report makes grim reading for all those who want improvements for women in Afghanistan. It shows that despite early promises, things are getting worse in many areas. More girls are going to school (around 2.7 million) but there has been no real progress on the political front. 'In Parliament, the quota system put into place in 2005 guarantees 68 female MPs – there are now 69. However, there is now just one female minister compared to three in 2004. The number of women in the civil service has dropped from 31 per cent in 2006 to 18.5 percent in 2010.'

More worryingly, the threat to women from male violence or archaic laws has grown:

'In addition, the government's ground-breaking Elimination of Violence Against Women law, which criminalises traditional practices such as honour killing, child marriage and giving away girls to settle disputes, is being enforced in only ten of Afghanistan's 34 provinces. In the second quarter of 2011 alone, the Afghan Independent Human Rights Commission registered 1,026 cases of violence against women. In 2010 as a whole, by contrast, there were 2,765 cases in total.'[28]

Despite political and legal pressures the lawmakers have acted in their own interests rather than those of Afghan women. In 2009, for short-term electoral gain, President Karzai backed the Sharia Personal Status Law whose provisions include entitling men to withhold food from their wives if they do not comply with their sexual demands and allowing rapists to avoid prosecution by paying blood money to women they have injured.[29] In 2012, he endorsed a religious code which would allow men to beat their wives and make it harder for women to socialise in public with men.[30] These violations of women's rights with legal backing are taking place under the rule, and often with the blessing, of the Western-backed President. The presence of Western troops is not preventing this.

Amnesty International USA launched a campaign in 2012, at the NATO summit in Chicago, placing adverts on bus shelters saying: 'NATO: Keep the Progress Going'. One of their panellists at an alternative summit was former Secretary of State Madeleine Albright, who said of Iraq sanctions that half a million children's deaths were 'worth it'. The current executive director of Amnesty USA is a former government insider, who worked as Deputy Assistant Secretary for International Organizations at the Department of State.[31] This position has been highly controversial, including among women and women's organisations.[32] As Mitra Qayoom says, the posters show

> 'Afghan women in their blue burqas promoting NATO's occupation of Afghanistan and further encouraging the public to support the propaganda that the US and its NATO allies are in Afghanistan to help liberate the Afghan women. We see Hillary Clinton shaking hands with Afghan women promising to help them in their fight for justice and women's rights in Afghanistan. But when it comes time to do so, she ignores the voices of these women. She could not care less. I am tired of seeing the Afghan women being used as an excuse to continue this senseless war.'[33]

An equally depressing story can be told about the aftermath of the invasion and war in Iraq. Similar claims for the liberation of women were made in the run-up to the war and in its early years. Funding, political backing and media exposure were provided for new women's organisations who would recount the horrors of life under Saddam Hussein. After the overthrow of the regime, millions of US dollars were allocated to women's NGOs in Iraq. Some of these played the role of what Haifa Zangana calls 'soft occupiers'.[34]

Before the war a number of initiatives were taken in the United States to create organisations that would support war on the basis of women's rights. In February 2003 the Foundation in Defense of Democracies, a Zionist think-tank with some of the leading US neo-cons as its advisers, 'brought together fifty Iraqi women (most of them US citizens) to establish Women for a Free Iraq (WFFI)'. At the inaugural gathering were key representatives of the Bush administration, including Dick Cheney, Condoleezza Rice and Paul Wolfowitz. At its press launch the same day, the statement from WFFI made clear its stand, citing approvingly 'the determination of the American government to disarm Saddam, and its commitment to help liberate the people of Iraq'.[35]

This and other women's organisations, and their spokespeople, were valuable to the belligerent governments in the run-up to and immediate aftermath of the invasion. However, the plan to use the treatment of women to justify the war on the grounds of humanitarian intervention soon came unstuck. The situation in Iraq quickly deteriorated for those who were trying to justify humanitarian intervention: they immediately encountered Iraqi resistance; they were unable to find the weapons of mass destruction with which they had justified the war and incidents involving the killing or abuse of Iraqis caused widespread opposition to the occupation.

A series of landmark events highlighted the true nature of the war and occupation. These included the siege and bombardment by US troops of the resistance stronghold of Fallujah in 2004, in which around 600 civilians were killed, most of them women, children and the elderly.[36] Other atrocities included the massacre at Haditha, the 2004 scandal of the torture and abuse of prisoners by US military guards in Abu Ghraib prison, and the rape and murder of a young Iraqi girl, A'beer Qassim Hamza, and the killing of her family by US soldiers.[37]

The consequences of the war were measured in ever-higher figures of devastation: hundreds of thousands, perhaps as many as a million, Iraqi dead and over four million refugees. A survey by psychologists in 2006 found 92 per cent of children had learning difficulties, largely as a result of insecurity and fear.[38] Documented rapes by occupying troops and Iraqi security forces numbered 1,053 between 2003 and early 2007.[39] A rapid increase in sectarian tensions and killings had been exacerbated by the policies of the occupiers.[40] All this weakened the claim that the occupation was helping to bring any of the supposed benefits of 'humanitarian intervention'. International opposition to the occupation was fuelled by several other factors: the legacy of a very strong anti-war movement which had built up before the invasion, but which was now sustained in Britain, the United States and elsewhere; the continued campaigning against the occupation by women and men in Iraq, which gave the lie to the subservience of Iraqi women; and the rising numbers of deaths resulting from the war and occupation.

So the experience of war in both Afghanistan and Iraq has done much to discredit the claim of humanitarian intervention. That has not prevented its supporters, including Blair, from trying to revive the doctrine to justify air strikes and intervention in Libya in 2011 and a possible intervention in Syria. Such interventions may result in short-term changes, most obviously the overthrow of an unpopular regime. But the balance sheet shows that the chaos caused by the interventions impacts negatively on ordinary people and that the real gains accrue to the imperialists and a small number of the local elite who benefit politically or financially from regime change.

The dilemma supporters of humanitarian intervention face is that it is relatively easy for the United States and its allies to stage the initial attack, especially when it takes the form of an air war. It helps the argument for war to be able to point to real or potential human rights atrocities, but doing something about the problems in the longer term is a different matter. Reconstructing a society cannot be undertaken by invaders, by people who have previously been a colonial power or by military machines. Reconstruction therefore becomes closely tied to military plans and is bedevilled by corruption. This reflects the fact that rebuilding the country is never the main aim of the operation. That is to create a client regime subservient to Western interests, not to improve the lives of ordinary people.

The effect of war on whole countries tends to be to destroy stable civil society and devastate the lives of millions, regardless of their role in the process. Elaheh Rostami Povey, a London-based Iranian who has studied women in Afghanistan, explains that there were hopes that the 2001 overthrow of the Taliban would change things:

'I don't think Afghanistan is different in terms of the impact of war on people's lives. When I first went to Afghanistan in 2002 just after the Taliban fell people were very hopeful that the Taliban had gone and they could end those years of war. Afghan people had had war for three decades.'

Povey makes clear, however, that the impact of war itself has an effect on civilians regardless of the protagonists.

> 'When I started interviewing Afghan people for my project I was quite amazed when the women said that although they rejoiced at the overthrow of the Taliban they thought the pre-Taliban period of civil war was even worse. Under the civil war, which was a result of the US intervention and the Russian intervention, both sides used different communities for their own ends. The situation was so bad that brothers and neighbours were killing each other.'

She had little doubt that foreign intervention heightened the tensions rather than reducing them:

> 'There are so many ethnic and religious groups in the country and no one is denying that they have been in conflict before, but they were saying that the conflicts always became worse when there was foreign intervention. This was true in the British period in the nineteenth century and of the Soviet Union and the civil war of the 1980s.'[41]

A similar point was made by Nicola Pratt:

> 'With the possible exception of the wives of war profiteers, war has been an almost universally negative thing for women [in the Middle East]. It makes everyday household and family maintenance difficult and this dispropor-tionately impacts upon women. It makes going to work or school/university or getting involved in politics dangerous and this also disproportionately impacts upon women. This is largely a result of the changing nature of warfare, where the 'battle front' and the 'home front' are now practically the same. But even during the era of conventional warfare, scarce resources were located to the military at the expense of civilian welfare and men who served were often physically and mentally scarred for life, if they survived.'[42]

So war in itself has severe consequences for the civilian population irrespective of their involvement. The terrible death toll and refugee numbers in Afghanistan and Iraq, the breakdown of civil society and the impact that has on education, health and social problems, are all part of the wider cost of war which cannot be quantified simply by looking at the immediate casualties of the conflict. Those trying to live in such a society are faced with a host of problems beyond mere survival.

Despite very high levels of military spending, the Western powers have found themselves in a quagmire in both Iraq and Afghanistan. The wars have essentially been failures, achieving the first stage of regime change, but then unable to impose stable pro-Western rule. That is why all predictions of a rapid transition to peace and security have been confounded and why the imperialist powers are spending more human and financial resources on trying to win the wars, but with few visible results.

Current projections for Afghan troops to have taken over from NATO forces in 2014 are hampered by the rising number of attacks on NATO troops by Afghani soldiers or police. The impasse is not leading to a clear strategy of withdrawal. Instead, there is a downward spiral not just in the war-torn countries themselves but in the Western countries. For the wars have not dealt with terrorism; they have exacerbated it. They have alienated large sections of the British population, especially Muslims. They have also created a rising tide of Islamophobia in Europe and North America, directly attributable to the War on Terror, which is leading to escalating racism against Muslims. Once again, women are on the front line.

Muslim Women: What Not to Wear

In 2006, the then Foreign Secretary Jack Straw caused a furore when he told his constituency newspaper, the *Lancashire Evening Telegraph*, that he felt 'uncomfortable' when women wearing the face veil or niqab visited his constituency surgery and that he asked them to remove their veils. He said he wanted a debate about the issue.[43] Straw's remarks caused outrage among Muslims and non-Muslims alike. His constituency, Blackburn, has a large Muslim population, and he had never raised the issue before, presumably happy for Muslim women to vote for him regardless of how they were dressed. But within a few years his views would be voiced more widely across the political spectrum. The right-wing UK Independence Party had as one of its 2010 election pledges a commitment to 'ban the burqa'. The media repeatedly suggests that women who wear face coverings or veils may be a 'security risk'. There are even allegations that male terrorists dress in burqas in order to avoid detection. The English Defence League also claims that people commit robberies dressed in burqas.[44]

This growing attack on Muslims has been one of the consequences of the War on Terror. 'Since September 11, every EU country has introduced citizenship reforms, revised integration policies and brought in immigration laws that limit the rights of existing citizens and long-term residents to family reunification.'[45] After 9/11 the government tried to prevent attacks on mosques, at least to pay lip service to the idea that British Muslims were not to blame for terrorism, and to integrate sections of the Muslim community into a regular relationship and dialogue. That approach has changed as successive wars have failed and the international situation appears more intractable. Especially since the London bombings of 2005, there have been increasingly peremptory calls for Muslims to get their house in order.

Criticism of cultural questions, especially of women wearing religious dress, has become more strident. There have been proposed or actual bans on the hijab, the niqab and on the burqa. The terror laws are more draconian than anything passed during the much deadlier and more coordinated IRA bombing campaign of the 1970s and 1980s though these were bad enough, resulting in a high number of miscarriages of justice.

Some sections of the media are running a relentless campaign, equating Muslims with extremists and even terrorists. Government ministers repeatedly attempt to force 'Muslim representatives' to condemn anyone deemed an 'extremist'. There are also demands that Muslims 'integrate' into Western society: dressing differently, speaking different languages, wearing symbols of religion are all seen as remaining apart from a society into which many Muslims have been born. Naseem Akhtar, a founder of the Saheli Women's group, said: 'I have grown up in Britain, having come to Birmingham from Kashmir, Pakistan as a one-year-old toddler. I see myself as a British Muslim of Kashmiri origin. But now I am asked, "Are you British first or Muslim first." No one asks the question of Catholics or Jews.'[46] Rania Khan says:

'We now face a new dilemma, if we as British Muslim women do not get involved we are labelled as "outsiders", "excluders" or "do not wish to conform to British way of life", and when we do get involved we are then given a different title – "infiltrators" – and that really hurts. As a young British Muslim all my family and I have done is to build bridges between different communities, and support the most vulnerable.

As young Muslim women we do not just have a glass ceiling to break but rather a glass box; fighting sexism (one which effects all women in general), racism and Islamophobia. I call this the triple whammy.'[47]

The obsession with integration has led to a wave of Islamophobia in the guise of liberal concern. In reality the demand for assimilation into Western culture is an attempt to enforce political conformity and acceptance of the right of the West to intervene anywhere in the world. Women from Muslim backgrounds who favour total assimilation have been given media platforms to present a view of Islam which stresses violence towards women and oppressive attitudes, while women with different viewpoints have been ignored.[48]

Across Europe there are signs of a legislative crackdown against a relatively flimsy piece of cloth which is invested with heavy symbolism. In April 2010, a near-unanimous vote of Belgium's Lower House voted to outlaw the burqa even though no more than a few dozen women there wear it. The following month the French Parliament approved a resolution deploring full-face cover[49] – this after a law passed in September 2004 which bans religious symbols in schools on the grounds of secularism, but which is clearly aimed at Muslim girls.[50] The Swiss Parliament voted for a nationwide ban on the burqa, following a referendum which prohibited the building of any more mosques in Switzerland.

The French ban on wearing the burqa in public places was passed in 2011, although, as in most of the countries concerned, only a small number of women were thought to wear this form of dress. The *Guardian*, which investigated its effect, reported:

'But five months after the law was introduced, the result is a mixture of confusion and apathy. Muslim groups report a worrying increase in discrimination and verbal and physical violence against women in veils. There have been instances of people in the street taking the law into their hands and trying to rip off full-face veils, of bus drivers refusing to carry women in niqab or of shop-owners trying to bar entry. A few women have taken to wearing bird-flu-style medical masks to keep their face covered; some describe a climate of divisiveness, mistrust and fear. One politician who backed the law said that women still going out in niqab were simply being "provocative".'[51]

The French law can be said to have created confrontation between Muslims and non-Muslims, with women in burqas or niqabs attacked for no other reason than that their clothing denotes a certain religion – and, of course, a certain race since the overwhelming majority of French Muslims are of north African origin.[52] In the Netherlands the anti-Muslim politician Geert Wilders greeted as 'fantastic news' the Dutch Cabinet decision to agree to ban the burqa along with other items that cover the face such as ski masks. Again, the legislation will be largely symbolic, since only about 300 women in the Netherlands wear the burqa and most of them rarely leave their homes. In a population of 17 million, this can hardly be seen as a threat.[53] But to see these laws as sledgehammers to crack nuts misses the point. In virtually every case the legislation is passed as a result of pressure by the Far Right. Their aim is to use liberal sentiments to ban certain forms of dress on the grounds that they are oppressive to women, in the process exacerbating racism and tension.

Right-wing parties and organisations, from UKIP, the BNP and EDL in Britain to the anti-immigrant Northern League in Italy, are seizing the question to mobilise an anti-Muslim climate. A Tunisian Muslim woman was fined €500 in the Italian town of Novara for wearing a veil while on her way to prayers in a mosque, under a law which stops people from covering their faces near public buildings. The mayor, a member of the anti-immigration Northern League, justified this by saying, 'We cannot accept cultures that destroy women's dignity.'[54] There was apparently no hint of embarrassment at his party's support for the then Prime Minister Silvio Berlusconi.

A report from Amnesty International showed that one of the consequences of these European laws has been to make it harder for Muslim women to integrate in the way that so many Western societies are demanding. Amnesty's expert on discrimination, Marco Perolini, said: 'Muslim women are being denied jobs and girls prevented from attending regular classes just because they wear traditional forms of dress, such as the headscarf.' He added, 'General bans [on religious symbols in schools] risk adversely Muslim girls' access to education and violating their rights to freedom of expression and to manifest their beliefs.'[55]

This series of ideological attacks, which focuses on Muslims as 'the enemy within', is itself a product of the War on Terror. When there is an onslaught by the major Western powers against countries with a majority Muslim population, justification for these attacks depends in part on demonising the people who are under attack. This is why governments and the media have been spreading hatred against Muslims. They also try to use anti-Muslim sentiment in populist campaigns to bolster their support in periods of austerity. This tactic has a long and ignoble history dating back to the scapegoating of the Irish in the 1880s, of the Jews in the 1930s and of the Afro-Caribbeans in the 1970s. On every occasion, politicians and the media have sought to divert criticism over unemployment and poverty by trying to get those affected to blame their neighbours of different races and religions.

While this has given succour to racists and fascists who take advantage of Islamophobia, sections of the Left and liberal intelligentsia have also joined the attack. Islamophobia takes many forms; perhaps the most insidious is the one which seeks to rescue Muslim women from their supposedly oppressive religion, families and societies. One of the main arguments in the lexicon of Islamophobia is that Islam, and therefore many Muslims, oppress women. According to this view, Islam is a particularly misogynistic religion, which forces women into an inferior position. Women are not allowed to take part in many aspects of public life, they have to cover their heads and bodies so that they are not seen by men other than their husbands and families, and in certain Islamic regimes women are discriminated against by being denied access to education. This distorts how Islam is actually practised in most parts of the world and requires a convenient amnesia about the oppression of women in the Judeo-Christian tradition. It also treats Muslim women as unable to think for themselves, seen as totally submissive and passive if they cover themselves.

It also fails to address two important points. The first is that many Muslim women wear the hijab either as a free choice or as a statement about themselves and their identity. The second is that the actual experience and practice of many Muslim women, especially younger Muslim women, directly contradicts this view of passivity.

It is impossible to understand why the racists focus on the burqa to attack Muslim women without seeing the connection to the War on Terror and without linking their argument to that of the victors in 2001, who associated liberation with unveiling and showing the face. If freedom for women in Afghanistan can be ushered in by disrobing, how much more important is that unveiling in Western countries which are deemed more 'civilised'?

A 2005 study showed there were complex reasons why women wear the hijab, including making a political choice in a sometimes hostile environment: 'they are publicly branding themselves as Muslims at a time when such a label carries the potential fear of making them vulnerable to open hostility.'[56] A young British Muslim woman, Naeema, put it this way:

'People ask about the hijab, they always ask "Does your mum make you wear that?" They can't imagine we choose it. In our house we read people like John Pilger, we study what is happening in the world. Our opposition to what Bush and Blair are doing is informed. We are politically aware, but they just think we have no education, that Muslim women are stupid.'

Zenib, from Newham, said:

'I choose to wear the hijab in Britain, but in villages in Pakistan and India and developing countries, women are traditionally covered up in public places . . . It isn't the main thing in their lives. Of course women should not be forced to do it. But women in the West are forced in a way to fit in. When I did my fashion degree you learn about what styles are in, which labels to wear and trends are set which psychologically women feel they have to follow and then they have to be a size zero. And who chooses that? It's mainly men that design these trends and uncover women the way they want to see them.'[57]

In a country such as Britain, with its colonial past, its belligerent present and its long history of racism, it should be a source of pride rather than approbation that those who suffer some of the worst effects of oppression are campaigning and organising to challenge them.

Muslim Women: Fighting Back

It is hard to imagine the degree of confidence in dressing as they choose and in challenging racism and Islamophobia which young Muslim women in Britain have developed without the political education of opposition to war. The nature of the anti-war movement has played a very important role in this process. Partly through design but partly through accident the movement developed in such a way that it was habitable to Muslims, including Muslim women. This involvement alongside non-Muslims led to ideas changing and to an understanding not just of war but of other questions of liberation.

Yvonne Ridley became a Muslim in the course of her anti-war campaigning. She is a popular figure in the Muslim community for her work in opposing war and fund-raising for Palestine:

'I think the women got the anti-war message straight away and it took a lot, not all, but a lot of men to catch up to the horrors and brutality of war. It's possibly easier for a woman to stand up and call for an end to fighting than it is a man. In the Muslim community I know a lot of men felt intimidated by the movement and thought they would be targeted for arrest if they joined in because of the Islamophobia being whipped up.'[58]

Women and girls who were growing up at the time of 9/11 found this a key turning point in their lives. Henna Malik, at school in 2001, describes how it affected her:

> 'I remember September 11 clear as day, I had just returned from sixth form, my mother was watching the news, smoke was billowing out of the Twin Towers, and the news was suggesting that Muslims were responsible. I was in utter shock. My first instinct was to write a letter to read out in my media studies class the next day. It referred to the Oklahoma bombing, being initially blamed on "Islamists", which is a bizarre phrase. It then went on to state that even the name Islam is derived from the word peace. I was genuinely scared about the reaction I would face as a young Muslim woman walking into school the next day – Would I be perceived as a terrorist? Would people stop talking to me? This then led me to think about the wider societal perceptions of all Muslims.'[59]

Much changed for Henna as a result of the wars and her involvement in the movement, which began with a Palestine demonstration in 2002:

> 'The anti-war movement [was] my university education in war and peace ... I started to study world politics as a result of the ramifications of September 11, however I did not understand fully concepts such as imperialism until I was engaged in the anti-war movement. Before being faced head on with the ripple effect of being an "other", a Muslim, I hadn't had to think so much about war, or even peace, until my own peace was threatened.'[60]
>
> 'I was empowered by the anti-war movement, as much as I was attempting to fight for the liberation and free the people of Iraq. They were in turn freeing me from the shackles of mental slavery.
>
> 'The steering committee of the School Student Stop the War Coalition was made up of nine members, eight of whom were women. The student anti-war movement was led by young women, and women were leading the demonstrations. The anti-war movement was also an equality movement, and it showed without society's barriers women are very capable of being highly successful leaders.'[61]

Rania Khan, from Tower Hamlets, believes the movement

> 'has politicised and mobilised a new generation of British Muslim women who otherwise would have had minimal interest in local and international

politics. For me, I was inspired by the various speakers like Lindsey German, Salma Yaqoob and my mother Lutfa Begum to get involved.

'As we began to feel the pain and suffering of those who lost their lives during the Iraq war on both sides – the 500,000 Iraqis, the majority of whom were innocent civilians, or young British soldiers – I began to realise that whichever way you look at it, it is the poor, the working class who suffer the most on the back of multinational companies who make billions during a war. And it is truly shameful! I was also inspired by the young people of St Paul's Way school [in Tower Hamlets] who attended the protest demanding why our government had gone to war in Iraq when that money could be better spent fixing their broken schools, better spent on their housing needs.

'The anti-war moment gave women like me a platform and a voice to speak against injustice. Solidarity and empathy of supporters of the STW movement with those suffering was humbling.'[62]

Non-Muslim women were also on a sharp learning curve in the anti-war movement. Penny Hicks, a key player in STW in Coventry and later in Manchester, tells of how she overcame some reservations about engaging in political activity with Muslim women wearing the hijab:

'The principle of uniting around a set of demands while being tolerant of others wanting to pursue more specific goals has taught me how to build united fronts. The different traditions of organising and conducting discussions were a rich education. I had worked with Muslims in my trade union but the anti-war movement opened up a new and more political relationship with diverse groups of Muslims. I remember, for example, still around 1992 being anti the hijab, seeing it as an oppressive symbol. The patient discussions Muslim women held with me were a revelation. The fact that women were choosing to wear it was a new conversation for me.'[63]

Dahabo Isse describes the importance of the anti-war movement for her:

'My experience of the anti-war movement was very good, inspiring and helpful to the people where war continues on their lands. It motivated us and [we] felt that there are . . . some people who care about us and have concerns about the effect and the destruction war causes . . . [it] also included slogans about Somalia ... My involvement also included attending steering committee meetings of the Stop the War Coalition, events and also make speeches in conferences.'[64]

Yvonne Ridley says:

'In Britain I think it would be fair to say that Muslim women have become part of the backbone of the anti-war movement. For the first time in their lives they have been invited to join a movement which is dynamic, integrated, multicultural for all people of faith and no faith. Unlike the feminism of the '70s, they're not excluded because of their culture or beliefs. Given a chance to prove themselves, they have impressed so many people with their organisational skills and ability to help mobilise their communities.

'As for the Muslim women in Palestine; they are in a league of their own when it comes to suffering, enduring and resisting. One of the biggest mistakes the men of war have made is to underestimate the Muslim women and they continue to do it time and time again.'[65]

It became clear that the mobilisation of Muslim women was not going to end after the war in Iraq, but was to have a major politicising influence and help energise future campaigns. Palestine had long been a key issue and now flared up again. A new generation of Muslim women came into the movement, protesting at Israel's invasion of Lebanon in 2006 and then again at Israel's bombing of Gaza in late 2008 and during the early weeks of 2009.

Huge mobilisations shook the capital and Britain's major cities as night after night bombs rained down, killing between 1,000 and 2,000 people. Again the involvement of women and children was noticeable, with Muslim women in particular fundraising, organising vigils and protests, and speaking. The movement was very broad, encompassing wide sections of the Left and the traditional peace movement. The explosion of activity over Gaza took organising on the issue of Palestine to a new plane.

Young people were particularly affected by the vicious brutality of the British police. Demonstrators near the Israeli embassy were kettled, attacked and arrested. Those convicted received harsh sentences. This helped to radicalise a new generation. It also saw the rebirth of a student movement with a wave of occupations in solidarity with Gaza. These took place at over 30 colleges in Britain, were the first occupations for many years and were all the more remarkable being over an international issue. Large colleges such as Queen Mary and Royal Holloway were occupied, with a new cohort of women activists coming to the fore.

Many of the students were too young to have marched against the Iraq war, but opposition to these wars had helped create a strong anti-war and pro-Palestine consciousness. Women played a leading role again, and Muslim women – some Palestinians, but many from South Asian backgrounds – were prominent. They stayed in the universities, defied the college authorities and were at least partly successful in highlighting the issue and winning demands about investment and scholarships for Palestinians from the authorities.

This marked the changing attitudes of young Muslim women too; like their non-Muslim counterparts they saw their future in becoming educated to equip them for jobs outside the home. They organised round issues to do with war and Palestine, but also became part of the movement against higher tuition fees and against the abolition of the Educational Maintenance Allowance for sixth form students. Anti-war students made the connections with the trade union movement, the Occupy movement and the campaigns against austerity.

In 2005 the anti-war party Respect won record swings against Labour in four parliamentary constituencies with large Muslim populations. George Galloway won a parliamentary seat in Tower Hamlets and a number of councillors were elected in Tower Hamlets, Newham and Birmingham the following year. The role of women as activists and supporters was noticeable to those involved in the campaigns.[66] Similarly, the dramatic result of the Bradford West by-election in March 2012 was widely attributed to the mobilisation of young people and women. The result underlined the radicalisation of Muslim women, their willingness to vote against their husbands and fathers, and their continued concerns about the war.[67]

Rania Khan is typical of the young Muslim women radicalised by war, and describes how the movement affected her:

'Yes I am a product of the anti-war movement, which has given me so much in terms of confidence; encouragement, knowledge of local and global issues, a voice when I felt voiceless and most importantly, I received a lot of love and support from my comrades in the movement, which I am truly grateful for.'[68]

8
Changes: War and Women's Consciousness

In this book I have considered the role of war in politics and society in Britain over the past 100 years and its impact on women. But why has campaigning against war become so important to women, and what has motivated them? In this chapter I explore the views of a number of the women I interviewed, who spoke about their influences, experiences and what especially made them organise, demonstrate and campaign. They also discussed the role of men in war, the difference between male and female attitudes, the role of women in the movement and what implications these have for future politics and organisation.

Women's heightened consciousness against war, which I have traced through a period when war has impinged more and more on everyday life, only partly explains why some women become so involved. There are many and sometimes complex reasons why they get involved while others do not. But it is clear that opposition to war is heightened by exposure to its costs.

Elaheh Rostami Povey was exiled from her home country of Iran under the Shah's repressive rule in the late 1960s. She came from a highly political family but left for personal reasons. She became involved in Iranian student activity in London in the early 1970s, so was already a socialist and anti-war when she returned to Iran after the revolution in 1979. Living in Tehran during the Iran–Iraq war in the 1980s, she had direct experience of being in a country at war and what that means. She describes the relentless worry and fear which seize hold of everyone:

'Although the war never extended to Tehran where I lived there were a few times it was bombed and every night there were sirens going, anti-aircraft guns. My daughter Tara was three. The experience of living, dragging children from the top of the building to the bottom, trying to hide under staircases or whatever, desperately feeling any moment a bomb will hit you . . . that was how I experienced the horrors of war, how war could affect people. Tara even now is still scared of fireworks. It reminds her of then.

'We were among the lucky ones, we weren't hurt, and so many people, one million, died in Iran, half a million in Iraq. The impact of the war on Iranians and Iraqis was huge. It was unbelievable. Wars are horrible things. The impact stays with you for a very long time . . . It really is one of the most horrendous things human beings can experience.'[1]

Jenny Jones, a longstanding Green Party member of the London Assembly, argues that this generalised sense of living in a world dominated by war has a very powerful effect:

'The world wars have of course made a huge difference. But there are other wars, wars in Africa for example, or the war in Afghanistan, where supposedly things are getting better for women but actually they are not – or so marginally it's not worth the pain and stress. In Africa women are raped and brutalised and their kids are brutalised so there it's going backwards. Rape is about subjugating the population.'[2]

Nicola Pratt, a Middle East expert and lecturer at Warwick University, argues that war is always disastrous for women:

'Having studied the impact of war on women, it has not changed my mind about opposing war but it does enable you to tell a more detailed story about why war is never the answer – including so-called humanitarian wars, such as the recent NATO bombing of Libya.'

She continues: 'Although war, like other processes, is gendered, that is not the same as saying that gender inequalities cause war. Indeed, it is rather the other way round – that war causes gender inequalities. Or, at least, war exacerbates gender inequalities.'[3]

Many politicians who make the decision to wage war believe that any anti-war sentiment will fade fairly rapidly once hostilities have started. Politicians can even gain popularity as a result of going to war. Margaret Thatcher's war in the Falklands in 1982 is an example. However, the era of neoliberal wars and the new imperialism has made it harder for nations to wage short, politically 'successful' wars. Instead, wars tend to turn into lengthy and intractable conflicts where superior armed force is met with opposition from irregular forces who are able to mount effective and often popular campaigns.

The resilience of anti-war and peace campaigning in the major imperialist countries underlines deep and long-term opposition to war. Commitment to campaigning stays with many people all their lives. Over the years, a cumulative consciousness about war develops. The experience of the War on Terror over the past decade has been to increase scepticism about war as well as specific knowledge about the nature of warfare.

Nicola Pratt suggests the need to force politicians to take responsibility for their actions:

'I do believe that capitalism is a major cause of wars. However, I hope that we can be successful in holding politicians to account about the wars that they wage and making them think twice before they launch the next one. I really hope that Tony Blair will be tried for war crimes. But I also recognise that Europe and the US are waging war in new, more dangerous ways – through drones. Unfortunately, this makes war more likely in the future. But I believe that you must always speak out against war because not to do so would make you complicit with war.'[4]

The increase in drone warfare and other types of remote combat is creating new areas of protest. Helen John, a Greenham veteran, has become involved in a campaign against drones, which she sees as a continuation of her earlier campaigning:

'Tragically now, in 2012, the drones, a family member of cruise missiles, are killing by stealth thousands of innocent victims globally for oil, land, minerals or water.

'For the first time British Royal Airforce pilots will be guiding these weapons from British soil. The reaper drones will be based at RAF Waddington in Lincolnshire, the home of Bomber Command, which itself committed war crimes by a deliberate policy of killing so many German civilians [in the Second World War]. We are not at war and any use of drones by the RAF will be a war crime.'[5]

Angela Sinclair, at university when first radicalised during the Second World War, worked for the Friends' Ambulance Service in the East End. Now she campaigns against all wars:

'As long as there were marches and demos I went on as many as I could. Pacifism was my main thing. I wrote letters to the papers. My motives were both religious and political. I used to be shy, but I'm not shy any more. It's lovely seeing . . . now the number of people who are against Afghanistan. One war just leads to another.'[6]

Campaigning spans the generations, as a number of the young women I talked to explained. Tansy Hoskins came from a family of peace campaigners:

'I have a long family history of being involved in peace movements. My grandmother was very much involved in CND and inter-faith peace work and conscientious objector organisations. My parents were also very much involved with CND and I was taken on all the CND demos as a baby and child. As a child I was also involved with the campaign against the first Iraq war, I remember being at a candle-lit vigil at our local war memorial, but that was quite small.'[7]

Sinead Kirwan's parents were both socialists, and her maternal family were Irish republicans:

'I heard a lot of stories from my grandmother, like her dad having to hide in an open grave all night to avoid the Black and Tans who were out in the town.

'When my mum's grandmother was buried, the British army made them open up the coffin because they thought there were guns inside.'

She was also influenced as a child by books about the Second World War: 'One of my favourite stories was *When Hitler Stole the Pink Rabbit*, which is about a Jewish child who is forced to become a refugee and move to London. I remember thinking how terrible that was.'[8]

Carmel Brown from Liverpool believes the full impact on the next generation of campaigning against the War on Terror is unquantifiable: 'My own daughters have taken themselves off on demos against racism and I'm sure some of that's from the example we give. If we have to do it again, we'll do it again. As women we have to be teachers and teach our kids fair play.'[9]

War and Work

War is a brutal and forceful factor in bringing about social change. Wars have been and are a major source of danger and dislocation, which impacts disproportionately on women. But they can also mark a breakdown of traditional values and allow women more freedom, ushering in changes in their lives. Furthermore, the impact of modern wars on a domestic audience can lead to heightened consciousness on the issue.

Kate Connelly, who became involved against the Iraq war as a school student in Cambridge, stresses the double-edged impacts of wars:

'Some feminists argue that war emancipates women at the expense of men by enabling women to enter a wider range of jobs and allowing them greater freedoms. Of course, it would be true to say that many women's horizons have been hugely broadened by the opportunities created by war and that many women have experienced 'enjoyable' wars. However, I think this is a problematic argument because it fails to acknowledge that many women lose their loved ones in war, and that although historically the work available to them has been broadened, employers have usually tried to pay them less than they paid men and often the work has been very unsafe – for example the munitions work undertaken by the TNT women ("canaries") in the First World War. On top of holding down jobs, women in war time are often forced to cope with food shortages and childcare, usually with little or no help from the state pursuing that war. Women's roles can be broadened by war, but they can also be broadened as a consequence of mass movements and campaigns for equality.'[10]

Billie Figg, who was a young woman during the Second World War, believes the roots of modern consumer society lie in the changing role of women then:

'The war affected women enormously. This exposure of women to a great big world outside was a great motor to the consumer society. We took jobs, we fancied the things that would simplify domestic life so we could go to work, we were dazzled by the new designs coming along, so we contributed enormously to the growth of the consumer society.

'I was very excited because I worked in an advertising agency and wrote copy about these things. [My husband] Jack spotted early on in the '60s more women going to work and he said "that will become the norm, two-salary households, and women won't be able to stay home". We didn't stop to look at that at the time. It's a very big change which is still affecting us; the era when women lost the choice of whether they would stay home. The results of that we live with today. War gave women the taste of jobs outside the home.'[11]

Women entering the workforce helped the trend towards a consumer society. At the same time, many would argue that this has increasingly negative effects: families identify their success or failure in terms of consumption, so that women have little choice but to work outside the home. While the majority of women have certainly welcomed this, and alongside it more educational opportunities and greater financial independence, they have very often come up against the limits of a society which now chooses to exploit them on the same basis as men. The horizons opened up by war have only partly been achieved.

Rae Street considers the changes brought about by war to be very double-edged:

'So often it was one step forward and two steps back. Women still do not have equality and I hardly think the recent wars in the Middle East or the Falklands or the Balkans have changed women's positions in society here in the UK. Sadly, in the Middle East women are losing out again. Maybe there are more hopeful signs in Africa – Rwanda and Congo spring to mind after their wars – and Latin America, with the new socialist governments, but that is a complex picture.'[12]

Jenny Jones makes a similar point: 'We've been lucky perhaps in the West for women to take some advantage of the wars, but you need a certain level of democracy and awareness for women to be able to do that.'[13]

Elaheh Rostami Povey describes how the impact of war can sometimes be judged by the responses when it ends. The absence of war and the sense of relief that permeates society help to create a space where social movements can begin to organise in ways which simply were impossible, practically and politically, during the war:

'It's interesting after eight years of war how people immediately try to reconstruct their lives. The end of the war gave hope to those in the women's movement and democracy movement. They began to find a new life not just at personal levels but at society level and began to organise round these issues. The experience since the 1990s to today, despite the problems, shows how Iranian society changed after the war. Sometimes when I compare Iran's situation with, say, Iraq and Afghanistan – despite all the problems that exist – you see movements can develop much more when there is no war, even when there are political, economic and cultural difficulties.'[14]

Women and the Movement

The women's liberation movement evolved in part from the movement against the Vietnam war. Greenham Common was specifically a women's protest. The movement since 2001 has been notable for women's involvement. Some of this is clearly cumulative. Women have developed a more general confidence and political consciousness through anti-war campaigning. Rae Street thinks that joining up

'with so many friends through the Greenham link, working with like-minded women gave me a sense of freedom that was completely new and refreshing. And, of course, it gave me confidence. The diffident young girl who had been constantly told by her father to "keep quiet" suddenly found she could cope with small, maybe awkward audiences or large gatherings. So when I went to Japan for CND (I went three times) to the huge thousands-strong gatherings organised by Gensuikyo [Japan Council against Atomic and Hydrogen Bombs], I was amazed at myself.'[15]

Kate Hudson did not find it easy to identify one factor behind women's involvement, although she feels that maybe fewer formal structures make the movement more open to women:

'Why have women played such an important role in the new movements? I really don't know. Does it have something to do with the fact that women are just more public in the movement and in education, that they are working and that there is a changing role?

'Women have always been disproportionately significant in CND; nearly all of the recent chairs of CND were women. Women are more involved in CND than in the labour movement. For the first three years of me being chair the whole of the officers group was women. Is it because it's less structured?'

'. . . I don't feel I'm doing it because I'm a woman.'[16]

'Women activists have an exceptional approach to campaigning against war and on many other issues that breach life and death,' argues Helen John. 'The high proportion of women involved in the peace movement reflects the fact that women think and act from a well-considered point of view. They have a greater understanding that we cannot resolve issues by killing people, whereas men tend not to wish to appear foolish or soft, particularly in the eyes of other men'[17]

Sinead Kirwan points to Muslim women's involvement:

'Muslim women have played a massive role. Young Muslim women see Muslim men arrested and this has massive impact. The men are less able to participate in politics directly. On the Gaza protests and at meetings there have been a lot of mothers and sisters of those arrested. People can relate to it because of Iraq. Also the arguments around Afghanistan about doing things for women made people want to stand up against it.'[18]

Some of the women interviewed felt that involvement in anti-war protesting was part of a wider social movement challenging oppressive ideas. Kate Connelly argues:

'It is partly because the anti-war movement challenged powerful governments who have been quite uninterested in women's rights and have actually overseen a decade of regressive attitudes towards women, which have seen the return of practices previously dismissed as oppressive (pole dancing, beauty competitions) now dressed up as "liberation". Therefore, many women feel no "loyalty" to the governments that we have today. In most social movements which challenge hitherto dominant ideas oppressed groups often come to the fore because they have been given new confidence to challenge their oppression by the experience of a mass movement.'[19]

Rae Street makes similar points and also stresses that some women are much more informed and knowledgeable about the truth of war and related issues:

'Clearly women are now in our society able to speak out more; they have increased opportunities. They are also ready in difficult situations to give strength to one another. But this is not new. Look at the suffragists.

'Added to this I believe that many women are more ready to see clearly through the smokescreen of lies and propaganda put out by governments, which in turn has been devised by the military manufacturers and the corporate organisations for their own ends, that is militarism.

'I find this particularly true of NATO . . . This clarity of thinking extends too to seeing global security from the wide view – standing in other people's shoes. I think it is possible that more women can see the danger of, for example, having military and nuclear-armed bases in the UK and across Europe; or have a more rounded view of the Israel/Palestine situation; or see more clearly that wars in the Middle East are making the world more dangerous or that the UK's Trident system brings only danger not security, and so much more.'[20]

She believes that many 'women are often more prepared to stand outside the "establishment" viewpoint'. In addition, 'women are less likely to see a distinction between academic "war and peace studies" and campaigning. So if they are "academics", they are less likely to distance themselves from campaigning and if they are mainly campaigners they can write and research themselves authoritatively.'[21]

Jane Shallice believes that 'women are much more engaged' and that in the last ten years Muslim women are freer to organise: 'There are big gender differences in terms of social attitudes. Women are the people who provide, and who organise in the family. They are also more open emotionally about expressing fear, horror or anguish.'[22] Many women stressed that they have been inspired to take a more active role in campaigning after seeing women speaking, being interviewed, leading demonstrations and writing articles. For Tansy Hoskins these role models are very important:

'I think this is probably down to the fact that there have been strong role models in the anti-war movement that other women have been able to look to for inspiration. I think that having Lindsey German as convenor of Stop the War has been very important because it has meant that there has been a woman's voice talking sense on television and radio and at rallies and demonstrations. In addition, women like Kate Hudson, Rose Gentle and Salma Yaqoob have been inspirational role models. Also internationally, women like Cindy Sheehan and Malalai Joya have been role models for women. In addition to Rose Gentle other women have come from Military Families against the War.'

At the same time, her own activity has been changed by women (and some men) urging her to play a different role:

'As a Steering Committee member I started speaking at lots of public meetings across the country. I was constantly encouraged to do more and more. I remember Chris Nineham not giving me much choice about speaking from the stage at an anti-arms fair demo at Excel, because there hadn't been enough female speakers. However, ending up speaking in front of a big crowd turned out to be really great and something I enjoyed and it stood me in good stead for future public speaking as I had lost all fear.'[23]

Sinead Kirwan explains what it meant to her:

'I had to learn tactics, like how to walk out. I'd already campaigned against the Balkans war with a group of school students who went on the demonstrations when I was at Kingsland School, and we'd had a walkout over education cuts. But this time it was part of being a mass thing. What really changed me was not making assumptions about what people will do in changed circumstances. I spoke at one of the demos in Hyde Park. We'd got lots of people from school because we did a leaflet.'[24]

For Kate Connelly discovering politics while still at school was a formative experience:

> 'I definitely feel that I have been given more confidence as a result of the anti-war movement. Through the anti-war movement I have spoken in public numerous times, I have gained an enormous amount of experience as an organiser that I would never otherwise have obtained, especially at the age of 16 when most young people are dismissed and marginalised by mainstream politics. The anti-war movement has educated me about imperialism, racism, terrorism, the media, oppression, nationalism, resistance and social movements. The understanding I gained from the lessons of the War on Terror have provided a prism through which I view the world.'[25]

Are Women More Peace-Loving?

Traditionally, war was the business of men: men joined armies, travelled often long distances to fight and died on the battlefield. There were civilian casualties too among those who found themselves directly in the path of the war. The victims of sieges suffered, as did those who could not cultivate their crops or had their food pillaged by armies.

Women suffered rape and abuse.[26] They also became 'camp followers', expected to perform domestic and sexual services. But whereas women in the past played a passive and often a victim role, the twentieth century saw women playing more positive and active roles in wartime.

Sexual stereotyping means that armies, militarism and war are male-dominated. They expound 'masculine' values – toughness, discipline, aggression and a disdain for emotional responses. The role of armies is to maintain force and to fight. For this, a level of brutalisation is necessary to inure those who have to engage in battle and kill the 'enemy'. Rape has long been a weapon of war, used to subjugate the population. Women by contrast have been considered more peace-loving. However, these stereotypes do not reflect the views of many women and men.

Warfare and armies are integral to capitalist society and reflect the values of that society at its extremes. Armies are masculine and often brutal, reinforcing and taking to their logical conclusion bullying, hierarchical discipline and the use of force. Susan Brownmiller describes this process:

> 'The very maleness of the military – the brute power of weaponry exclusive to their hands, the spiritual bonding of men at arms, the manly discipline of orders given and orders obeyed, the simple logic of the hierarchical command – confirms for men what they long suspect, that women are peripheral, irrelevant to the world that counts, passive spectators to the action in the centre ring.'[27]

While Brownmiller overstates the purely male aspect of the armed forces and does not take into account how women are prepared to adapt to the bonding and discipline, the military remains highly male-dominated and maintains an aggressive ethos. The widespread use of rape in war underlines the military values and the way in which women are regarded as both peripheral and trophies or spoils of war. Brownmiller again: 'Men who rape are ordinary Joes, made unordinary by entry into the most exclusive male-only club in the world.'[28]

Now, of course, the armed forces have ceased to be an exclusively male club: women have been able to enlist. But when they do they are often consigned to 'caring' or auxiliary roles, as was the case during the two world wars. When women have been able to join the army and other military forces in combat roles, they have been expected to abandon their 'feminine' attributes and fight alongside the men on an equal basis.

Joining the army and doing the same work as men has not protected women from shocking levels of sexual abuse and rape. The US military had 3,158 cases of sexual assault reported in 2011 within the military. The US Defense Department estimated that in 2010 there were over 19,000 sexual assaults in the military.

The Service Women's Action Network describes the attacks as Military Sexual Trauma (MST): 'MST is the leading cause of PTSD [post-traumatic stress disorder] among women veterans, while combat trauma is the leading cause of PTSD among men.[29]

'Feminine' values are seen as the antithesis of military values.[30] Susan Faludi documents how trainee cadets at the Citadel military academy in South Carolina insulted and abused new recruits in language referring to their supposedly female traits.[31] A young woman who took legal action to become the first female cadet there was repeatedly harassed.[32] While more women have been attracted to the army in recent decades, they are unlikely to play a combat role. There is also some evidence that they are much less likely to support recent wars than men.[33] Many complex reasons are put forward to explain this. One is that men are predisposed to fighting and aggression, and that the military is a prime vehicle for expressing a masculine ethos in modern capitalist society. More generally, many feminists subscribe to the view that the system of weapons and war which so dominates our lives is a product of 'male values'. As one group argued: 'The arms race and women's oppression are very clearly linked.' 'We see nuclear weapons and nuclear power as particularly horrendous results of male domination.'[34]

The connection between men, 'masculinity' and war is a strong one. Yvonne Ridley says: 'I think women are less gung-ho than male war correspondents and not as interested as the so-called "boys with toys". With wars I always look for the human angle and quite often the women's angle because they are the ones who really suffer in a conflict.'[35] Billie Figg sees strikingly different attitudes between men and women:

> 'I suppose men are warlike – they are programmed to want to fight. They take very early on to guns and on TV and computer games, even football. You see sweet little boy children, and the mothers say "he loves soldiers and toys", although she doesn't want him to and doesn't encourage him. Do you think we could ever get rid of that and persuade mothers and fathers never to let children have military toys? Could we get anywhere?'[36]

Angela Sinclair echoes this view:

> 'Unemployment leads to war and maybe it's fair enough if you believe in it for the MoD to go round sixth forms getting people to join the army. The casualties are so young they don't know what war is about. I hope they tell them current affairs but I think they stress travel, life abroad, learning a

trade. How tempting for young men. How can we possibly train people to kill? You give a little boy a gun, he loves it. Guns make them feel powerful.'[37]

Chanie Rosenberg comments that 'Women are sadder about wars, more upset by the fact. They're not so accepting of it. Death seems to mean more to a woman.'[38] Yet there are others who point to problems with ignoring the role of some – admittedly a minority – of women in warmongering. Conversely, it is impossible to ignore the very strong opposition to war and militarism voiced by many men. Jackie Mulhallen points out that 'the WSPU [suffragettes] famously supported the war. Some women imagine the world would be more peaceful if women were in power, but I never thought so. After Mrs Golda Meir, Mrs Indira Ghandi and Mrs Margaret Thatcher, no one could say that women did not start wars.'[39] Nicola Pratt makes a similar point:

> 'I think that some women believe in the notion that "womanhood" leads you to be anti-war. I have heard women say, "How can a woman give life and then allow it to be destroyed in a war?" Of course, such an idea can be leveraged strategically – for example, by the mothers of soldiers in Iraq and Afghanistan. They might get more media attention for their anti-war positions than if they were men. But it is also a dangerous idea that stereotypes women as peace-loving and maternal. I only have to mention Margaret Thatcher, Condoleezza Rice, Hillary Clinton . . . as a counter-argument!'[40]

Rae Street agrees: 'Working for peace is not just a woman's issue. There are rabid reactionary women – Mrs Thatcher springs to mind – just as there are genuinely compassionate men.'[41]

The counter-examples of belligerent women have multiplied in recent decades. Condoleezza Rice, Madeleine Albright and Hillary Clinton have all played central roles as US Secretaries of State, directing wars and interventions which have been as bloody as any orchestrated by their male counterparts. They head a world system based on economic and military competition in which war plays an increasing and deadly part, and where research centres, universities, multinational companies, armies and governments all devote massive resources to developing weapons and fighting wars.

We should see this not as a biological urge to kill on the part of men, but the underpinning of military power and the culture which accompanies it. Susan Brownmiller long ago pointed out that rape is less about sexual desire than it is about the exercise of power.[42] Military organisations, in their aim and internal structure, exercise power in its most brutal form. Given the oppression of women in the wider society it should be no surprise that the exercise of power in this context is mostly perpetrated by men and that sexual assault is part of that process. But as we have seen, in a minority of cases where women become part of the military or are in political control of military machines – that is, where women exercise power – they are capable of the same kind of brutality.

The sexual and gender stereotypes which pervade capitalist society, and which are reinforced in myriad ways through images, media and ideology, are the product of a society which funds, promotes and glorifies war. In such circumstances it is remarkable how many men reject militarism and aggression. The training which young men and women undergo in order to become part of the military is designed to create hardened, aggressive individuals who regard killing as a normal part of life. But when they leave this environment they often suffer severe social and psychological problems as they try to adjust to civilian life. There is therefore nothing innate in men that leads them to kill and wound others; this is a socially constructed process. However, there are other questions, some of which those I interviewed touched on. Henna Malik explained that she and her mother, who both played an active role in campaigning against war in Iraq, were more motivated to do so than the men in her family:

'If I just look at my household as a very small example . . . it was my mother and I who were most emotionally affected by the war. It made us want to be part of effectively opposing the war and we were incredibly active in doing so. My brother and father on the other hand, although not in support of the war, were more ambivalent, less interested in attending the rallies, meetings and demonstrations.'

She argues that at least part of this was biological: 'I think there are a few reasons why women react differently to men. The first in my opinion is linked to biology. Women bring life into the world, this is something a man will never experience, I believe as a result we are programmed to look at taking life away as highly problematic.' But she also points out that women are also more likely to identify with others suffering oppression:

> 'War is also an incredibly male-dominated sphere – there is no room for emotion or consideration in war. Not that women are driven by emotion, but we do take it into consideration, which does not negate any rationality in our decision-making. Women are also an oppressed segment of the population themselves. We can relate to others' struggles because as women we face them ourselves against inequality to this day.'[43]

Henna's point is highly controversial. Many men play caring roles in looking after children and many reject the traditional masculine role. Yet while most of the people I talked to rejected the idea that all men are belligerent, they also recognised that women were often motivated in different ways from men and that there were special concerns which women felt. Henna's final point – that attitudes to war may be developed as part of awareness of women's own oppression – makes sense in terms of the development of a number of women activists. For Jackie Mulhallen too, 'Certainly my own attitudes changed, since opposing the Vietnam war meant I learnt a lot about imperialism and capitalism and I decided I would always oppose an imperialist war,'[44] while Kate Connelly has

> 'always been interested and inspired by women's movements, and the figures I found most inspirational were those who linked fighting against women's oppression with wider issues of emancipation. Sylvia Pankhurst, for example, was one of my early political heroines . . . Nevertheless, I do not think that being a woman was the determining factor in my opposition to war.'[45]

Nicola Pratt agrees:

> 'I don't think that being a woman has affected my attitude to war. I joined the Women's International League for Peace and Freedom in 2006. This was motivated not by any notion that women are particularly anti-war or that "womanhood" is essentially anti-war. I don't believe in that at all. Rather, I

joined WILPF as an antidote to the instrumentalisation of "women's rights" by the Bush administration in its "War on Terror". I recognised that women are particularly impacted by war and that mobilisations for war, including the "War on Terror", are gendered processes. I was concerned that the Bush administration's rhetorical support for women's rights and women's empowerment was giving feminism a bad name. WILPF enabled me to explore these processes in ways that were not possible within STWC.'[46]

While most of the women interviewed had come to anti-war conclusions through a variety of means and while many stressed that their gender had no bearing on their politics in the sense of making major political decisions over issues of world politics, they often referred to the issue of women as motivating them to do certain things or become active over certain specific issues. Their consciousness of themselves as women meant that while they became politically aware over a range of issues, they felt particularly strongly about women's position in war. Tansy Hoskins puts this forcefully:

'I suppose I have been made angrier each time women have been made into the excuse for war like in Afghanistan, where women have been the excuse for the war and occupation there, but in fact the US and UK have not done anything to improve the lives of women and don't give a damn how many women they kill in their airstrikes or how much money they spend on bombs rather than hospitals or schools. The hypocrisy of using women as an excuse for war is sickening. In addition, women always suffer most from the lawlessness that comes from war and occupation, and it is hard to know that if it was you in that country you would be as unprotected as the women there are now.'[47]

Feminism was not necessarily the motivation behind some women becoming anti-war, but it helped to deepen anti-war feeling, especially in reaction to supposedly feminist justifications for war.

Political Choices

The anti-war movement is noted for its diversity, its openness and its effectiveness in campaigning. Meetings are still likely to attract more people from ethnic minorities than most left-wing campaigns, and usually more women. It points to new forms of organisation, free from the bureaucratisation which affects some trade unions and political parties. It also means that meetings, protests and other activities are more habitable to women. Jackie Mulhallen's experience in King's Lynn is that:

> 'Women organising means that whole families become involved. I think women should organise politically with men and with children, not separately, and this is what they are doing in Stop the War. One of its strengths is that families join and it brings both sexes and all ages together. We have children at our meetings and on demos, and the children who came on the demos in 2003 occupied the colleges in 2009.'[48]

But how far can the experience of the anti-war movement be generalised into other campaigns and movements? Nicola Pratt thinks that it can provide a model for organising specifically round feminist issues, in particular avoiding some of the pitfalls of the 1960s and 1970s movement, which tended to attract support from a fairly narrow group and did not relate sufficiently to working-class, black and Asian women:

> 'The anti-war movement in the UK provides a good example of a coalition of previously disparate groups, but particularly bringing together some on the Left and some Muslim organisations. I would like to see women's organising similarly bridge racial as well as class divides in the UK. At the moment, I see the majority of young women's organising, through groups such as UK Feminista, as being predominantly about "white middle-class" women. It looks like a replay of second-wave feminism. All the criticisms made by black feminists in the 1970s and 1980s seem to be largely forgotten. On the other hand, young Muslim women are also organising, but within their own "communities" or through the anti-war movement.
>
> 'My ongoing support for the Women's International League for Peace and Freedom is because it does go beyond second-wave feminist concerns and looks at global economic injustices and war, although there is occasionally a tendency towards an "imperial feminism" among some members. Unfortunately, WILPF is not growing at the rate of other UK women's organisations and does not attract large numbers of Muslim women.

'The resistance to austerity may bring about women's organising across race and class because it is working-class women that are disproportionately impacted by austerity measures, but middle-class women too [are affected] and, of course, these women are not just white.'[49]

Rania Khan agrees:

'In so far as the anti-war movement is a model, its significance lies in its absolute opposition to racism and Islamophobia. This is an essential prerequisite. In order to engage effectively with Muslim women and to facilitate their involvement, it is essential we understand the difficulties.'[50]

Tansy Hoskins stresses that involving women in movement and organisations is never a finished process:

'I hope that any future movements use the anti-war movement as a model and have women in leadership roles. The Stop the War Coalition has been representative of its membership and has set a standard of reflecting membership in its leadership. It is up to the leadership of each movement to keep encouraging new women to come forward and take on new roles and to find new women speakers both nationally and internationally.'[51]

It is not simply a question of saying that women should be involved, but of constructing a culture of openness and encouragement that can give women the confidence to play leading roles:

'I also hope that STW will set the standard for women themselves as well. Because movements come from a flawed society they are never going to be perfect and I think it is up to women to push themselves and each other as well. Too often young women in particular are too self-conscious or self-deprecating, whereas men are taught to be confident and to believe that what they are saying is important. Women need to speak up more and take responsibility for ensuring that movements are led by women as well as men and that there are always new women able to step into leadership roles. They need to encourage each other and not be modest, otherwise nothing will change.'[52]

The Stop the War Coalition is a grassroots campaign. It opposes war but does not have direct political representation, although it counts elected representatives such as Caroline Lucas among its supporters. The Green Party London Assembly member Jenny Jones believes that if more women were elected to office it would help change the attitude to war:

> 'The whole issue of the war would be helped if women were elected more into prominent positions. Here at City Hall we have very little power from the point of view of direct executive power. I can't help feeling that if we had more women in positions of power the world would be a whole lot better . . . I feel women would make it a fairer world.'[53]

But there is also the question of women organising separately from men, an issue long debated in the women's movement when discussing how women become involved in politics and how they develop roles which go beyond supportive or a secretary. Some peace and anti-war organisations are specifically women-only, for example, some of the peace camps, WILPF and Women in Black. The rationale for this is that it helps women develop confidence and organisation, and allows them a space as women which they would not otherwise have.

Despite advances within the political parties and trade unions, women's participation in mass organisations usually remains a minority role. The Stop the War Coalition made steps to change that and involved women locally and nationally who developed skills in campaigning and organising.

Yvonne Ridley considers whether women would be more thoughtful and considerate about other women:

> 'I've often wondered why we don't launch women-only political parties or political movements. Clearly, the men aren't listening and they just give lip service to women when it suits. The way the plight of the Afghan women has been used and abused as a political football is breath-taking. Women simply would not do that to women.'[54]

Most of the women I spoke to had mainly experienced politics and organising as part of mixed organisations and wanted to 'feminise' those structures rather than step outside them. Jenny Jones argues:

'Politics is not very female because you need a fair amount of aggression and you need a thick skin. 'Women often wait to be asked and don't push themselves forward. The Greens are an exception. More than half our nationally elected representatives are women – three out of five. There are issues like food which we've taken up which appeal to women. There's more cooperation in campaigns and women can fit that sort of politics into looking after their kids, as most women still have to do.'[55]

For Billie Figg, electing women as councillors is important, but she doubts that this will change the attitude of men:

'Women don't get into areas like councillors enough, and when they do it's been my experience that the men just stroke their hair and explain to them in avuncular terms what they don't understand. There's still a superior attitude towards women's ideas on the part of males.

'When women felt liberated by the war that's what they went for – glamorous roles outside the home. Perhaps they should have looked for roles by going into councils into areas where we could influence how we build houses or develop schools. There are women council leaders now, but I suspect I would find them carbon-copy males.'[56]

Her last point will resonate with many who have voted for a woman as a more caring and peace-loving alternative, only to find that women in high office act within the terms of the structures of power, rather than reflecting the interests of those who elected them. The women Labour MPs elected as part of Tony Blair's landslide election victory in 1997 did not distinguish themselves from their male counterparts when voting for war with Iraq in 2003, despite the largest mass movement in British history.

Feminism as a movement has always divided along class lines, and mainstream feminism today does not distinguish itself from mainstream politics in any fundamental sense, including backing the drive to war which is so fundamental to capitalism. Feminism has indeed been integrated into the drive to war, with Condoleezza Rice and Hillary Clinton helping to rebrand the most powerful military machine in the world as a humanitarian lifesaver. They are the political descendants of Emmeline and Christabel Pankhurst, who embraced the cause of the First World War with such enthusiasm. Many women take a very different approach, echoing the division over previous wars. Just as many suffragists and suffragettes opposed war in 1914 because they linked winning the vote for women with much wider social change, so many women in the movement today see the connection between opposing war, fighting for their rights as women and campaigning for a more equal society.

The experience of mainstream feminism has been extremely limited. Women's representation in public life is still woefully small, but it is evident that it is also incapable alone of bringing real change to women.

The demand for more women in public office has led to a handful of women ministers and one prime minister in Britain. 'Democracy' in Afghanistan, imposed by the US occupation, had to include a quota of women in the Afghan Parliament. This helped to satisfy domestic concerns about women – one of the main justifications for going to war – while doing nothing to overturn the oppressive structure of Afghan society.

While most feminists support more women in public office, it is clear after 30 years of feminism and neoliberalism marching hand in hand that women in these positions have little inclination and even less power to alter society in any fundamental way.

The anti-war movement has not succeeded in its aim of stopping the war, but it has helped to create a grassroots movement and consciousness among women about the need for change. It has also challenged one of the main pillars of neoliberal capitalism – its militarism and warmongering. The more democratic and open the movement has been, the more it has attracted women. It is part of a wider global justice and anti-capitalist movement which has grown powerfully over the past decade and a half and has been a crucial factor not only in mobilising but in educating new generations who have also campaigned against attacks on education, austerity and racism. Real, activist, fighting movements which involve large numbers of women have ideas of equality embedded in them, none more so than ideas of women's liberation.

Rania Khan has become involved in a range of campaigns:

'I don't think there is any one model of how women should organise. There are a multitude of organisations and campaigning groups out there doing fantastic work. When I attended the Occupy protest at St Paul's I was really struck by its open and democratic forms of organising; they sought to reach out and involve the widest numbers of people possible. I really like that. You can see the same dynamic with UK-Uncut. In general, I think the new movements and campaigns are more mindful about the centrality of women's involvement than perhaps campaigns and movements from the past.'[57]

For a number of women who have become politicised as a result of war, the nature of war today raises the question of how to end it and whether peace can be achieved without society changing much more fundamentally. Nicola Pratt argues:

'I do believe that war is fuelled by capitalism, although I wouldn't want to be too deterministic, as war existed before capitalism. However, the necessary expansionary nature of capitalism, its constant need for new markets and new resources, as well as its need to protect existing markets and resources, make war almost inevitable.'

This drive to war also opens up the possibility of campaigning against war and the austerity it imposes: 'On the other hand, I also think that the current economic crisis makes it easier to speak to people about opposing war.'[58]

Many people in the anti-war movement are also anti-imperialist in the sense that they see the connection between war, intervention and capitalism, and reject the role of the United States and its allies in launching these wars. While the Stop the War Coalition always refused to take an explicitly anti-imperialist stand, arguing that all who supported its main demands were welcome in the movement, many of its leading figures are identified with this view. In terms of its size and political impact, Stop the War became more than a single-issue movement, embracing a range of other causes, and funnelling activists into other campaigns.

The Future

Young women in Britain today have very different lives from those of their grandmothers. Most are in paid employment. They are better educated, more independent and have greater control over their lives than ever before. They can decide when, if and how many children to have. They play a role in society and in political life. Many of these changes were brought about, directly or indirectly, as a result of two world wars which helped create modern British society. Chanie Rosenberg describes how the Second World War was instrumental in changing women's attitude to work:

> 'The fact that women had to go to work to do what the men had previously done, that was a major factor in changing women's lives. The Ford equal pay strike in 1968 was a big thing in society – I remember it because it was women. That was a major political change. People would say, 'It's women.' Women working has been the key to change. All the things women didn't do before they now did. The women who worked in engineering factories wanted to continue or wanted their daughters to have those opportunities.'[59]

It also helped to create the conditions for second-wave feminism which broke in the late 1960s. This reflected women's continued frustration at what they came to recognise was their own oppression. It also reflected the modernisation of society which, as women went out to work and into higher education, began to challenge some aspects of the family. Legislation was introduced which made divorce, abortion and contraception more easily available. The more obvious manifestations of inequality were made illegal.

Attitudes changed partly as a result of these social advances. Chanie Rosenberg (born in 1922) says: 'When I was a kid the attitude was the girls get married while the boys go to work. Now kids are treated more equally. When I started teaching . . . one mother said to me, "Why does she need geometry when she's going to grow up and get married?"'[60]

It is impossible for society to go back to a time when women were considered mainly as wives and mothers, or where it is seriously argued, as it was less than 100 years ago, that women should be denied the vote or, as it was less than 50 years ago, that higher education is 'wasted' on a woman because she is destined to be a housewife not a wage earner.

But there are many paradoxes in women's position today. While our lives are better in many respects, in others there appears to be regression. The welfare state is under attack, young people face uncertain futures in employment, and threats of war and ecological disaster are ever-present. Women are still unequal in terms of how much they earn, the sorts of jobs they do, their role in the family and attitudes towards them.

The need for anti-war and peace movements, as well as the other social movements, is as strong as ever. Women's role in them has been decisive in raising their political involvement and in changing consciousness about war. As Chanie Rosenberg puts it:

'Women's attitude to death is becoming much more the general attitude to death. Every time a British soldier dies you see the pictures, you feel for the family. That is the common attitude. Lots of men take on that attitude also. I always think that one English soldier who died – [you see] his funeral and everything – and there were one million in Iraq. I'm sure I'm not the only one who thinks that. Stop the War became the general attitude, not just the progressive attitude. A lot of that is women's attitude.'[61]

This is a major change in society and one which should cause concern to the military and those who support them because it represents a low level of acceptance of war and killing. However, one way in which this feeling is negated is by exporting the killing from the rich imperialist countries to the poorest parts of the world, whose women often bear the brunt of the consequences.

Jenny Jones is on the Metropolitan Police Authority:

'I've followed the area of the trafficking of women. Many of them can't go back, are severely traumatised, abused by several men every day – and how dare men fuck society so much. These women come often from war zones: there were a lot from the Balkans, now there are a lot from various

African countries and some from Asia. It's another downside of war. It's not just poverty that drives them out, it is when society has broken down, often through wars. When you get the breakdown of community and family that happens. . . . War means environmental devastation, refugees – it's all connected.'[62]

Globalised society has made the world a smaller yet more dangerous place. So while consciousness of war has changed, so has the threat. These two aspects are reflected in the role of women as campaigners. They can see the terrible consequences of wars and are motivated to do something about it. Women have become involved in anti-war movements as their political confidence and involvement have grown. That so many have chosen to do so suggests a particular concern about war itself, but also a fear that the likelihood of future wars is growing. There is a recognition that war is an integral part of the world system and that it cannot simply be opposed on a case-by-case basis. This recognition can also help to create the idea that the system which creates wars also helps create and maintain the basis for women's oppression. Bringing together those ideas, and a commitment to fighting both, can create a new movement of women, working alongside men but as their equals, able to fight for a more peaceful and equal world.

9
Conclusion

'My kids see women who go and get things done, there is a ripple effect. It's way too early to tell what the impact will be.'

Carmel Brown[1]

Any mass movement represents the coming together of large numbers of people over a specific issue or cause with the aim of changing opinion and putting political pressure on the government or other authorities. It includes people who might not agree on other issues; those who would never have previously considered working with the people whose goal they now share; those who are prepared to commit to a campaign for a limited amount of time. The movement which developed after 9/11 even at its outset came as a surprise: there were those who claimed that no movement could be built given the scale of the destruction caused by the 9/11 attacks. There were others who felt that the movement was necessary but would be difficult to build, and that its scope would be limited. Both these predictions were confounded early on when tens of thousands turned out in 2001 to protest at the war in Afghanistan.

There were three main components to this mobilisation: the traditional Left, which had a good record of opposing wars; the peace movement, which had been built out of the two phases of CND in the late 1950s–early 1960s and again in the early 1980s; and the Muslim community, which had previously mobilised on a range of issues from Bosnia to Chechnya, but had done so independently of the other parts of the movement.

This changed in 2001, and then more dramatically in 2002, when the threat of war in Iraq began to galvanise protesters on a mass scale. It peaked in 2003, maintained a mass presence as the wars ground on and lasted until Tony Blair left office in 2007 and British troops withdrew from Iraq. Today, Stop the War continues to campaign against the war in Afghanistan and to prevent future wars in countries such as Iran or Syria.

Most movements do not succeed in their immediate aim; and that is true of Stop the War. But it is a mistake to look too narrowly at mass movements. The campaign for women's suffrage lasted over a decade, split in 1914 when war was declared and eventually achieved its full goal over a decade later. The US civil rights movement began in the 1950s and campaigned for more than a decade to achieve its basic demand of desegregation. The movement against apartheid in South Africa took decades to succeed. In all those cases, many of those involved felt that they had only achieved part of what they wanted and few today would argue that the problems of racism and inequality had been solved. At the same time, these movements are generally recognised as having brought about major change and progress, and to have represented the coming together of those wanting equality as a powerful force. These movements helped to change history; they also changed the people involved, who often retained a commitment to campaigning over other issues.

This is true with the Stop the War Coalition. It grew into a mass movement but was always based in the grassroots. Organised from two small offices, with limited financial resources and only a handful of staff, it took on the government, the police and the state machine, all of which at various times tried to prevent marches or reroute them. It took on a Labour government which was taking Britain to war. This meant that the Labour Party, and so the Left, was divided. This made it harder to mobilise than in Spain or Italy where the major Left parties were in opposition and opposed to the war. The media were also biased against the movement, with the Murdoch press rabidly pro-war and the BBC doing everything to promote the government's case and stopping its employees from demonstrating. Only the *Independent* and the *Daily Mirror* took a strong anti-war stance, to the extent that the *Mirror* became involved in mobilising for the 15 February demonstration.[2]

In these circumstances it is remarkable that the movement achieved what it did. But it also made a longer-term contribution: it altered the consciousness of many people, including large numbers of women. It was a force for change in society. It was also part of a wider process of asserting the necessity of protest and the development of a strong anti-war sentiment.

A mass movement on this scale becomes much more than a single-issue campaign. It was a school of tactics and strategy; it led to a welter of campaigns around civil liberties, Islamophobia, Palestine and many other issues. It created a mass anti-war consciousness, which still exists in Britain where many oppose the war in Afghanistan and where the invasion and occupation of Iraq are and always were widely regarded as a failure. The movement also taught skills: speaking, writing, organising, demonstrating. It brought the first political experience to many thousands of school students who walked out of school in 2003 in protest at the war. Just six years later many of these same students occupied their colleges in protest at Israel's bombing of Gaza. It also changed politics in Britain in relation to the Muslim community.

Many women have made the transition from anti-war campaigning to anti-capitalist and anti-globalisation protests. The new campaigns which have developed – UK-Uncut, Occupy, the student movement, the anti-austerity movement – were influenced by the anti-war movement. The sheer scale of demonstrations in 2002–3, the sit-ins, road blockades, walkouts, banner drops, have all been carried through and elaborated since then. This has helped to create movements where anti-war consciousness is high on the agenda and where the connections between opposition to spending on wars and opposing austerity are easily made. The anti-war movement also maintains a national presence. Some people, including many women, began to make connections between protest and wider politics, joining left-wing organisations and developing their ideas.

Muslim women now play a far bigger role in politics (even the ex-Tory chairman [sic], now Minister for Faith and Communities, Baroness Warsi, emphasises her Muslim credentials). There are now Muslim women MPs, councillors, trade union activists, political writers, political campaigners, fundraisers and TV and radio presenters. There were very few before 2001. These are important developments for which the anti-war movement should take some credit.

The process is not over yet and is too early to quantify the full impact of the anti-war movement. It has had a profound effect on British society – remarkably so in the face of opposition not just from the traditional right-wing pro-war party, but from Labour, which took us into the wars. The importance of this cannot be overstated, because war is not just about the past but about the present and future. And we are a very long way from seeing the end to wars involving our government and its allies.

Permanent War

We live in an era of permanent war. The long-term effect of the two world wars was to create ever-more sophisticated weapons of mass destruction and to increase the proportion of the wealth produced in the world which is given over to armaments. Since 1945 we have seen a series of wars which have led to vast numbers of civilian deaths, terrible atrocities and the creation of wastelands with dreadful effects on the environment and health.

It is impossible to calculate exactly how many have died. One estimate gives the number of deaths between 1945 and 2000 at 51 million worldwide.[3] The historian Eric Hobsbawm puts the figure for those killed or 'allowed to die by human decision' in the 'short twentieth century' (1914–91) at 187 million.[4] This excludes those who succumbed to disease or famine brought about or exacerbated by war. Modern wars have produced terrible casualty figures, with an estimated 3–4 million dead in the Korean war (1950–53) and more than two million in the Vietnam war.[5]

Many regions of the world are rarely free from conflict. Somalia, Iraq and Afghanistan have seen repeated wars, as have the Congo and Rwanda. In the first decade of the twenty-first century, wars were waged from Africa through the Middle East to South Asia. More countries amassed stockpiles of weapons, encouraged by arms sales from multinational companies. Since the Second World

War, successive US governments have waged wars in or bombed Korea, Guatemala, Indonesia, Cuba, the Congo, Peru, Laos, Vietnam, Cambodia, Grenada, Libya, El Salvador, Nicaragua, Panama, Iraq, Bosnia, Yugoslavia, Sudan and Afghanistan.

Arundhati Roy describes the richest countries in the world as a cabal who

'between them . . . manufacture and sell almost all of the world's weapons [and] possess the largest stockpile of weapons of mass destruction – chemical, biological and nuclear. They have fought the most wars, account for most of the genocide, subjection, ethnic cleansing and human rights violations in modern history, and have sponsored, armed and financed untold numbers of dictators and despots.'[6]

The role of the United States is crucial to organising this cabal. Its military might and economic power since 1945 have ensured its dominance in very large parts of the world. Societies like the United States – and to a lesser extent Britain – are highly militarised. War is part of everyday consciousness in modern Western society. Images of war are shown daily in the media. People can watch films and television programmes based on real or imagined wars too numerous to mention. There is a major industry of books about war. Millions of people have personal experience of war or know someone who has. The history of the First and Second World Wars is taught widely in schools.

Much reaction to this culture of war is to support it, sometimes even to glorify it. In Britain, church and state unite to present any war that the government is involved in as just and to highlight the sacrifices of past wars in order to vindicate future ones. At the same time, it is inevitable that greater exposure to war creates greater opposition to it. Even the usually sanitised depiction of war presented in the news media conveys the horrors of war.

It is this paradox which explains how the widespread and now permanent organisation against war is a feature of political life in the United States and in many European countries. Consciousness about questions of war and peace is consequently very high. As we have seen, strong and longstanding peace and anti-war organisations, including CND and the Stop the War Coalition in Britain, and a wide range of smaller organisations, maintain a presence which goes far beyond immediate mobilisations.

Opposition to war has seeped into popular culture, ranging from poetry to song, film and theatre. In many cases, culture has created awareness of war and helped build the movement, perhaps most notably with the protest songs of the Vietnam war. While during periods of war serious attempts are made to marginalise anti-war voices, and while campaigning to create disaffection in the armed forces is illegal,[7] permanent war has also created permanent peace campaigning.

The historian of war Gabriel Kolko explains the way in which war affects more people and makes it much harder for governments and generals to be certain of how wars will develop:

> 'The fundamental contradiction of modern war since it has become totally mechanised is that it extends combat to many more people than ever before, protracts the length of time it requires, and vastly augments the material price of any effort, so that when its innumerable demographic, human, and social costs are combined its outcome ceases to be predictable.'[8]

So eleven years after what George Bush thought would be a rapid and relatively cost-free war in Afghanistan, the United States still has over 100,000 troops there and is committed to keeping its bases and some presence until at least 2024. US troops were forced to withdraw from Iraq, having failed to create a stable society or one whose government and people are friendly to the West.

The United States: Decline and Fall?

If the capitalist system has embedded within it the drive to war, it is hardly surprising that the largest and most powerful capitalist country is at the heart of this war drive. As we have seen, the United States has intervened directly in dozens of countries since the Second World War. Indirect military intervention (funding opposition groups, arming rebels, CIA assistance in engineering coups) and US 'soft power' are widespread.

The United States' ability to protect its markets and impose control on other countries was at its height in the decades after the

Second World War. Western Europe was rebuilt with money from the Marshall Plan, and the United States' political influence went alongside its economic influence. The United States maintained its hegemony during the Cold War, but since the collapse of its rival superpower in the late 1980s its weaknesses have become more transparent.

First, while the collapse of the Eastern Bloc opened up new markets to the United States and its allies, the spread of global capital has given rise to major new developing economies. The United States' economic power has declined in relation to its rivals, especially the new giant, China, and to a lesser extent India and Brazil. China produces goods which are sold in the United States and which the United States pays for with money borrowed from, among others, China. The United States faces competition in a whole range of industries and areas.

Second, the United States has to assert its dominance militarily more frequently, not less. The mismatch between its waning economic power and its military might is what forces it to wage more wars, not fewer. The United States increasingly relies on military force – and the political clout which accompanies it – to achieve strategic and political control of crucial areas of the world and to gain access to natural resources, most obviously oil, on which it depends.

Third, as a consequence, the United States is forced to spend vast amounts on the military. A full 17.9 per cent of all central government spending goes on the military.[9] Those in the Republican Party who complain about 'big government' could solve this problem at a stroke with dramatic cuts to the military and the wars in which it is involved.

The United States heads the league of countries in every aspect of military might and power. None of its rivals comes close. A substantial part of the spending deficit which the United States now faces is a result of fighting costly and protracted wars in Iraq and Afghanistan in order to gain and maintain this strategic control.

The decline of US power has not led to a reduction in spending. In 2011, world military spending totalled of $1,630 billion. Of this, the United States accounted for 41 per cent ($711 billion), nearly 5 per cent of its total wealth. Its nearest rival, China, spent $143 billion or 8.2 per cent of its GDP, followed by Russia ($71.9 billion) and in fourth place Britain ($62.7 billion).[10]

The United States and its allies, mired in political problems because of their determination to force austerity onto the poorest while protecting the richest, regard their arms budgets as untouchable. Greece still spends 2 per cent of its GDP on arms, including buying submarines from Germany whose government and media denounce the Greeks as lazy and spendthrift. Britain spends 2.6 per cent of its GDP on defence and a full 5.8 per cent of central government spending on it.[11] So even when government spending is the subject of austerity and welfare cuts, it is thought essential to maintain spending when it comes to 'defence'.

These high levels of spending suggest growing rivalry. In the next decades we are likely to see military tensions between the major economic powers, especially in times of recession and economic crisis. However, while all the economic factors point to a sharp US military decline, they also suggest that the United States may feel the need to continue to exercise its military might.

But its military superiority does not always lead to victory. It has not succeeded in imposing hegemonic control on those countries it has invaded and occupied. Forced out of Iraq because it was unable to agree a Status of Forces agreement with the government in 2011, trying to maintain a presence in Afghanistan while disengaging from a bloody and unpopular war, losing some of its closest allies in the Middle East, its foreign policy is in crisis. Iran has become the dominant power in the Middle East since the overthrow of Saddam Hussein, and it is Iran which the United States now has to deal with.

It is forced to wage proxy wars, relying on allies in the form of regional powers, most notably Turkey and Saudi Arabia, who are arming and giving military assistance to the anti-government forces in Syria. But proxies can be unreliable: they have their own interests which only partly coincide with those of the United States; they are not always successful in achieving smooth regime change; and they are subject to their own political opposition and dynamic, as we saw in Egypt and Tunisia. Therefore, while the

United States and its Western allies may be reluctant to intervene directly in Syria or Iran, they may be forced to do so in order to achieve the outcome they desire. This is, after all, what they did in Libya in 2011 in order to overthrow Colonel Gaddafi.

It is foolish to read from the United States' decline, or its lack of success in current wars, that it will not and cannot intervene elsewhere. US power and military reach allow it to do so. While the twenty-first century is clearly not the American century as the twentieth century was, large empires take a long time to decline or collapse. We have the example of the British Empire as proof of that.

Future Wars

One peace organisation at the turn of the millennium spelt out some of the dangers of future wars:

> 'The calendar end to the "century of war" has not automatically ushered in a century of peace and humanity. Our world is still darkened not only by the direct violence of local conflicts and civil wars, but also by innumerable other forms of violence, including environmental destruction, violence-promoting publications, images, and games. Now, through advanced science and technology, some are trying to extend battlefields into space.'[12]

Since then, we have seen the development of surveillance techniques, remote control warfare (for example, bombing by drone) on an increasing scale and the use of information technology to make weapons even deadlier and more precise. Drone attacks have killed thousands in Pakistan and are now being used in the Middle East. We have looked at the continued threat of war in that region, with the likelihood of this spreading if there is an air strike on Iran's nuclear power plants, which Israel wants to carry out with US backing. The growing rivalry between the major powers threatens to escalate into open military conflict.

There is also the wider background. At the beginning of the twenty-first century it is clear that the world faces ever-more polarised choices over inequality, the environment, war and peace, rights at work. These issues are connected. The drive to make a profit and the exploitative nature of the economic system in which we live create inequalities, injustice and environmental hazards. Multinational companies relentlessly strive to spread their influence and operations throughout the world. Globalisation in the past three decades has extended the market system across the world, destroying communities and violently assaulting traditional ways of life.

Far from equalising some of the poorer societies and people, the glaring inequalities brought about by this process are widening, but are largely ignored by the people who benefit from them. In a race to the bottom which has had a great impact on women, wages in developing countries are held down. They produce goods which were once produced in the developed countries, where workers were paid more and production costs were greater. These goods are sold in the wealthy countries at premium prices.

Concerns for the environment are also subordinate to the needs of profit, so energy consumption and pollution continue to increase to the benefit of a handful of companies and the governments over which they have so much influence. Climate change, leading to shortages of food and water, may create conflict over commodities or migration of whole populations.

The contradictions facing the new imperialist powers mean that we can expect more wars and more protests. And at the centre of those protests will be women.

In this book I have shown how war has changed women's lives and how that in turn has created a new consciousness among women. When the First and Second World Wars broke out, few could have predicted how women's view of themselves would change. Wars never go strictly according to plan. The casualties suffered by men in the First World War created opportunities for women to work in jobs from which they had previously been barred. The total war of 1939–45 led to a radicalised consciousness among women which resurfaced among their daughters' generation in the 1960s. Wars in the twentieth century have always thrown up unanticipated situations and raised issues to do with how society is organised.

The world wars ended in social turmoil. From 1917 to 1919 the prospects of revolution opened up across Europe, and revolution was successful for a time in Russia. After the Second World War, major welfare reforms were introduced in Britain, and those countries which had been occupied now settled scores not just with the Germans but with their own collaborationist leaders.

The disruption and horror of war lead to society being questioned and growing numbers of people who become disillusioned with a system that produces war and so try to change it. Wars can be ended by revolution because of the great strains they exert on the old societies and their political and economic systems.

Total war has created mass movements and the mass involvement of women. One of the features of globalisation has been the packaging of Western politics as a form of egalitarian human rights democracy, which is presented as an example to the whole world. This form of democracy cannot live up to its promise however, because it does not deliver genuine equality or democratic grassroots control.

At the same time, the process of globalisation has seen women across the world drawn into education and work, and therefore expectations of equality are much greater than at any time in history. Women are much more central to public life and to society outside the home. It is clear to many that the continued fight for their liberation will require a much wider-ranging social change, one that challenges the basis on which society is organised and not just surface inequalities.

The experience of women in opposing war has been central to their developing ideas about equality and liberation. To have a chance at stopping war – and successfully realising genuine women's liberation – will require challenging the market and its profit motive.

Notes

Chapter 1

1. Olive May Taylor, quoted in Joyce Marlow (ed.), *The Virago Book of Women and the Great War* (London, 2009), p. 35.
2. George Dangerfield, *The Strange Death of Liberal England* (London, 1970).
3. Maud Pember Reeves, *Round About a Pound a Week* (London, 1994), p. 21.
4. Barbara Drake, *Women in Trade Unions* (London, 1984), p. 46.
5. Ibid., pp. 47–8.
6. Ibid., p. 50.
7. Eric Hobsbawm, *The Age of Empire 1875–1914* (London, 1989), pp. 192–218.
8. Philip S. Foner (ed.), *Clara Zetkin: Selected Writings* (New York, 1984).
9. Christine Collette, *For Labour and for Women* (Manchester, 1989), p. 72.
10. Ibid., p. 71.
11. Ibid., p. 73.
12. Ibid., p. 145.
13. Ibid., p. 148.
14. Sylvia Pankhurst, *The Suffragette Movement* (London 1977), pp. 501–2.
15. Andrew Rosen, *Rise Up, Women* (London, 1974), p. 211.
16. Ibid., pp. 173–4.
17. Drake (1984), p. 82.
18. Pankhurst (1977), p. 592.
19. Susan Grayzel, *Women and the First World War* (London, 2002), p. 27.
20. Quoted in Marlow (1999), p. 103.
21. Quoted in Lyn Smith, *Voices against War* (London, 2009), p. 26.
22. June Hannam and Karen Hunt, *Socialist Women: Britain, 1880s to 1920s* (London, 2002), p. 124.
23. Hannah Mitchell, *The Hard Way Up* (London, 1977), pp. 183–8.
24. Ibid., p. 183.
25. Ibid., p. 187.

26. Quoted in Smith (2009), p. 41.
27. Mary Sargant Florence, Catherine Marshall and C. K. Ogden, *Militarism versus Feminism, Writings on Women and War* (London, 1987), p. 5.
28. Colette (1989), pp. 142–3.
29. Sheila Rowbotham, *Friends of Alice Wheeldon* (London, 1986), p. 34.
30. Ada Nield Chew, *The Life and Writings of a Working Woman* (London, 1982), p. 57.
31. Rowbotham, (1986), pp. 36, 40.
32. Marlow (1999), pp. 99–111.
33. See Sarah Evans, *Personal Politics* (New York, 1987), pp. 133–45; Grayzel (2002), p. 80.
34. Colette (1989), p. 173.
35. Foner (1984), p. 130.
36. Amy Lillington, *The Clarion*, 14 May 1915, quoted in Marlow (1999), pp. 104–5.
37. Florence, Marshall and Ogden (1987), pp. 14–16.
38. Ibid., pp. 3–42, 55ff.
39. Collette (1989), p. 166.
40. Ibid., p. 163.
41. Grayzel (2002), p. 84.
42. Ibid., p. 87; Rowbotham (1986), pp. 1–3.
43. Collette (1989), p. 174.
44. Drake (1984), p. 68.
45. Sarah Boston, *Women Workers and the Trade Unions* (London, 1980), pp. 96–8.
46. Grayzel (2002) p. 28; Drake (1984), p. 68.
47. Drake (1984), p. 69.
48. *Manchester Guardian*, 23 October 1917, quoted in Marlow (1999), p. 244.
49. Marlow (1999), pp. 244–6.
50. Ibid., pp. 176–91.
51. Grayzel (2002), p. 40.
52. Drake (1984), pp. 237–9, table 1.
53. Gail Braybon and Penny Summerfield, *Out of the Cage* (London, 1987), p. 39.
54. Grayzel (2002), p. 29.
55. Marlow (1999), p. 171.
56. Braybon and Summerfield (1987), p. 41.
57. Marlow (1999), pp. 85–6.
58. Quoted in Angela Holdsworth, *Out of the Doll's House* (London, 1988), pp. 64–7.

59. Braybon and Summerfield (1987), p. 51.
60. James Hinton, *The First Shop Stewards' Movement* (London, 1973), p. 63.
61. Drake (1984), p. 69; Lindsey German, *Sex, Class and Socialism* (London, 1989), pp. 129–31.
62. Collette (1989), p. 169.
63. Andrew Murray, *The T & G Story* (London, 2008), p. 39.
64. Grayzel (2002), p. 23.
65. Ibid., p. 36.
66. As reported in Central London branch of the Women's Labour League annual report, 31 March 1915. See Collette (1989), pp. 160–1.
67. Ibid., p. 162.
68. Grayzel (2002), pp. 83–4.
69. Harry McShane and Joan Smith, *No Mean Fighter* (London, 1978), pp. 74–5.
70. June Hannam and Karen Hunt, *Socialist Women: Britain, 1880s to 1920s* (London, 2002), p. 149.
71. *Women's Dreadnought*, quoted in ibid., p. 150.
72. Deirdre Beddoe, *Back to Home and Duty* (London, 1989), p. 90.
73. Collette (1989), p. 162.
74. McShane and Smith (1978), pp. 75–6.
75. Nield Chew (1982), pp. 55–6.
76. Collette (1989), pp. 162–3.
77. Hannam and Hunt (2002), p. 144.
78. Ibid., p. 140; Sheila Rowbotham, *Dreamers of a New Day* (London, 2010), pp. 158–9.
79. Grayzel (2002), p. 63.
80. Ibid., p. 64.
81. Rowbotham (2010), pp. 89–102.
82. Diana Gittins, *Fair Sex* (London, 1982), p. 33.
83. Marlow (1999), pp. 204–5.
84. Mrs C. S. Peel, quoted in ibid., p. 220.
85. Grayzel (2002), pp. 65–6.
86. Ibid., pp. 70–1.
87. *Daily Express*, 26 September 1918, quoted in Marlow (1999), pp. 369–71.
88. Quoted in ibid., pp. 372–3.
89. Grayzel (2002), p. 71; see p. 143 for Regulation 40D.
90. Rowbotham (2010), p. 106.
91. Ibid., p. 111.
92. Rosen (1974), pp. 89–90.
93. Hannam and Hunt (2002), p. 125.

94. Ibid., p. 126.
95. Grayzel (2002), p. 104.
96. Paul Foot, *The Politics of Harold Wilson* (Harmondsworth, 2004), pp. 231–7.
97. Juliet Nicolson, *The Great Silence 1918–20* (London, 2009), chapter 5.
98. G. D. H. Cole, *A History of the Labour Party from 1914* (New York, 1969), p. 141.
99. Collette (1989), p. 190.
100. Beddoe (1989) p. 49; Grayzel (2002), p. 106.
101. Richard Croucher, *We Refuse to Starve in Silence* (London, 1987), pp. 15–16.
102. Pamela Graves, 'Labour Women in Britain', in Helmut Gruber and Pamela Graves (eds), *Women and Socialism/Socialism and Women* (Oxford, 1998), p. 190.
103. Beddoe (1989), p. 49.
104. Ibid., pp. 5–2.
105. Ibid., p. 50.
106. Rowbotham (2010), p. 187.
107. Ibid., p. 161.
108. German (1989), pp. 94ff.
109. Nicolson (2009), pp. 258–9.
110. Mitchell (1977), pp. 208–9.
111. Grayzel (2002), p. 110.
112. Gruber and Graves (1998), pp. 191–8.
113. Noreen Branson, *Poplarism 1919–1925* (London, 1980); Rowbotham (2010), pp. 165–6.
114. Virginia Nicholson, *Singled Out* (London, 2008), p. 2.
115. Braybon and Summerfield (1987), p. 151.

Chapter 2

1. Ian Kershaw, *Making Friends with Hitler* (London, 2004), pp. 70–4.
2. Noreen Branson, *History of the Communist Party of Great Britain 1927–1941* (London, 1985), p. 229.
3. Ibid., p. 225.
4. Ibid., p. 227.
5. Germany relied on slave and conscript labour from occupied countries to replace men in its army, although women played a major role in agriculture. Thanks to Michael Williams for this point.

6. Alan Milward, *War, Economy and Society* (Harmondsworth, 1977), p. 219.
7. Juliet Gardiner, *Wartime* (London, 2004), p. 18.
8. Ibid., p. 35.
9. Dorothy Sheridan (ed.), *Wartime Women* (London, 2000), pp. 64–5.
10. Paul Addison and Jeremy Crang, *Listening to Britain* (London, 2010), p. 55.
11. Ibid., p. 119.
12. Ibid., p. 137.
13. Ibid., p. 183.
14. Ibid., p. 342.
15. Gail Braybon and Penny Summerfield, *Out of the Cage* (London, 1987), p. 160.
16. Clive Ponting, *1940: Myth and Reality* (London, 1990), p. 148.
17. Vera Brittain, *England's Hour* (London, 2005), pp. 49–58.
18. Ponting (1990), p. 167.
19. Addison and Crang (2010), p. 264.
20. Gardiner (2004), pp. 346–51.
21. Addison and Crang (2010), p. 201.
22. Gardiner (2004), pp. 151–2.
23. Ibid., p. 149.
24. Addison and Crang (2010), p. 252.
25. Gardiner (2004), pp. 153–4; Angus Calder, *The Myth of the Blitz* (London, 1992), pp. 385–7.
26. Addison and Crang (2010) pp. 90, 126, 127.
27. Braybon and Summerfield (1987), p. 156.
28. Sheridan (2000), pp. 112, 120.
29. Ibid., p. 114.
30. Addison and Crang (2010), p. 32.
31. Ibid., p. 115.
32. A. J. P. Taylor, *English History 1914–1945* (Oxford, 1992), p. 458.
33. Addison and Crang (2010), pp. 125, 137.
34. Gardiner (2004), p. 323.
35. Addison and Crang (2010), pp. 164, 273.
36. Ibid., p. 279.
37. Ibid., p. 392.
38. Gardiner (2004), p. 290.
39. Ibid., p. 291.
40. Ibid., p. 292.
41. Addison and Crang (2010), pp. 407–11.
42. Ibid., pp. 416–17.
43. Angela Sinclair interview with the author, 20 September 2009.

44. Gardiner (2004), pp. 336–7.
45. Ibid., pp. 324, 325; Bernard Kops, *The World is a Wedding* (London, 1963), pp. 67–8.
46. Phil Piratin, *Our Flag Stays Red* (London, 1978), p. 73.
47. Gardiner (2004), p. 327.
48. Angela Sinclair interview with the author, 20 September 2009.
49. Ibid.
50. Gardiner (2004), p. 303.
51. Sheridan (2000), p. 111.
52. Ibid., p. 94.
53. Ibid., p. 111.
54. Braybon and Summerfield (1987), p. 181.
55. Sheridan (2000), p. 108.
56. Brittain (2005), pp. 201–4.
57. Gardiner (2004) p. 364 and picture caption facing p. 498.
58. Jackie Mulhallen interview with the author, 21 August 2010.
59. Interview with Florence Davy, in Jennifer Golden, *Hackney at War* (Stroud, 2009), p. 74.
60. Interview with Mrs Barrett in ibid., pp. 101–3.
61. Billie Figg interview with the author, 14 April 2010.
62. Ibid.
63. Penny Summerfield, *Women Workers in the Second World War* (Beckenham, 1984), p. 10.
64. Ibid., p. 29.
65. Braybon and Summerfield (1987), p. 155.
66. Addison and Crang (2010), p. 324.
67. Ibid., pp. 178, 192.
68. Brittain (2005), p. 131.
69. Addison and Crang (2010), p. 220.
70. Brittain (2005), p. 134.
71. Braybon and Summerfield (1987) pp. 158–9; Lindsey German, *Material Girls* (London, 2007), pp. 78–9.
72. Braybon and Summerfield (1987), p. 167.
73. Ibid., pp. 163–6.
74. Gardiner (2004), pp. 432–42.
75. Ibid., pp. 445, 448.
76. Ibid., p. 443.
77. Summerfield (1984), p. 94.
78. Ibid., p. 84.
79. Braybon and Summerfield (1987), p. 238.
80. Sheridan (2000), pp. 158–9.
81. Summerfield (1984), p. 82.

82. Mass Observation report, quoted in Braybon and Summerfield (1987), p. 245.
83. Richard Croucher, *We Refuse to Starve in Silence* (London, 1982), p. 255.
84. Sheila Lewenhak, *Women and Trade Unions* (London, 1977), p. 225.
85. Braybon and Summerfield (1987), pp. 176–7.
86. AEU memorandum to the Royal Commission on Equal Pay 1944–46, *Statistics Relating to the War Effort*, Cmnd 6564 (London, 1946), Appendix 8.
87. Braybon and Summerfield (1987), pp. 180–1.
88. Gardiner (2004) p. 472.
89. Paul Du Noyer, *In the City* (London, 2010), p. 59.
90. Billie Figg interview with the author, 14 October 2010.
91. Sheridan (2000), pp. 196–200.
92. Poster, Imperial War Museum.
93. Picture of Billie Figg in her 'Make Do and Mend' hat.
94. Pat Kirkham, 'Beauty or Duty', in Pat Kirkham and Deborah Thom (eds), *War Culture* (London, 1995), pp. 15–17.
95. Gardiner (2004), pp. 497–8.
96. Billie Figg interview with the author, 14 April 2010.
97. Quoted in Braybon and Summerfield (1987), p. 210.
98. Ibid., p. 205.
99. German (2007), p. 33.
100. Braybon and Summerfield (1987), p. 216.
101. Historic Divorce Tables. www.statistics.gov.uk/StatBase/Product. asp?vlnk=581.
102. Gardiner (2004), p. 476.
103. Penny Hicks interview with the author, 22 August 2010.
104. Jenny Jones interview with the author, 3 July 2010.
105. Brittain (2005), p. 68.
106. Angela Sinclair interview with the author, 20 September 2009.
107. Addison and Crang (2010), p. 118.
108. *Picture Post,* gale.cengage.co.uk/product-highlights/history/picture-post-historical-archive.aspx.
109. Gardiner (2004), p. 499.
110. Anonymous, *A Woman in Berlin* (2004).
111. Angela Sinclair interview with the author, 20 September 2009.

Chapter 3

1. Sven Lindqvist, *A History of Bombing* (London, 2002), ss. 232–4.
2. For a full discussion of this, see Gabriel Kolko, *The Politics of War* (New York, 1990), chapters 22 and 24.

3. Quoted in Lindqvist (2002), s. 241.
4. Bruce Kent, quoted in Lyn Smith, *Voices against War* (London, 2009), p. 176.
5. Pat Arrowsmith interview with the author, 9 December 2011.
6. Ibid.
7. Chie Yuasa, quoted in Smith (2009), p. 173.
8. Gabriel Kolko, *Century of War* (New York, 1994), pp. 416–17.
9. Ibid., p. 397.
10. Ibid., p. 413.
11. Ibid.
12. For a cogent explanation, see Michael Kidron, *Western Capitalism since the War* (London, 1968).
13. Kenneth Morgan, *The People's Peace* (Oxford, 1992), pp. 53–4.
14. Christopher Booker, *The Neophiliacs* (London, 1992), p. 121.
15. Morgan (1992), pp. 166–8.
16. For a full account of this local campaign, see Jill Liddington, *The Long Road to Greenham* (London, 1989), pp. 176–88.
17. Pat Arrowsmith interview with the author, 9 December 2011.
18. Quoted in Kate Hudson, *CND: Now More than Ever* (London, 2005), p. 28.
19. Ibid., p. 76.
20. Ibid., p. 40.
21. Pat Arrowsmith interview with the author, 9 December 2011.
22. Hudson (2005), p. 41.
23. Liddington (1989), pp. 187–8.
24. Booker (1992), p. 127.
25. Quoted in Hudson (2005), pp. 42–3.
26. Booker (1992), pp. 128–9.
27. Hudson (2005), pp. 44–5.
28. David Widgery, *The Left in Britain 1956–1968* (Harmondsworth, 1976), pp. 102–3.
29. Pat Arrowsmith interview with the author, 9 December 2011.
30. Hudson (2005), p. 55.
31. Widgery (1976), p. 103.
32. For a description, see Martin Grainger, 'We Marched against Britain's Death Factory', *Newsletter*, 12 April 1958, in ibid.
33. Pat Arrowsmith interview with the author, 9 December 2011.
34. Hudson (2005), p. 57.
35. Sheila Rowbotham, *Promise of a Dream* (London, 2000), p. 65.
36. Morgan (1992), p. 182.
37. Sheila Rowbotham, *A Century of Women* (London, 1997), p. 290.
38. See Andrew Murray, *The T & G Story* (London, 2008), pp. 122–3.
39. Hudson (2005) pp. 64–5.

40. Booker (1992), p. 152.
41. Ibid., p. 169.
42. For details, see Hudson (2005), pp. 69–75.
43. Pat Arrowsmith interview with the author, 9 December 2011.
44. Widgery (1976), p. 111.
45. Pat Arrowsmith interview with the author, 9 December 2011.
46. Chanie Rosenberg interview with the author, 12 October 2010.
47. Rowbotham (2000), p. xii.
48. Rae Street interview with the author, 24 August 2010.
49. Ibid.
50. Hudson (2005), p. 81.
51. Jane Shallice interview with the author, 23 April 2012.
52. Booker (1992), p. 184.
53. Jackie Mulhallen interview with the author, 21 August 2010.
54. Rowbotham (2000), p. 66.
55. Jane Shallice interview with the author, 23 April 2012.
56. Rowbotham (2000), p. 67.
57. Widgery (1976), pp. 112–13.
58. Jackie Mulhallen interview with the author, 21 August 2010.
59. Hudson (2005), pp. 85–6.
60. Angela Sinclair interview with the author, 20 September 2009.
61. Jane Shallice interview with the author, 23 April 2012.
62. Rowbotham (2000), p. 68.

Chapter 4

1. John Rees, *Timelines* (Abingdon, 2012), pp. 102–10.
2. Jonathan Neale, *The American War: Vietnam 1960–1975* (London, 2001), pp. 89–91.
3. Rees (2012), p. 105.
4. Sven Lindqvist, *History of Bombing* (London, 2002), s. 325.
5. Ibid.
6. Paul Foot, *The Politics of Harold Wilson* (Harmondsworth, 1968), p. 214.
7. Gabriel Kolko, *Century of War* (New York, 1994), p. 432.
8. Jane Shallice interview with the author, 23 April 2012.
9. Sheila Rowbotham, *Promise of a Dream* (London, 2000).
10. Chris Harman, *The Fire Last Time* (London, 1998), p. 145.
11. Rowbotham (2000), p. 155.
12. Jackie Mulhallen interview with the author, 21 August 2010.
13. See Hester Eisenstein, *Feminism Seduced* (Boulder, CO, 2009), pp. 48–54.
14. Lise Vogel, *Woman Questions* (London, 1995), p. 6.

15. Ibid., p. 14.
16. Quoted in Sara Evans, *Personal Politics* (New York, 1979), p. 62.
17. Ibid., p. 63.
18. Ibid., p. 78.
19. Ibid., pp. 84–7.
20. Ibid., p. 87.
21. Quoted in ibid., p. 190.
22. Jo Freeman, *The Politics of Women's Liberation* (New York, 1975), pp. 59–60.
23. Evans (1979), p. 192.
24. Ibid., p. 201n.
25. *Liberation Now* (1971) pp. 335–6.
26. Vogel (1995), p. 12.
27. Jane Shallice interview with the author, 23 April 2012.
28. Rowbotham (2000), p. 164.
29. Ibid., p. 171.
30. See Harman (1998), pp. 146–7.
31. Rowbotham (2000), pp. 170–1.
32. Quoted in David Widgery, *The Left in Britain 1956–1968* (Harmondsworth, 1976), p. 379.
33. Roger Protz, letter to *The Times*, 30 October 1968, quoted in Widgery (1976), pp. 387–8.
34. Rowbotham (2000), p. 203.
35. See Sheila Rowbotham, 'The Beginnings of Women's Liberation in Britain', in *The Body Politic* (1972), p. 97.
36. *Shrew*, vol. 4, no. 1 (1972).
37. Rowbotham (1972), p. 93.
38. Eric Hobsbawm, *The Age of Extremes* (London, 1994), p. 452.
39. Kolko (1994), p. 437.
40. Rees (2012), p. 109.
41. For more on this, see Lindsey German, *Material Girls* (London, 2007), pp. 147–67.

Chapter 5

1. See Kate Hudson, *CND: Now More than Ever* (London, 2005), p. 122.
2. E. P. Thompson, quoted in ibid., p. 131.
3. Eileen Daffern (Clough), quoted in Lyn Smith, *Voices against War* (London, 2009), p. 195.
4. Personal recollection of the author.
5. 'Talking with Tony Benn', *Spare Rib*, 100, November 1980.
6. Kate Hudson interview with the author, 15 June 2010.

7. Ann Pettitt, *Walking to Greenham* (South Glamorgan, 2006), p. 13.
8. Ibid., pp. 26–9.
9. Ibid., p. 37.
10. Helen John interview with the author, 12 June 2012.
11. Ibid.
12. Lynne Jones, 'On Common Ground: the Women's Peace Camp at Greenham Common', in Lynne Jones (ed.), *Keeping the Peace* (London, 1983), pp. 79–97.
13. Angela Sinclair interview with the author, 20 September 2009.
14. Kate Hudson interview with the author 15 June 2010.
15. Rae Street interview with the author 24 August 2010.
16. Chanie Rosenberg interview with the author, 12 October 2010.
17. Kate Connelly interview with the author, 21 August 2010.
18. Jackie Mulhallen interview with the author, 21August 2010.
19. Kate Hudson interview with the author, 15 June 2010.
20. Jane Shallice interview with the author, 23 April 2012.
21. Kate Hudson interview with the author, 15 June 2010.
22. Nicola Pratt interview with the author, 21 December 2011.
23. Interview with Jane Dennett (Rowley), in Smith (2009), p. 217.
24. Swade, Tamar 'Babies against the Bomb', in Jones (1983), p. 65.
25. Mary Daly, *Gyn/Ecology* (London, 1979), pp. 392–4.
26. For an overview of some of the debates, see Jill Liddington, *The Long Road to Greenham* (London, 1989), pp. 255–63.
27. Kate Hudson interview with the author, 15 June 2010.
28. Helen John interview with the author 12 June 2012.
29. Nicola Pratt interview with the author 21 December 2011.
30. Kate Hudson interview with the author, 15 June 2010.
31. Nicola Pratt interview with the author, 21 December 2011.
32. For a more detailed explanation of the role of imperialism in the neoliberal world, see John Rees, *Imperialism and Resistance* (London, 2006); Andrew Murray, *The Imperial Controversy* (London, 2009).
33. Rees (2006), pp. 20–5.
34. For background to the break-up, see Duncan Blackie, 'The Road to Hell', *International Socialism*, 53, Winter 1991.
35. For a general background to this process in the Balkans, see Tariq Ali (ed.), *Masters of the Universe* (London, 2000); Misha Glenny, *The Balkans 1804–1999: War and the Great Powers* (London, 1999); Lindsey German, 'The Balkan War: Can There Be Peace?', *International Socialism*, 69, Winter 1995.
36. See Ellen Meiksins Wood, 'Kosovo and the New Imperialism', in Ali (2000), pp. 190–1.

37. Tony Blair's speech to the Economic Club of Chicago, 'Doctrine of International Community', 22 April 1999, www.pbs.org/newshour/bb/international/jan-june99/blair–doctrine4-23.html; also www.fco.gov.uk.
38. For good assessments of this, see John Rees, 'NATO and the New Imperialism', *Socialist Review*, June 1999; Robin Blackburn, 'Kosovo: The War of NATO Expansion', in Ali (2000), pp. 360–80.
39. Interview with Eve-Ann Prentice, in Smith (2009), p. 267.
40. For a very good, brief description of the Genoa demonstrations and their consequences, see T. Behan, 'Nothing Can Be the Same Again', *International Socialism*, 92, Autumn 2001, p. 3.

Chapter 6

1. Helen John, 'Dear Brothers and Sisters, Onward!' in Andrew Murray and Lindsey German, *Stop the War* (London, 2005), p. 69.
2. Salma Yaqoob, 'Muslim Women and War on Terror', *Feminist Review*, 88, 2008, p. 153.
3. Ibid.
4. Quoted in John Kampfner, *Blair's Wars* (London, 2004), pp. 114–15.
5. Jane Shallice interview with the author, 23 April 2012.
6. Carol Turner interview with the author, 13 June 2012.
7. Rania Khan interview with the author, 6 June 2012.
8. Eliza Manningham Buller, former head of MI5, gave evidence to the Chilcot Inquiry in July 2010 where she made clear that many 'insiders' believed from 2003 that the war in Iraq would increase the threat of home-grown terrorism. See www.guardian.co.uk/uk/2010/jul/20/iraq-inquiry-eliza-manningham-buller.
9. Jane Shallice interview with the author, 23 April 2012.
10. Kate Hudson interview with the author, 15 June 2010.
11. Dahabo Isse interview with the author, 21 December 2009.
12. Yvonne Ridley interview with the author, 11 April 2012.
13. Ibid.
14. Tansy Hoskins interview with the author, 20 July 2010.
15. Kate Connelly interview with the author, 21 August 2010.
16. See Murray and German (2005), p. 6.
17. Penny Hicks interview with the author, 22 August 2010.
18. Kate Hudson interview with the author, 15 June 2010.
19. Carmel Brown interview with the author, 23 August 2010.
20. Nicola Pratt interview with the author, 21 December 2011.
21. Salma Yaqoob, 'Solidarity in Practice', in Murray and German (2005), p. 60.

22. Murray and German (2005), p. 60.

23. S. Saleem, 'A New Era', in Murray and German (2005), p. 59.

24. Quoted in Bob Woodward, *Plan of Attack* (London, 2004), p. 119.

25. Kampfner (2004), p. 168.

26. 'The Secret Downing Street Memo', *The Sunday Times* 1 May 2005.

27. Carol Turner interview with the author 13 June 2012.

28. The present author was one of only two (I think) women speakers on the Jenin demonstration and we wanted to put across the idea that more women could and should be speaking. The MAB list of speakers for 28 September was almost exclusively male, although they had no objection to women speakers proposed by others. However, we effectively won this argument and by 15 February MAB was proposing a number of women speakers.

29. Penny Hicks interview with the author, 22 August 2010.

30. Jackie Mulhallen interview with the author, 21 August 2010.

31. Kate Hudson interview with the author, 15 June 2010.

32. Tansy Hoskins interview with the author, 20 July 2010.

33. Carmel Brown interview with the author, 23 August 2010.

34. Rae Street interview with the author, 24 August 2010.

35. Sinead Kirwan interview with the author, 20 April 2010.

36. Ibid.

37. Henna Malik, in Murray and German (2005), p. 190.

38. Mark Winter, 'A Form of Enrichment', in Murray and German (2005), p. 182.

39. Joanne Stevenson, 'Going Underground', in ibid., p. 184.

40. Kate Connelly interview with the author, 21 August 2010.

41. Elane Heffernan, 'Sometimes it Feels Like the Twin Towers Fell on Our Heads Too', *Feminist Review*, 88, 2008, p. 129.

42. For a discussion of the figures, see Murray and German (2005), p. 163, which cites an ICM poll showing that at least one person from 1.25 million households in Britain went on the march in London.

43. See Stefaan Walgrave and Dieter Rucht, *The World Says No to War* (Minneapolis, 2010), p. 83.

44. See Murray and German (2005), pp. 155–61.

45. Carmel Brown interview with the author, 23 August 2010.

46. Ibid.

47. Tansy Hoskins interview with the author, 20 July 2010.

48. Kampfner (2004), pp. 290–1.

49. Patrick E. Tyler, 'A New Power in the Streets', *New York Times*, 17 February 2003, www.nytimes.com/2003/02/17/international/middleeast/17ASSE.html?pagewanted=all.

50. For a comprehensive but not exclusive list, see Murray and German (2005), pp. 192–6.
51. Rose Gentle interview with the author, 16 August 2011.
52. Recollection by the author who accompanied her.
53. Joan Humphries interview with the author, 20 May 2012.
54. Rose Gentle interview with the author, 16 August 2011.
55. Walgrave and Rucht (2010), p. 90, Table 5.1.
56. Ibid., p. 95, Table 5.4.
57. Pippa Norris, *Democratic Phoenix* (Cambridge, 2002) pp. 200–2.
58. Samuel Henry Barnes and Max Kaase, *Political Action: Mass Participation in Five Western Democracies* (Beverly Hills, CA, 1979), p. 134.
59. A 1970s study by Verba, Nie and Kim showed men more active politically than women; see Norris (2002), p. 90. A contrasting view is Christy (1987) in ibid.
60. www.cawp.rutgers.edu/research/topics/voting_behavior.php.
61. Murray and German (2005), p. 99.
62. International IDEA survey Stockholm 1999, quoted in Norris (2002), pp. 89–90.
63. Norris (2002), p. 24.
64. Ibid., p. 197.
65. Ibid., pp. 197–8.
66. Ibid., p. 195.
67. Pippa Norris, Stefaan Walgrave and Peter Van Aelst, 'Who Demonstrates? Antistate Rebels, Conventional Participants, or Everyone?' *Comparative Politics*, Vol. 37, No. 2, January 2005, pp. 189–205, PhD Program in Political Science, City University of New York.
68. F. Parkin (1968), quoted in Norris, Walgrave and Van Aelst (2005).
69. Walgrave and Rucht (2010), p. 152.
70. Ibid., p. 150, Table 8.1.
71. Ibid., p. 127, Table 7.2.
72. Ibid., p. 157, Table 8.4.
73. Ibid.
74. See, for example, Kevin Gillan, Jenny Pickerill and Frank Webster, *Anti-War Activism: New Media and Protest in the Information Age* (Basingstoke, 2008), pp. 19–40.
75. Angela Davis, 'A Vocabulary for Feminist Praxis: On War and Radical Critique', in Robin Riley, Chandra Mohanty and Minnie Bruce Pratt (eds.), *Feminism and War* (London and New York, 2008), p. 23.

Chapter 7

1. blog.amnestyusa.org/women/u-s-don't-abandon-afghan-women. www.washingtontimes.com/news/2010/may/13/karzai-visits-graves-us-fallen-afghan-war/?page=all. Accessed 4 April 2012.
2. See Samuel Huntingdon, *The Clash of Civilisations: And the Remaking of the World Order* (London, 1997), pp. 255–8.
3. Liz Fekete, 'Enlightened Fundamentalism?' *Race and Class*, Vol. 48. No. 2, 2006, p. 2.
4. International Commission on Intervention and State Sovereignty, *The Responsibility to Protect* (Ottawa, 2001), p. xi.
5. Laura Bush, radio address, www.whitehouse.gov/news/releases/2001/11/20011117.html.
6. 'Cherie Blair Attacks Taliban "Cruelty"', BBC News, 19 November 2001, news.bbc.co.uk/2/hi/uk–news/politics/1663300.stm.
7. Hester Eisenstein, *Feminism Seduced* (Boulder, CO, 2009), p. 174.
8. Cited in Iris Marion Young, 'The Logic of Masculinist Protection: Reflections on the Current Security State', Signs, vol. 29, no. 1, 2003, p. 18.
9. Quoted in Eisenstein (2009), pp. 175–6.
10. Ibid., p. 175.
11. See Malalai Joya, *Raising My Voice* (London, 2009) for the story of a highly courageous Afghan woman who opposes both the occupation and the Taliban and warlords.
12. 'Statement: Worldwide Sisterhood against Terrorism and War', republished in Ammu Joseph and Kalpana Sharma, *Terror Counter-Terror: Women Speak Out* (London, 2003).
13. Amnesty International USA, Testimony before the Subcommittee on International Operations and Human Rights, House Committee on International Relations, 31 October 2001, avalon.law.yale.edu/sept11/kumar–001.asp. Accessed 8 April 2012.
14. Huibin Amelia Chew, 'What's Left? After "Imperial Feminist" Hijackings', in Robin Riley, Chandra Talpade Mohanty and Minnie Bruce Pratt (eds.), *Feminism and War* (London and New York, 2008), p. 82.
15. Laura Flanders, *Bushwomen* (London, 2004), pp. 268–9.
16. Quoted in Elaheh Rostami Povey, 'Gender, Agency and Identity: The Case of Afghan Women in Afghanistan, Iran and Pakistan', *Journal of Development Studies*, 2004.
17. Commentary: Liberation, *Business Week*, 3 December 2001, www.businessweek.com/magazine/content/01–49/b3760701.htm. Accessed 6 April 2012.
18. Dahabo Isse interview with the author, 21 December 2009.

19. UN Development Report (Geneva, 2008).
20. www.reuters.com/article/2011/06/15/us-women-danger-idUSTRE75E31R20110615.
21. Rostami Povey (2007), p. 75.
22. Joya (2009) p. 2.
23. Ibid., p. 5.
24. Ibid., pp. 254–62.
25. Mitra Qayoom, 'Real Lives: Imperil Fictions and Afghan Facts', www.counterfire.org/index.php/articles/international/15977-real-lives-imperial-fictions-and-afghan-facts. Accessed 28 August 2012.
26. Canadian Women for Women in Afghanistan, *Policy Statement – What Do Afghan Women Want?* October 2010, www.cw4wafghan.ca/PolicyStatement. Accessed 4 April 2012.
27. www.oxfam.org.uk/applications/blogs/pressoffice/2011/10/03/ten-years-of-gains-for-afghan-women-under-threat-warns-oxfam. Accessed 4 April 2012.
28. Ibid. For the full report, see www.oxfam.org/.../place-table-safeguarding-women-rights-afghanistan.
29. See Human Rights Watch, www.hrw.org/.../afghanistan-law-curbing-women-s-rights-takes-effec. Accessed 6 April 2012.
30. Hamid Karzai Backs Clerics' Move to Limit Afghan Women's Rights', *The Guardian*, 6 March 2012, www.guardian.co.uk/.../2012/.../hamid-karzai-afghanistan-womens-ri...
31. Ann Wright and Coleen Rowley, 'Amnesty's Shilling for US Wars', 18 June 2012,consortiumnews.com/2012/06/18/amnestys-shilling-for-us-wars. Accessed 29 August 2012.
32. Lisa Savage, 'At Afghanistan Summit This Week, Will Afghan Women be at the Table? *Common Dreams*, 3 July 2012, www.commondreams.org/view/2012/07/03-7. Accessed 28 August 2012.
33. Mitra Qayoom, 'Real Lives: Imperial Fictions and Afghan Facts', www.counterfire.org/index.php/articles/international/15977-real-lives-imperial-fictions-and-afghan-facts. Accessed 28 August 2012.
34. Haifa Zangana, *City of Widows* (New York, 2009), p. 95.
35. Ibid., pp. 97–8.
36. Ibid., p. 108.
37. Ibid., pp. 129–31.
38. Cited in Nadia Al-Ali and Nicola Pratt, *What Kind of Liberation?* (London, 2009), p. 77.
39. Zangana (2009), p. 33.
40. For two extremely good accounts of life in Iraq, see ibid. and Al-Ali and Pratt (2009).
41. Elaheh Rostami Povey interview with the author, 14 October 2010.
42. Nicola Pratt interview with the author, 21 December 2011.

43. *Lancashire Evening Telegraph*, 6 October 2006.
44. Tommy Robinson, BBC Big Question, 1 April 2012.
45. Liz Fekete, 'Enlightened Fundamentalism? Immigration, Feminism and the Right', *Race and Class*, vol. 48, no. 1, 2006, p. 2.
46. Quoted in Liz Fekete, *Integration, Islamophobia and Civil Rights in Europe* (London, 2008), pp. 15–16.
47. Rania Khan interview with the author, 6 June 2012.
48. See Fekete (2008), pp. 28–33.
49. *The Economist*, 13 May 2010.
50. news.bbc.co.uk/2/hi/3619988.stm.
51. www.guardian.co.uk/world/2011/sep/19/battle-for-the-burqa.
52. On the French law, see Sylvie Tissot, 'Excluding Muslim Women: From Hijab to Niqab, From School to Public Space', *Public Culture*, 23 January 2011.
53. www.huffingtonpost.com/2012/01/27/dutch-burqa-ban-–n–1236625.html.
54. www.guardian.co.uk/world/2010/may/04/italian-police-fine-muslim-woman.
55. Amnesty Report, 23 April 2012, www.amnesty.org/en/news/muslims-discriminated-against-demonstrating-their-faith-2012-04-23. Accessed 25 April 2012.
56. Haleh Afshar, Rob Aitken and Myfanwy Franks, 'Feminism, Islamophobia and Identities', *Political Studies*, vol. 53, 2005.
57. Quoted in E. Heffernan, 'Sometimes it Feels Like the Twin Towers Fell on Our Heads Too', in *Feminist Review*, no. 88, 2008, pp. 131, 133.
58. Yvonne Ridley interview with the author, 11 April 2012.
59. Henna Malik interview with the author, 4 April 2012.
60. Ibid.
61. Ibid.
62. Rania Khan interview with the author, 6 June 2012.
63. Penny Hicks interview with the author, 22 August 2010.
64. Dahabo Isse interview with the author 21 December 2009.
65. Yvonne Ridley interview with the author, 11 April 2012.
66. Personal recollection by the author who stood in West Ham, came second to Labour with 20 per cent of the vote and had one of the four biggest swings in the election.
67. Helen Pidd, 'He Made Us Feel Important', *Guardian*, 5 April 2012.
68. Rania Khan interview with the author, 6 June 2012.

Chapter 8

1. Elaheh Rostami Povey interview with the author, 14 October 2010.
2. Jenny Jones interview with the author, 7 June 2010.

3. Nicola Pratt interview with the author, 21 December 2011.
4. Ibid.
5. Helen John letter to the author, 12 June 2012.
6. Angela Sinclair interview with the author, 20 September 2009.
7. Tansy Hoskins interview with the author, 20 July 2010.
8. Sinead Kirwan interview with the author, 10 April 2010.
9. Carmel Brown interview with the author, 23 August 2010.
10. Kate Connelly interview with the author, 21 August 2010.
11. Billie Figg interview with the author, 14 April 2010.
12. Rae Street interview with the author, 24 August 2010.
13. Jenny Jones interview with the author, 7 June 2010.
14. Elaheh Rostami Povey interview with the author, 14 October 2010.
15. Rae Street interview with the author, 24 August 2010.
16. Kate Hudson interview with the author, 31 May 2010.
17. Helen John interview with the author, 12 June 2012.
18. Sinead Kirwan interview with the author, 10 April 2010.
19. Kate Connelly interview with the author, 21 August 2010.
20. Rae Street interview with the author, 24 August 2010.
21. Ibid.
22. Jane Shallice interview with the author, 23 April 2012.
23. Tansy Hoskins interview with the author, 20 July 2010.
24. Sinead Kirwan interview with the author, 10 April 2010.
25. Kate Connelly interview with the author, 21 August 2010.
26. For a comprehensive account of rape in war, see Susan Brownmiller, *Against Our Will* (London, 1976).
27. Ibid., p. 32.
28. Ibid.
29. Naomi Wolf, 'A Culture of Cover-up: Rape in the Ranks of the US Military', *The Guardian*, 14 June 2012.
30. Colleen Burke, 'Women and Militarism', www.wilpfinternational.org/publications/womenmilitarism.htm.
31. Susan Faludi, *Stiffed: the Betrayal of the Modern Man* (London, 1999), pp. 143–51.
32. Ibid., pp. 121–32.
33. blogs.lse.ac.uk/politicsandpolicy/2011/12/27/public-opinion-military-intervention.
34. 'Working as a Group: Nottingham Women Oppose the Nuclear Threat', in Lynne Jones (ed.), *Keeping the Peace* (London, 1983), pp. 28–9.
35. Yvonne Ridley interview with the author, 11 April 2012.
36. Billie Figg interview with the author, 14 April 2010.
37. Angela Sinclair interview with the author, 20 September 2009.
38. Chanie Rosenberg interview with the author, 20 October 2010.
39. Jackie Mulhallen interview with the author, 21 August 2010.

40. Nicola Pratt interview with the author, 21 December 2011.
41. Rae Street interview with the author, 24 August 2010.
42. Brownmiller (1976), pp. 14–15.
43. Henna Malik interview with the author, 4 April 2012.
44. Jackie Mulhallen interview with the author, 21 August 2010.
45. Kate Connelly interview with the author, 21 August 2010.
46. Nicola Pratt interview with the author, 21 December 2011.
47. Tansy Hoskins interview with the author, 20 July 2010.
48. Jackie Mulhallen interview with the author, 21 August 2010.
49. Nicola Pratt interview with the author, 21 December 2011.
50. Rania Khan interview with the author, 6 June 2012.
51. Tansy Hoskins interview with the author, 20 July 2010.
52. Ibid.
53. Jenny Jones interview with the author, 7 June 2010.
54. Yvonne Ridley interview with the author, 11 April 2012.
55. Jenny Jones interview with the author, 7 June 2010.
56. Billie Figg interview with the author, 14 April 2010.
57. Rania Khan interview with the author, 6 June 2012.
58. Nicola Pratt interview with the author, 21 December 2011.
59. Chanie Rosenberg interview with the author, 20 October 2010.
60. Ibid.
61. Ibid.
62. Jenny Jones interview with the author, 7 June 2010.

Chapter 9

1. Carmel Brown, interview with the author, 23 August 2010.
2. Ibid.
3. www.worldmapper.org/display.php?selected=287.
4. Eric Hobsbawm, *The Age of Extremes* (London, 1994), p. 12.
5. Ibid., pp. 434–5.
6. Arundhati Roy, 'War is Peace', *Spokesman*, 73, 2001, p. 18.
7. For example, Pat Arrowsmith was tried and imprisoned during the 1970s for leafleting troops about their withdrawal from Northern Ireland.
8. Gabriel Kolko, *Century of War* (New York, 1994), p. 471.
9. World Bank data.worldbank.org/indicator/MS.MIL.XPND.ZS.
10. L. Wittner, *Common Dreams*, 23 April 2012. Data from SIPRI, www.stopwar.org.uk/index.php/cost-of-war/1363-insanity-of-worlds-highest-ever-military-spending-as-governments-slash-vital-social-services. Accessed 1 September 2012.
11. World Bank data.worldbank.org/indicator/MS.MIL.XPND.ZS.
12. Hiroshima Declaration, 6 August 2001, reprinted in Roy (2001).

Suggested Reading

As well as the books referenced in the notes, there are many others which I have drawn on to write this book, and there are a number of issues, such as questions of imperialism, which I could not deal with in great detail but which it would be well worth readers pursuing if they are interested in why wars happen.

First, an overview. The following books cover the whole period I have written about and are in different ways all worth reading. *The Age of Empire 1875–1914* (London, 1989) and *The Age of Extremes* (London, 1994), both by the Marxist historian Eric Hobsbawm, tell the story of colonialism and empire in the past century and a half. They are rich in detail and, while they cover all sorts of other issues as well as war, give the background and analysis of why the wars broke out, with which I am broadly in agreement. The American writer Gabriel Kolko covers much of the same period in *Century of War* (New York, 1994) but as the title suggests, concentrates exclusively on wars. Kolko also wrote *The Politics of War* (New York, 1990) about the military and political consequences of the Second World War, which is a more focused and rewarding book, but both are important. Also worth reading is A. D. Harvey, *Collision of Empires* (London, 1992). Sheila Rowbotham's *A Century of Women* (London, 1997) does what it says and looks at women's experience in the twentieth century from a socialist feminist point of view. Lyn Smith's oral history *Voices against War* (London, 2009) is a great resource.

I see the root of modern warfare in the economic system of imperialism. Some contemporary accounts of imperialism have been valuable in different ways. They include: Michael Kidron, *Western Capitalism Since the War* (London, 1968); Andrew Murray, *The Imperial Controversy* (London, 2009); John Rees, *Imperialism and Resistance* (London, 2006) and *Timelines* (London, 2012). John Newsinger, *The Blood Never Dried* (London, 1997) tells the bloody history of the British Empire. Tariq Ali's *Masters of the Universe* (London, 2000) and Perry Anderson's *The New Old World* (London, 2009) attempt to come to terms with the New World Order, as does David Harvey's *The New Imperialism* (Oxford, 2003).

There are many writings by Marxist thinkers and much commentary on them. A good starting point is S. F. Kissin, *War and the Marxists*, volumes 1 and 2 (London, 1988, 1989). He studies the thinking of Marx and Engels on the wars they lived through between 1848 and 1895, and how their successors developed ideas of imperialism. Hal Draper and E. Haberkern look at *Karl Marx's Theory of Revolution. Volume V: War and Revolution* (New York, 2005). Karl Marx and Friedrich Engels wrote extensively and at various times about wars and revolutions, including their writings on 1848 and 1849 in Germany, and the American Civil War, 1861–65. These can be found in the various volumes of their *Collected Works* and in the Penguin editions of some of their earlier writings edited by David Fernbach, for example *The First International and After* (1974) and *Surveys from Exile* (1973). Fernbach's introductions to these volumes are lengthy but accessible and informative.

There are also the numerous debates arising from the crisis of the Left around the First World War. Rosa Luxemburg, Leon Trotsky and Vladimir Lenin, who wrote his book *Imperialism, Highest Stage of Capitalism*, as a result of this crisis, all have contributions in their various collections of writings, published by Monthly Review, Pathfinder and Lawrence and Wishart, respectively. The war produced revolution and the attempt to organise internationally, including debates on war, is documented brilliantly in a number of works. These include John Riddell's series *The Communist International in Lenin's Time*, especially volume 1, *Lenin's Struggle for a Revolutionary International* (New York, 1984), and volume 4, *To See the Dawn*, which is about the Congress of the Peoples of the East and discusses attitudes to Islam in an anti-colonial context. The period is also covered by Fernando Claudin, *The Communist Movement*, volumes 1 and 2 (New York and London, 1975) and Leon Trotsky, *The First Five Years of the Communist International*, volumes 1 and 2 (London, 1973 and 1974). A fascinating collection on women in the communist movement internationally in this period is Helmut Gruber and Pamela Graves (eds.), *Women and Socialism/Socialism and Women* (Oxford, 1998).

A good starting point for writings on women and the two world wars are the more general histories. I have drawn on wider reading over a range of subjects concerning women, including much on the social unrest in the years leading up to the First World War. Caroline Benn's *Keir Hardie* (London, 1997) looks at this period in some detail, as does Ralph Miliband, *Parliamentary Socialism* (London, 1972) and Keith Laybourn, *The Rise of Socialism in Britain* (Stroud, 1997). A wonderfully written and evocative account is George Dangerfield, *The Strange Death of Liberal England* (London, 1970). Wider issues of the New Woman in these years are addressed by June Hannam and Karen Hunt, *Socialist Women* (London, 2002) and Walter Kendall looks at socialist politics in *The Revolutionary Movement in Britain* (London, 1989).

There are many excellent sociological studies of women's social and economic position at the time, lots of them rediscovered by feminists and published by Virago. They include Clementina Black, *Married Women's Work* (London, 1983), Maud Pember Reeves, *Round about a Pound a Week* (London, 1994) and Barbara Drake, *Women in Trade Unions* (London, 1984). Hannah Mitchell and Ada Nield Chew tell working-class women's stories in *The Hard Way Up* (London, 1977) and *The Life and Writings of a Working Woman* (London, 1982). Sylvia Pankhurst's *The Suffragette Movement* (London, 1977) is a great jumping off point for the story of the most important women's movement in Britain, and can be supplemented by Shirley Harrison, *Sylvia Pankhurst: A Maverick Life* (London, 2004), Andrew Rosen, *Rise Up, Women* (London, 1974) and Paul Foot's substantial chapter in *The Vote* (London, 2005). Jill Liddington and Jill Norris describe the remarkable lives of the northern-based working-class suffragists in *One Hand Tied Behind Us* (London, 1978) and Jill Liddington tells the story of one of them, Selina Cooper, in *The Life and Times of a Respectable Rebel* (London, 1984).

I found Gail Braybon and Penny Summerfield's account of both the first and second world wars, *Out of the Cage* (London, 1987), invaluable for its detailed accounts, personal reminiscences and interviews and accessible style. Susan R. Grayzel, *Women and the First World War* (London, 2002) looks at war's impact on different aspects of women's lives. Deirdre Beddoe, in *Back to Home and Duty* (London, 1989), covers the years between the wars, as do Virginia Nicholson, *Singled Out* (London, 2008) and Juliet Nicolson, *The Great Silence 1918–20* (London, 2009).

Sheila Lewenhak's *Women and Trade Unions* (London, 1977) and *Women and Work* (London, 1980) look at what wars meant for women, as does Sarah Boston, *Women Workers and the Trade Unions* (London, 1980). Vera Brittain writes movingly about the impact of two wars on her life in *Testament of Youth* (London, 1977) and *England's Hour* (London, 2005). From a British point of view, Angus Calder's brilliant *The People's War* (London, 1992) debunks many of the myths about what actually happened in the Second World War, as does his *The Myth of the Blitz* (London, 1992). Paul Addison and Jeremy Crang, *Listening to Britain* (London, 2010) is fascinating in its description of official eavesdropping on ordinary people in 1940. Other good accounts include Dorothy Sheridan's edited extracts from Mass Observation, *Wartime Women* (London, 2000), Penny Summerfield's *Women Workers in the Second World War* (Beckenham, 1984), and for a more modern and extremely detailed account Juliet Gardiner's *Wartime* (London, 2004).

Jennifer Golden, *Hackney at War* (Stroud, 2009) is one of many local histories about the Second World War, but Hackney has a lot of stories to tell, which again contradict established versions of the war narrative. For a very different perspective on the Second World War see the anonymously written *A Woman in Berlin* (London, 2004), which tells the terrible story of mass rape by Russian soldiers in the occupied city in 1945.

The 1950s and 1960s and questions of war and peace are well documented in Kate Hudson, *CND: Now More than Ever* (London, 2005). Chris Harman, *The Fire Last Time* (London, 1998) is a good historical analysis of the 1960s and 1968 in particular. Sheila Rowbotham's story of her 1960s, *Promise of a Dream* (London, 2000) is interesting on both CND and Vietnam. My favourite source on this period is David Widgery, *The Left in Britain 1956–1968* (Harmondsworth, 1976). I think when it first came out it was denounced by one reviewer as containing a number of inaccuracies. It might well, but they are minor and do not detract from a book which has a wealth of original sources from the period plus an analysis written by a socialist activist at the time. It gives a flavour of the time.

The Vietnam war profoundly influenced the modern women's movement, which began in the United States. There are some really good personal accounts. The most enlightening and informative is Sara Evans, *Personal Politics* (New York, 1979) which is a great description of the civil rights, anti-war and student movements and how women became disillusioned with their treatment. Another is Jo Freeman, *The Politics of Women's Liberation* (New York, 1975). *Liberation Now: Writings from the Women's Liberation Movement* (New York, 1971) gives a sense of what the movement was like; in Britain its counterpart was *The Body Politic* (London, 1972). On Greenham, Ann Pettitt, *Walking to Greenham* (South Glamorgan, 2006) is a contemporary account and Lynne Jones (ed.), *Keeping the Peace* (London, 1983) also gives a flavour of the politics at the time.

I have written on issues of women's liberation, and readers interested in some of the history and analysis should look at my *Material Girls* (London, 2007) and *Sex, Class and Socialism* (London, 1989). On women's current issues I have enjoyed Hester Eisenstein, *Feminism Seduced* (Boulder, CO, 2009) and Susan Faludi, *Stiffed* (London, 1999).

For what is happening in the countries that have been supposedly liberated, read Malalai Joya, *Raising My Voice* (London, 2009), Elaheh Rostami Povey, *Afghan Women* (London, 2007), Haifa Zangana, *City of Widows* (New York, 2009) and Nadia Al-Ali and Nicola Pratt, *What Kind of Liberation?* (London, 2009). Two of the most readable books on how the imperialists took us to war are John Kampfner, *Blair's Wars* (London, 2004) and Bob Woodward, *Plan of Attack* (London, 2004). For the real story of a mass movement which tried to challenge war, see the book I co-authored with Andrew Murray, *Stop the War* (London, 2005).

The following websites are a useful resource:

Bureau of Investigative Journalism
   http://www.thebureauinvestigates.com
Campaign Against the Arms Trade
   http://www.caat.org.uk
CND
   www.cnduk.org
Counterpunch
   http://www.counterpunch.org
Democracy Now
   http://www.democracynow.org
Global Research
   http://www.globalresearch.ca
Housmans Bookshop
   www.housmans.com
http://antiwar.com
http://www.commondreams.org
Information Clearing House
   http://www.informationclearinghouse.info
Institute for Policy Studies
   http://www.ips-dc.org
Stop the War Coalition
   http://stopwar.org.uk
Tom Dispatch
   http://www.tomdispatch.com
ZNet
   http://www.zcommunications.org/znet

Index